I HATE
FINANCIAL
PLANNING

In memory of Tom Hunstad
1954–2000
My brother, my friend

Contents

Acknowledgments / ix

Introduction / xi

CHAPTER 1 / 1
"Plan" Is a Four-Letter Word

CHAPTER 2 / 25
Do You Need a Kick in the Budget?

CHAPTER 3 / 43
The Good, the Bad, and the Ugly

CHAPTER 4 / 59
You Gotta Play This Numbers Game

CHAPTER 5 / 73
The Only Constant Is Change

CHAPTER 6 / 105
Home, Sweet Investment

CHAPTER 7 / 131
*Saving for Retirement—And Other
Never-Ending Jobs*

CHAPTER 8 / 159
*Past Performance Is No Guarantee
of Future Results*

CHAPTER 9 / 189
Sickness, Disaster, Death, and Other Fun Topics

CHAPTER 10 / 211
Lifestyles of the Ready and Willing

CHAPTER 11 / 233
Financial Insecurity

CHAPTER 12 / 249
What Makes You Do That Thing You Do?

Guide to Financial Jargon / 267

Index / 283

Acknowledgments

There's a long list of people who helped make this book possible, starting with my colleagues at what was then ReliaStar Financial Corp. who had the vision to create a safe haven for consumers who are intimidated by the idea of financial planning. It was a bold move for a financial services company to go public with the message that we know people don't usually like what we have to offer. The Web address ihatefinancialplanning.com is a stroke of genius because it breaks down a barrier and helps people be open to learning. Actually *doing* something with what they've learned is another thing altogether, but then our procrastination antidote is still in development.

I could not have written this book without Mary Audette, Grant Evans, and Darren McKeever. They're dedicated to making the Web site what it is, and they're also quite willing to taunt me on a daily basis. Thanks to the compliance and legal review team, especially Lorna Ravinski.

Thanks to my high school English teachers in Chetek, Wisconsin. I think of them frequently even though it's been decades since I sat in their classrooms. Sometimes I'm thinking how I wish I had paid more attention when they were talking about grammar and usage. But mostly I'm just thankful they were so willing to nurture my love of words and challenge me to work hard.

I thank my parents for instilling in me a sense of personal financial responsibility. (I'm guessing they really had no choice, considering we never had any money.) I still have the handwritten instructions for balancing a checkbook that my mom gave me when I left for college. She might be surprised to know I always know my bank balance. Thanks to my siblings for keeping me humble and for insisting my wit be sharp and at-the-ready. Thanks to my nieces and nephews for giving me joy. And to my husband, Kirk, thanks for continuing your search until you found me.

Introduction

We launched a Web site in 2000 for the three out of four people who hate financial planning. That statistic came out of exhaustive research by a highly paid consulting firm hired by our employer. That was back in the day when corporations had budgets to pay for things like consultants to research obvious truths. What a revelation: people hate financial planning.

We hate this stuff as much as you do. We'll make that clear so you know we're not trying to convert you into a budget-loving, stock-ticker-studying, number-crunching financial freak. We've got stuff about budgeting, sure, but we don't expect you to like it. Heck, we'll be surprised if you even read that chapter. Don't worry one bit about stock tickers. We don't want anyone getting motion sickness while reading this book. But number crunching? Technically numbers do need to be crunched when making sense of your personal finances, but nobody's going to check your answers. Just an equation here or there to help you see where you are or perhaps where you want to go.

And that's the tricky thing about planning. You've got to think about it, make some choices, and take a stab at achieving goals. We're here to help you dare to plot out those goals. Maybe it's not about daring so much as actually doing. You can keep putting it off and nobody will care. But something got you to open this book, and we're guessing it's that voice knocking around inside your head lambasting you to do something, *anything*, about your money situation.

Since ihatefinancialplanning.com came on the scene, millions of people have found the Web site. Some have even returned. One reader wrote in to tell us, "I love the candid way you speak to us. I feel like you're just normal people giving advice that you just happen to know about from personal experience." Strange comment, considering we're anything but normal.

Don't expect a page-turner. This is not one of those can't-put-it-down type of books. In fact, you'll probably be more likely to throw it across the room. You can read a chapter here or there and come back when your life circumstances demand that you do something about retirement planning or writing a will or protecting your assets or any number of the other topics we'll discuss. We think you'll find that the time is now for most of it. But we're not going to put any pressure on you. We're just glad you're here because that means you're ready to take personal responsibility for your financial well-being. And sometimes that's the hardest part.

I HATE FINANCIAL PLANNING

1

"Plan" Is a Four-Letter Word

We have a friend—let's call her Kim—who in her early thirties moved from Minnesota to Florida, searching for a better job and a fresh start. Sixteen months later she decided a change of scenery wasn't the solution she thought it would be and moved back. The geographic Ping-Pong game helped her conclude she wanted to settle down and buy a house. Which surprised even Kim, since she could barely pay her bills. She'd had surgery the year before, and thanks to some poor choices during employee benefits enrollment, she'd had to pay a big share of the bill. It was a quick recovery, not counting the doctor and hospital bills. Speaking of which, she was working two jobs just to make a dent in them, not to mention her rent, credit card debt, and car loan. Naturally it was time to take on a mortgage.

When her lease was up, Kim packed up her belongings and moved into the basement of some friends for a hundred bucks a month. It wasn't the ideal housing arrangement for a thirtysomething professional, but it helped her overcome the obstacles blocking her way to home ownership. For the next year she lived as cheaply as possible, all while diligently paying down her debt and putting cash in the bank for a down payment. On Valentine's Day she met with a mortgage broker to get preapproved for a loan, and two months later she took possession of a quaint starter home.

That's what financial planning is all about. You have a goal and set out to make it happen, even if it means sidestepping barriers along the way. It only took Kim two and a half years to realize her dream. There were sacrifices, but that's nothing unusual for a first-time homebuyer. Affordability and availability caused her to buy a house in an entirely different city than she had originally planned, but doing so cut her commute to work in half. She also chose an adjustable rate mortgage (ARM) with a lower introductory interest rate in hopes of landing a better house. In her excitement, she forgot the "introductory" part and wasn't prepared when the rate jumped a year later, pushing her mortgage payment up more than a hundred bucks. That increase presented her with yet another financial planning opportunity.

But Kim also picked up a few planning tools that will help her make the next goal happen. For starters she learned not to sacrifice solid health insurance coverage just to save a few dollars in premiums. Being young and in good health, she had selected the least amount of health insurance and highest deductibles, not planning on needing surgery. She paid dearly for that one. And she also learned that having credit card debt can be like swimming across a lake with your legs tied together. You may get there if the extra work doesn't drown you first. Even now, when she's tempted to charge up the cards, she forces herself to recall the cold, damp floor of her friends' basement.

CHECK YOUR PULSE

Let's break from Kim's saga and shift to yours by quickly checking your financial pulse. It may be surprising to learn you've actually got one. You may not have a bona fide plan, but you're doing more than you think. Your answers to these eight statements could help you figure out things aren't so bad. Or not. Perhaps you truly haven't done one thing right, but what are the odds of that? Just mark your answers—many are true or false, so it shouldn't take much time. And don't worry about your final score or being accountable. The only thing we're really testing is your patience.

1. At any given time, I know:
    A. My total assets and liabilities, within a couple hundred dollars.

    B.   That I own some stuff, but I also owe some money too.

    C.   That "assets" is a shorter word than "liabilities."

If you answered A: Wow! Pardon us for being shocked, but so few people are actively aware of their net worth that we almost didn't write a comment for A answers. It's wise to keep your finger on the pulse as your net worth increases over time. It's a solid indicator of where you're headed.

If you answered B: To gain a better understanding of where you are financially—so you might get a better look at where you're going—you might want to use the net worth worksheet later in this chapter to tally up your assets and liabilities. You'll be glad you did (and not just because you may be surprised to see how much you already own).

If you answered C: We're making a joke of something that deserves serious consideration, but that's only because it's more fun that way. Being aware of your assets and liabilities can provide a solid foundation on which to build your financial future. We'll steer you to the section in this chapter on getting motivated and the accompanying net worth worksheet.

  2. If the interest rate on my credit card goes up, I would

    A.   Immediately find a credit card with a lower rate.

    B.   Keep using that card because I can't be bothered with details.

    C.   Be living a dream because my credit is so bad I can't get any plastic.

If you answered A: You are a smart shopper who's always looking out for number one. Way to go! Perhaps you want to skim Chapter 4 for other helpful hints on how you can maintain a solid credit rating.

If you answered B: Don't put off reading this chapter, because we've got a section especially for you on procrastination. Read the credit chapter if you dare.

If you answered C: Not qualifying for credit cards is a fairly strong signal that your credit situation needs help. One of your financial planning goals should be to seek professional help. Perhaps our discussion of debt management programs in Chapter 4 will capture your attention.

3. I know whether I have disability income insurance through my employer.
   - ☐ True
   - ☐ False

If you answered TRUE: It's important to know this sort of information about yourself, so you're prepared in the event that you become disabled and you're unable to earn an income. Many employers offer disability income insurance, but it may not be sufficient coverage, especially if you are single, the sole breadwinner in your family, or unable to rely on other resources should you suddenly become unable to work.

If you answered FALSE: You owe it to yourself to be aware of all the employee benefits you get at work and how they correspond with individual insurance policies you may have. Your ability to earn an income is perhaps your most valuable asset. Disability income insurance is essential if you are single or unable to rely on other resources should you suddenly become unable to work.

4. I have a written will outlining my wishes.
   - ☐ True
   - ☐ False

If you answered TRUE: Good for you. Most people put off writing this important document because they want to put off thinking about death. Be sure to update your will over time as your financial picture and/or family circumstances change.

If you answered FALSE: At least you're willing to admit it, which is more than most people are willing to do. It's not easy thinking about death and dying, but it could be harder knowing your wishes will not be carried out because you haven't put them in writing.

5. I have something I'm saving for.
   - ☐ True
   - ☐ False

If you answered TRUE: If you chose "true," you have a goal (or many goals) you're striving for. Nothing can beat the feeling of working toward achieving a goal and then accomplishing it. Savings and investment goals are as unique as the person who has them. Whether it's a washing machine you want to buy or a retirement home you're planning to move to someday, at least you have a goal and you're doing something about it.

If you answered FALSE: If there's never any extra money left for saving or investing, maybe you should make it a priority to move saving to the top of your spending list. It's important to have goals—maybe yours should be to pay yourself first.

6. My personal checkbook is
    A. Always balanced to the penny.
    B. Only balanced when I get a bank statement.
    C. Under the seat of my car because it has no balance.

If you answered A: Do you know if anal retentive should be hyphenated? Seriously, you are really in charge of your money if you know what your balance is. You're in control of your spending and you're probably in control of other aspects of your finances as well.

If you answered B: At least you know the importance of being in sync with your bank. Money is nothing to mess with. Perhaps you want to skip ahead to the budgeting chapter.

If you answered C: It's important to be in control of your cash supply so you're equipped to make other financial decisions. Does your cash flow struggle affect your life? It must, but there is something you can do about it. Read the budgeting chapter, but first, do some math and figure out your checkbook.

7. I know how much life insurance coverage I have.
    ☐ True
    ☐ False

If you answered TRUE: Congratulations! Depending on whom you talk to (not counting life insurance salespeople), life insurance is an essential component in any financial plan. If, by chance, you know how much life insurance you have and it's zero, hat's off for trying to confuse us.

If you answered FALSE: There are two schools of thought on life insurance. Some believe it's a waste of money and others insist life insurance is an essential component in any financial plan. In either case, you should be aware of the benefits life insurance can offer you and your loved ones.

   8. The person I rely on for financial advice is
       A. My spouse or partner
       B. My brother-in-law
       C. My financial professional

If you answered A: It's good you communicate with your significant other. However, unless he or she is knowledgeable about taxes and investments, you may be sacrificing your collective financial future. There's a section at the end of the chapter that can help you decide if you should be consulting a financial professional.

If you answered B: You're smart enough to not be going it alone where your money is concerned, but you're probably barking up the wrong tree. Check out the section later in this chapter to decide if you should be consulting a financial professional.

If you answered C: You're too busy to worry about P/E ratios or if your investments are diversified enough to help you achieve your financial goals. There's a reason these people are called "professionals" and you're choosing to rely on them.

We promise not to grade your quiz on a curve. In fact, it's never going to be graded, so you can rest easy. Our intent is to help you see where you are and steer you in the direction you need to go—financially speaking, at least. It's easy to joke about credit ratings and checkbook balances, but those numbers can help you determine a lot about yourself. Sort of like a compass showing you the way. If this quiz to check your pulse shows you one thing you could be planning better or one area you need to learn more about, we've done our job.

GOT GOALS?

One reason it's tempting to avoid financial planning or even skip a simple pulse check is that it forces you to get in touch with your goals. That involves thinking and plotting and following through—none of which is all too appealing, especially if there's a chance you won't accomplish the goal. But don't let the perceived enormity of the task overwhelm you. Our friend Kim's medical bills were the only excuse she would have needed to put off her home ownership goal. She was working nights to pay them off, and she had no business thinking she could afford a house payment when it was a stretch to pay rent and other bills. It's easy to assume your goals aren't achievable and give up working toward them altogether. But what's the point of that?

When thinking about your goals, be realistic. Oh heck, be unrealistic. Of all the aspects of financial planning, goal setting is the adventurous part. It's a time to think big, dream on, plan wildly—even though there will inevitably be plenty of circumstances to inject the appropriate dose of reality into your planning along the way. Think small too because it may take achieving several little things before you can tackle a big one. For instance, don't get hung up in a retirement-villa fantasy if what you really want to accomplish is an extra mortgage payment this year. Ask yourself these sorts of questions:

- Gee, what have I always wanted out of life? (And why do I use words like "gee"?)
- I want to travel around the world. How much will it cost to put my belongings in storage?
- Can I/we send the kids to college? Can I finally earn my degree? How much will it cost?
- Can I/we ever afford to buy a house? A cabin? A yacht? Maybe a kayak?
- I know I need to save more money, but to do so I need to earn more. What do I need to do to get a job that pays better?
- I want to retire at 55. How crazy is that?
- If I quit my job to launch my own business, will I have to work on holidays?

WRITE 'EM DOWN

Write down your goals, no matter how goofy it sounds. You've got to own the goal for it to have any chance, and seeing it in black and white can't hurt. No one is going to read over your shoulder, unless you've got a significant other. Don't exaggerate your goals just so they look good on paper. If it's credit card debt you want to pay off but you owe half your annual income to creditors, don't commit in writing to making the debt disappear in six months. It's going to take longer than that. Only you can make your goal happen, so stretch the truth with yourself and there's only one person who will hold you accountable. Sometimes we're our own worst enemy.

BE POSITIVE

Once you have your goals in writing, it should be pretty easy to identify what you need to do. Well, "easy" may not be the right word, but "pain in the neck" doesn't roll off the tongue quite as well. Just keep in mind that this is all about you, so at least you're in good company. And be positive. "I will buy a house" is a positive goal while "I will not spend any money" is negative. Keep your eye on the positive goal, and you just might stop spending money because you want to buy that house. Or work two jobs or live in a basement or both.

SET A DATE

Unless you establish a deadline, you won't accomplish a goal—ask anyone who promises to "get so much done around the house." Just be reasonable and don't be too hard on yourself if you miss your deadline. (See "Be Positive," above.) Or maybe a just-in-time deadline like Kim set will work best for you. She wasn't sure of the exact time frame for her home purchase, but when she got the bills paid and money saved turned out to be the perfect time.

STAY FOCUSED

If we installed an escape hatch in the whole planning process, this is where you'd probably make your exit in the financial ride of your life. Hey, it's not that hard if you just take your goals one at a time. Is it debt you want to get rid of? Then be proactive—check the due date on statements when they arrive, plan how much you'll pay and put your credit cards in a witness protection program. No matter what your goal, you might find yourself setting and achieving all sorts of miniature ones en route. Just don't let them distract you from your main goal.

EVALUATE PROGRESS

If you actively pay down your debt, you owe it to yourself to take note of the progress you're making on that goal. Just be sure to stop short of throwing yourself an expensive party. Feeling good about your goals will contribute to your success. Kim told friends she was going to buy a house, and their follow-up questions as time went on held her accountable to her goal.

What goal do you want to achieve? What's it going to take to get you there?

USE PAIN FOR YOUR FINANCIAL GAIN

You'll notice a common theme running through this financial planning chapter. And it's money. The reality is, the average dream requires cold, hard cash to see the light of day. That's why money can be such a pain. But in lieu of any other motivation, pain can be just the thing you need to start financial planning. Whether your pain comes from something as simple as an occasional overdraft or as disturbing as watching a loved one struggle financially during retirement, use it in your favor. Common sense says that real change comes only when real discomfort is upon you. So the first step, which may be the most personal and important, is to use your own discomfort as a motivator for change. We're going to show you how you can make the pain rewarding.

WHERE ARE YOU NOW?

First, take a serious look at where you are today, using the net worth worksheet that follows. A net worth statement will give you a black-and-white—or color, if you're in the red—picture of how your assets and liabilities shake out. You may cringe at the thought of listing what little you own and the lot you owe, but if you don't have a clue where you stand financially, you don't stand a chance of moving ahead. It's probably safe to say that most people have little or no idea where they stand financially. Assuming you fall into that category, it's also safe to say that once you do the inventory, you might be surprised to find out you're worth more than you thought.

Net Worth Worksheet

ASSETS	VALUE	LIABILITIES	BALANCE
POSSESSIONS		**PERSONAL DEBTS**	
Home		Home mortgage	
2nd Home		2nd Mortgage	
Car(s)		Car loan	
Furniture			
Collectibles		**CREDIT CARDS**	
Jewelry		Card #1	
Electronics		Card #2	
Computer equipment		Card #3	
		Card #4	
SAVINGS/INVESTMENTS		Card #5	
Bank accounts			
Emergency savings			

Assets		Liabilities	
CDs		**OTHER DEBT**	
Stocks		Personal loans	
Bonds		Unpaid bills	
Mutual funds		Income tax owed	
Real estate		**INVESTMENT DEBT**	
Annuities		Investment loan	
Life insurance cash value		401(k) loan	
Other		Life insurance loan	
RETIREMENT SAVINGS		Business loan	
Pension plan		**TOTAL LIABILITIES**	
Savings accounts			
401(k), 403(b), 457		**TOTAL ASSETS**	
IRAs		**TOTAL LIABILITIES**	
Other		**= TOTAL NET WORTH** (assets minus liabilities)	
TOTAL ASSETS			

Once you've tallied your net worth, take a look at the table below, which shows the average net worth for different age ranges and income levels nationwide. The data comes from a survey of American consumers conducted in February 2003 by SRI Consulting Business Intelligence. The whole thing about average, of course, is that there's lots of room above and below the figures listed. If you're above average, way to go. If not, you've gained some ground just by learning where you stand. Either way, repeat this task periodically as part of your overall financial plan, keeping in mind what every coach has ever said about the mutually beneficial relationship between pain and gain.

WE'VE PUT THIS OFF LONG ENOUGH

Our high school English teacher called it "approach avoidance," but putting off the task at hand is better known as plain old procrastination. Luckily you don't even have to excel at it to be an overachiever, especially when you combine the skill with financial planning. That's mainly due to the infamous time-equals-money equation. Who cares if you put off household chores? Ignore the mess in the basement, no big deal. But when it's a matter of putting off that financial plan, postponing the action verb in "retirement savings," or rationalizing escalating debt, procrastination could be a very big, expensive deal.

Average Net Worth by Age and Income Level

		AGE				
		<35	35–44	45–54	55–64	65+
I	Less than $25K	$5,605	$57,178	$56,065	$142,114	$135,527
N	$25K–$50K	28,211	59,388	157,788	249,245	441,646
C	$50K–$75K	71,556	147,881	219,883	361,499	552,542
O	$75K–$100K	181,111	224,819	295,083	585,647	831,004
M	$100K–$125K	288,350	373,622	571,522	915,977	1,256,834
E	$125K–$150K	92,659	481,751	604,858	1,082,008	1,060,180
	$150K+	319,987	878,497	1,529,564	1,493,051	2,388,261

Source: SRIC-BI Survey 2003

Why do you postpone progress? No matter what's standing in your way—whether it's a thoughtful reason or clever rationalization—it's still just an excuse. Are you too young? Is it too late? Don't you make enough money? Do you hate tax season? Maybe you're waiting to have a family. Or waiting for your partner to handle it. Are you hoping that the stock market will go up? That it will settle down? Confused by what you don't understand? Don't want to be told what to do? Don't know where to start? Perhaps you lost your checkbook. Or your mind.

The thing about financial planning is there's never a wrong time to start or a set amount of money you need. Planning can be as simple as organizing your bills so they get paid on time or as complex as adjusting your portfolio based on the P/E ratios of your holdings. Those examples aren't intended as a comment on your particular situation. They have merely been plucked from the gamut of financial planning possibilities. But if you put off whatever decisions you need to make, we can pretty much guarantee you're going to suffer the consequences. Procrastination of the financial kind could either make you or break you. And that's largely because of what we already mentioned.

Time equals money.

Take a look at four financially focused folks and see what would happen to their $100 monthly investment over time with a return of 8 percent, and then a lump-sum investment at various rates of return.

Poll

How much do you hate financial planning?

I also procrastinate, so I'll answer tomorrow	34%
On a scale of 1 to 10, I'm a 75	16%
"Hate" is a strong word, but I dislike it A LOT	24%
I love it	26%

Poll of visitors to ihatefinancialplanning.com

This graphic is just to give you a picture of what could happen if you don't procrastinate and what could happen when you do. In the real world, of course, income taxes and investment fees and expenses would reduce what you actually get to keep on a taxable investment, so don't ask Alan, Betty, Carol, or Dan for their cash.

These scenarios show that regardless of the rate of return, time has the potential to multiply an investment substantially. And when you add just a few points to that rate of return, the multiplication is downright amazing. Keep in mind that this example isn't intended to reflect

$100 Invested per Month at 8%

Investor	Start Age	No. of Years	Total Invested	Value at 65
Alan	25	40	$48,000	$351,428
Betty	35	30	$36,000	$150,030
Carol	45	20	$24,000	$59,295
Dan	55	10	$12,000	$18,417

Growth of $10,000 Lump-Sum Investment

Investor	Start Age	Value at age 65 at % return			
		4%	8%	10%	12%
Alan	25	$48,010	$217,245	$452,593	$930,510
Betty	35	$32,434	$100,627	$174,494	$299,599
Carol	45	$21,911	$46,610	$67,275	$96,463
Dan	55	$14,802	$21,589	$25,937	$31,058

the return of any particular investment. To keep our legal people happy, we're obligated to remind you that not all investments offer a guaranteed rate of return, and just because you invest consistently doesn't mean you're always going to make a profit. Sometimes you follow a plan and you still lose money, thanks to stuff you can't control, like when the market tanks.

If procrastination is standing in your way of financial progress, it's probably holding hands with impatience. Alan, Betty, Carol, and Dan all have one thing in common: They stuck with their savings plan. They didn't put a little money away for a few months and then stop for an impromptu vacation. Or in the case of the lump-sum investments, they didn't dump the money in, watch it grow for a couple of years, and pull it out for a trip around the world. They patiently let their money grow. We think that's quite a tribute to their stick-to-itiveness because whenever we've taken a hypothetical trip with imaginary friends, we've been left with sort of an empty feeling.

If you're still wondering whether procrastination really puts a kink in financial planning, just ask Dan in the illustration above if he'd rather have his or Alan's nest egg. Come to think of it, tracking down Dan could be just the excuse you're looking for to continue procrastinating. Meanwhile, we're going to put off the next section of this chapter a little longer by mentioning that potential investment returns aren't the only thing that could suffer if you procrastinate on financial matters. The other stuff isn't as easy to quantify in snappy graphics, but we can give you a few examples anyway. Failing to have adequate disability income insurance could be devastating if you suddenly find yourself unable to earn an income. Neglecting estate planning basics such as writing a will can leave questions that need to be settled by the courts instead of by surviving family members. And letting debt grow can stifle your plans to make progress in other areas of your financial life. If you've read this far you undoubtedly want to eliminate approach avoidance and move ahead.

PUT TIME ON YOUR SIDE

When discussing the art of procrastination, it's important to mention compound interest because it may be the antidote you need to prevent further avoidance. Most banks pay compound interest, which means that you earn interest not just on the dollars you put into your savings, but also on the interest already earned. At 6 percent interest, for example, a dollar saved today will double in 12 years, and it will be worth $4 in 24 years. With our innate math impairment, we're only allowed to use small figures like that in our illustrations, but imagine for a moment what $100 saved today could do. See how $1,000 would grow with compound interest:

$1,000 Earning Compound Interest		
Year	3% Return	6% Return
1	$1,030.00	$1,060.00
2	$1,060.90	$1,123.60
3	$1,092.93	$1,191.02
4	$1,125.51	$1,262.48
5	$1,159.28	$1,338.23

Left to work its magic, compound interest can have an amazing impact on your financial planning goals if you let it. But in order to let it, you've got to actually have some goals and then put some money toward achieving them. You'd be surprised how quickly the compounding amounts to some real cha-ching.

NEED HELP WITH THAT FINANCIAL PLAN?

We hope all that talk about procrastination provided just the break you needed from our banter about financial planning. You probably know you need some sort of a plan, so we're not telling you anything new. But that's never stopped us before. For the sake of argument, let's say we've convinced you to do something but you're not so sure you want to go about it by yourself. Perhaps you'll find some comfort in the fact that you're not alone in that thinking.

We would have thought that the market's demise earlier this decade would provide just the excuse most people needed to avoid organized planning, but it actually had the opposite effect. It was easy for average

RULE OF 72

The rule of 72 may look complicated, considering its reliance on math and all, but it's really simple. To figure out how long it's going to take for a lump-sum investment to double, simply divide 72 by the anticipated annual interest rate. This easy equation gives you a quick picture of not only what it takes for your money to double, but it shows that you can do it. Unless you put it off.

72 divided by 12% = 6 years until investment doubles
72 divided by 8% = 9 years until investment doubles
72 divided by 6% = 12 years until investment doubles
72 divided by 3% = 24 years until investment doubles

investors to consider themselves experts during the booming 1990s. Double-digit returns tend to boost everyone's ego and turn novices into gurus. Funny what a few years of serious losses will do. Investors are seeking professional help now more than ever, maybe because they saw during the economic slump that even so-called experts could lose money.

That's why we're not shy about saying you may want to seek advice from financial professionals. Don't misunderstand. There's plenty of room in the financial-planning universe for do-it-yourselfers. We commend anyone with the chutzpah to figure it out on their own, but more often than not, procrastinators like us need to hire professionals who can point us in the right direction. They can be your best agents for action and change, not only in getting you started, but also in providing objective evaluation of the realities of your plan, helping you maintain discipline, assisting with adjustments due to life changes, and keeping you on course during setbacks. Plus they tend to know about the complex financial products available and strategies to help you reach your goals.

A QUICK IDEA FOR DO-IT-YOURSELFERS

Hey, if you aren't interested in consulting a professional for assistance or you're on the fence about completing a financial plan, maybe QuickPlan—a nifty tool on our Web site—is for you. In three easy steps, you answer some quick questions (ergo, the name), and QuickPlan spits out a blueprint for the financial plan you've been resisting. It's not the least bit complicated, and you won't need to track down a bunch of numbers in order to answer the questions. It simply meets you where you are and recommends action steps you can follow. But be warned, as with the genuine financial plan we've been asking you to work on throughout this chapter, you're going to have to think about your goals before using QuickPlan to calculate what you'll have to do to make them happen. (Hint: it's probably going to involve saving some money.) But don't worry—just because we call it QuickPlan doesn't mean you have to accomplish everything immediately. Just take the plan and build your future one step at a time.

LOOKING FOR SOMEONE TO HIRE

These days you can't swing a dead cat without hitting someone who claims to do financial planning or consulting (animal lovers, please note it's just an expression). The fact that insurance agents, accountants, tax attorneys, brokers, and bank representatives all offer various and sundry financial planning services doesn't make it any easier. And to make things even more interesting, most states don't regulate or license financial professionals. Finding one you like and trust requires the same sort of care and effort you use in finding a doctor or an auto mechanic, for that matter.

And that may be reason enough for you to put it off, which is all right as long as you make an effort to move forward financially on your own. If you put any attempts at progress on hold while you wait for that certain someone to pop up who can make recommendations and sell you stuff for free (as long as we're dreaming), you'll miss out. So, the decision is yours. Set goals, study, analyze, invest, buy financial products, and do other time-consuming stuff on your own. Or take time to find someone you can work with who can help you make it happen.

At the risk of scaring off people who resist hard work, we'll bluntly state it's tough finding a financial professional. But think about it. Ideally, you'll work with this person for a long time, and you will be dealing with a very personal topic—your money. Throw in factors that neither you nor the person you hire can control, such as unpredictable market swings, and it's a tricky relationship. One that must be built on trust and mutual respect.

To that end, you're going to want to screen possible candidates thoroughly. You may want to get referrals from friends, relatives, work colleagues, or total strangers. And when we say total strangers, we're referring to ads you may see in your local area. But don't limit your search to professionals where you live, particularly if you're in a small town with few choices. You can establish a business relationship with someone in another city or state, if necessary. Once you have a few candidates in mind, set up interviews and ask each of them the following questions. Write down the answers for comparison purposes, and don't let candidates off the hook if they try to circle around a question without answering it.

1. What is your background, education, and experience? Any licenses, registrations, certifications? How do you stay current in the financial services industry?

2. If this is a second career for you, what did you do previously? (It's no secret people build on their experience, so if the financial professional used to be an accountant, you might get extra income tax–planning tips. A lawyer? Perhaps your pro will be savvy with estate planning. A teacher? You might get more lessons and background information to help you make financial decisions from a former teacher.)

3. Can you tell me one of your success stories?

4. How about a time when you really messed something up? (Let's face it, mistakes get made, and fessing up is about honesty and a willingness to learn. A person may not fall for the latest fad or supposed sure thing if he or she has been there, done that.)

5. How do you get paid? Be specific. (See what we've got to say below about how financial pros earn their keep. If you're screening a pro who charges a percentage of your assets, for example, but you don't have that much in assets, it may not be a good match, depending on the expectations of both of you.)

6. How much experience do you have working with clients whose income and circumstances are similar to mine?

7. My most urgent concerns are _____. Are there any conflicts between my interests and yours? How would you tackle that? (If you're a risk taker and you're interviewing someone who only believes in fixed investments, a long-term relationship may not be in the cards.)

8. Can I meet any other people in your office who would be working on my plan?

9. Are there other people or resources you might have access to on complex areas such as tax planning, individual stock selection, insurance policy evaluation, and estate planning? Can I meet with them?

10. If you sell insurance, investments, and other financial products, what companies do you represent? If not, can you help me obtain them if we determine I need them?

Review your notes from each interview, and make your decision based on how the prospective professionals answered the questions. Honestly consider how they talked to you. If their answers don't make sense to you, the person probably doesn't make sense *for* you. It's critical that you be confident with your choice and completely able to trust your professional, so don't feel bad for not hiring someone because you didn't have a rapport with them. Once this arduous task is complete, the real fun begins.

A Word about Designations

While the letters behind the names look good, they don't guarantee good advice and certainly not higher returns on any investments you may make. They do, however, let you know the professional you're dealing with has passed exams, undergone certification, and made the effort to obtain credentials. A certified financial planner (CFP) has a minimum of three years of experience and continuing education under his or her belt. A chartered life underwriter (CLU) or chartered financial consultant (ChFC) is generally a life insurance agent with additional training and certification. A CPA is a certified public accountant, and if the CPA is also a personal financial specialist (PFS), he or she has several hundred hours of financial planning experience. Steer clear ASAP of anyone claiming the designation PRL (Pure Rotten Luck).

HOW THEY EARN THEIR KEEP

Let's face it, you're going to pay for financial advice. It's a fact of life, much like paying to get a haircut. When you hire a professional to cut your hair, you're paying for his or her experience and training but also for the peace of mind you get knowing you aren't trimming those bangs yourself. You get what you pay for if you want something for free, as the saying goes.

Until recently there were basically four ways for financial professionals to earn their living: by charging a fee, a percentage of assets, earning a commission, or some combination of the other three.

- Fee-only pros charge either an hourly rate or a flat fee for their advice and take no commissions on the financial products you end up buying. Without the pressure to sell, sell, sell, they may devote more time to devising your plan and may be less likely to recommend a steady stream of solutions you need to buy.

- Commission-only pros, just as the name implies, depend on commissions on the products they sell to earn a living. They aren't compensated if you don't buy something from them.
- Fee-plus-commission pros charge a fee for the plan and then get a commission on the financial products they sell. Once you've paid for your plan, you can buy the recommended products from the professional or look elsewhere.
- Wealth managers typically charge a percentage of assets under management to strategize for you. They may work only with those clients who have a high net worth, however, and then charge an annual rate of up to about 1 percent of the client's assets.

A new trend among a growing number of financial professionals is to offer their services for a one-time financial plan. This new philosophy caters to do-it-yourselfers who want some help or need to solve a particular financial planning situation. Say you lose your job, inherit a windfall, or want to save for a college education. If this sounds like the sort of planning assistance you want, you can determine in the interviewing process whether a professional you're considering is willing to work within these parameters, but be mindful of one common problem. Once you get the plan, there's nobody there to ensure that you follow through, and most procrastinators we know don't exactly thrive in an environment like that.

There are pros and cons to each method, which makes your screening process all the more important. There are a few commission-only pros out there who are fixated on their bottom line more than anything else and may be tempted to offer products you don't necessarily need. These types give the industry a bad name. If you pay for a fee-only pro's time, on the other hand, but don't buy products from him or her, you may have to spend even more time seeking out products that can help you achieve your goals. These are extreme scenarios, mind you, so don't expect the worst. Just use caution when deciding which route will work best for you.

IT'S NOT THE END, IT'S THE BEGINNING

Financial planning is not something you do once and then forget about it. If you thought that, forget about it. We may be nearing the end of this chapter, but if the prevailing wisdom of financial planning holds true, it's just the beginning. That's probably because everything in this book is financial planning. If your goal is to buy a house, you'll need to check your credit rating before applying for a loan. Improving your credit may involve getting out of debt. And saving money may only be possible once you've created a budget you can live by. And then there's the whole issue of risk protection—insuring not just your ability to earn an income but also your home (and your life, if you're so inclined). Oh yes, and the more assets you acquire, the more essential it is for you to do some estate planning. At least write a will! See? Pick a goal, any goal, and you'll find that several chapters in this book apply to it. Except maybe if your goal is to stay right where you are and not make any progress.

Once you've gone through the hassle of creating some sort of financial plan—with or without a financial professional—you need to put it into action and review it regularly. The more you revisit your plan, the more you'll begin to consider it before making huge financial decisions. And small ones too. You'll be less apt to make rash spending choices and more inclined to balance decisions based on how they fit with your overall plan. As life changes occur—marriage, children, job loss, relocation, you name it—you will naturally modify your plan to include them. Become knowledgeable and remain active in your money matters. Because your money matters.

2

Do You Need a Kick in the Budget?

I t's both amazing and not surprising at all how often we're asked variations of the question, "How on earth can I possibly save any money?" How can you save enough money for retirement when you find yourself digging in the seat cushions for loose change between paychecks? Good questions both, and you aren't the only one asking them. People just like you are looking for answers that make their money situation more manageable. And people just like you are looking for ways to make it happen without creating a dreaded budget.

And we don't blame them. There is a long list of reasons to avoid budgeting. Budgets are boring and bad for your complexion. Like a new relationship, they demand a lot of attention in the beginning, but the results won't be known for a while and there are no guarantees. Besides, being honest about your own bottom line can be uncomfortable—it's what some would call "too much information." You may have avoided the budgeting process because you're afraid you won't be able to get all the numbers to line up in perfect rows. Well, that's not what a budget is for. A budget helps you get on track and stay on track with your financial goals. How's that for too much information?

If your budget, or lack thereof, is weighing on the minuscule part of your mind you've allocated to money issues, we're here to help. In this chapter alone, we've got tasks that will make you wish you'd bought that how-to book on dental hygiene for pet sharks. Our spending record and spending plan worksheets will remind you quickly why you have raised procrastination to a high art form. Throw in a thoughtful discussion of the difference between your gross and net income, and we'll understand if you want to let your pet shark use this book as a chew toy. Just remember to put a bookmark in this page, so you can find your place when you're ready to make some progress with your financial life.

FIRST, YOU SPEND

We have reached the point in this chapter when, against our own better judgment, we're going to ask you to do something. It's time to create a spending record, which is not to say you're going to set some new records in your spending. The fun part of doing a spending record is that you don't actually change your spending habits—at least for now. Just spend what you've been spending, but keep track of every penny you spend for a month. If you've got a partner in life, we recommend you work on this project together, especially if that person happens to be, say, an accountant. Or at least not afraid of numbers. And if the suggestion that you track your spending for an entire month makes you nervous, how about tracking it for a week? Nothing's going to change if you don't start somewhere.

Poll

Would your prefer to be physically fit or fiscally fit?

Physically Fit	43%
(I want a buff body)	
Fiscally Fit	54%
(I want a buff budget)	
Neither	3%
(I don't want to think about it)	

Poll conducted by ihatefinancialplanning.com

SEE HOW YOUR SPENDING COMPARES

Allow us to present a simple guideline of average spending. You're truly above average if you notice that the percentages don't add up to 100 percent. It's because budgeting and spending are not a perfect science. And please don't go off on us about the difference between math and science. Just take a look at these numbers and think about how they may compare to yours.

Housing (25% to 30%)

Rent/Mortgage

Property tax

Repairs/Improvements

Savings and Investments (5% to 15%)

Emergency savings account

Retirement savings

Debt (0% to ??)

Credit cards

School loans

Home equity loans

Major purchases payments

Utilities (5% to 10%)

Gas/Electric

Telephone/Internet/Cell phone

Water

Garbage

Cable/Satellite

Transportation (6% to 30%)

Car loan/Lease payments

Gas

Insurance

Maintenance/Repairs

Public transportation

Food (15% to 30%)

Groceries

Eating out

School lunch

Pet food

Medical (2% to 12%)

Insurance

Prescriptions/Medicines

Doctor/Dentist/Chiropractor

Hospital bills

Clothing (3% to 10%)

Purchases

Dry Cleaning/Laundry

Alterations

Necessities (2% to 10%)

Child care

Home furnishings

Hair care

Toiletries/Cosmetics

Postage/Stationery

Recreation and Entertainment (2% to 6%)

Games/Hobbies

School activity fees

Club dues

Special events

Miscellaneous (1% to 4%)

Everything else

And more

There are a few different ways to create a spending record. You're in luck if you have one of the popular software programs that records all your expenses, checks, and whatnot. All you have to do is hit a few report commands and—Presto!—you've got a spending record. This assumes that you have been diligently using the software to plug in your expenses on a regular basis, which we know from experience is a big assumption.

If you're not so software equipped, you're part of the majority. Simply keep a one-month record using the spending record worksheet that follows. We've included the typical categories and left spaces for you to add some of your own that fall outside of the "typical" kinds of expenses. Either use the worksheet in this book or the interactive one at our Web site. It saves your work securely, and you can update your work every time you spend.

Once you've got a month's worth of spending recorded, keep going. Track your spending record for three months or a full year if you dare. It goes back to what we said about budgeting not being a one-time ordeal. Playing this game for several months will help you track those expenses that don't occur monthly but require some very real coin, such as occasional car repairs, special medical or dental bills, year-end tax payments, quarterly insurance or utility payments. It's important to add these as categories to your spending record. You might as well

Spending Record Worksheet

Your Spending Record	Monthly	Yearly	Your Spending Record	Monthly	Yearly
HOUSING (Probably your biggest outlay)			**CHARITY**		
Mortgage/rent			Donations		
Real estate taxes			**MEDICAL/DENTAL**		
Gas			Premiums		
Electric			Copays		
Water/sewer			Prescriptions		
Phone/Internet			Vitamins		
Cable/satellite			**INSURANCE**		
Trash collection			Auto		
Home repairs/maintenance			Life		
AUTO (usually a close second)			Health		
Car loan			Home		
Gasoline			Disability		
License plates			Long-term care		
Repairs/maintenance			**PERSONAL (It adds up)**		
OTHER WHEELS			Haircuts, etc.		
Bus			Dry cleaning/laundry		

Train							
FOOD							
Groceries							
Eating out							
Work lunch							
CLOTHES							
Adult(s)							
Kid(s)							
ENTERTAINMENT							
Movies/sporting events							
Recreation							
Other							
KID'S ACTIVITIES (if you've got 'em)							
School							
School lunch							
Lessons							
Camp							
Sports							

Gifts							
Subscriptions							
SAVINGS							
Retirement savings *							
Vacations							
Emergency account							
DEBT PAYMENTS							
Student loans							
Home equity loans							
Credit card							
Credit card							
OTHER							
TOTAL							

*If your retirement savings are deducted from your paycheck, you don't need to include that amount here.

write them down because you end up spending the money anyway. Or at the very least, you panic about where the money is going to come from. And for the record, we're aware that we referred to budgeting as a game earlier in this paragraph. We're nothing without sarcasm.

IT CAN BE GROSS TO THINK ABOUT YOUR NET INCOME

Once you have a sense of where your money is going, it's important to balance that with how much money you actually earn. It's tempting to tell yourself, "I make $45,000 per year, so that must mean I've got 45K to spend." Allow us to warn you to save comments like that for the voices inside your head because it doesn't work that way. One of the most common budgeting mistakes, in fact, is to confuse your salary with your take-home pay. Of course, you *know* that income taxes, health insurance premiums, retirement savings, and the like are deducted from your check before you actually see the money, but you'd probably like to forget it.

Do yourself a favor and consider your actual take-home pay using the nifty net income worksheet that follows. You can then easily beef up the numbers next time you get a big raise.

WE'VE GOT A CALCULATOR FOR THAT

We're really stepping out on a limb here, but these budget worksheets just might get you in the mood for more. Consider our Balance Your Checkbook calculator, for example. Sometimes you don't know how much money you've got because you don't bother with the basics. Punch a few numbers into the calculator, and your checkbook register just might start making sense. Find it and other calculators at ihatefinancialplanning.com.

IT DOESN'T HAVE TO BE A STRETCH TO MAKE ENDS MEET

We wish we could say all the heavy lifting is done, but that isn't the case. If you have gotten this far, though, there's more incentive to keep going than to quit now. You may resist and you definitely procrastinate, but you don't quit. Do you? The good news is, you have some idea of how you're spending your money, and you have a solid number for your net income. Well, calling your income solid may be a stretch, but

Net Income Worksheet

MONTHLY INCOME		MONTHLY WITHHOLDING	
Your gross salary		Federal income tax	
Spouse's gross salary		State income tax	
Interest income		FICA	
Stock and bond income		Medical insurance	
Child support/alimony		Dental insurance	
Other income		Retirement plan	
Other income		Other deduction #1	
		Other deduction #2	
TOTAL GROSS INCOME		TOTAL WITHHOLDING	
		TOTAL GROSS INCOME	
		− TOTAL WITHHOLDING	
		= TOTAL NET INCOME	

you get the idea. Now all you've got to do is convert those numbers into a spending plan. When you understand how much money you really have—after taxes and the other nickels and dimes deducted from your income—and how you are really spending it, you'll understand just what you've got to work with for your budget. It's a project that will take time. But it's time well spent to benefit someone who's very important in your life. (YOU!)

Use the spending plan worksheet on pages 36 and 37 to create your spending plan. It's not perfect—you'll ignore some of the categories and may need to add a few of your own. Just use the categories that apply to you and fill in the amounts you need to spend on each. Change the categories and amounts as your situation changes. Ink smudges and messy papers are encouraged. The intent of a spending plan is to help you prepare for both the expenses you expect and those you don't anticipate. You'll be ready for your monthly energy bill and quarterly insurance premium and annual license plates. And with any luck at all, you'll have some cash ready for vacation. Unless, of course, the water heater rusts out the same week your pet stubs its paw.

YOU, TOO, CAN GET SWEPT UP BY DENIAL RIVER

It would surprise absolutely no one for us to state that budgeting is the gross underbelly of financial freedom. You know the task itself stinks, but you also know it's worth doing even if it makes your clothes smell and your hands messy. If you've gotten this far, you probably have also told yourself a few tales in the process. Stories such as "my cell phone is practically free" or "I only buy gifts once a year" or the tell-all, "I hardly ever eat out." If you made cracks like this to yourself during the spending record or spending plan phase of this odious exercise, we hope you were able to keep a straight face. We're here to tell you that those little white lies are a form of denial that will put your best budgetary intentions to the test. If you budget for a $29.99 monthly cell phone bill but you're actually spending $75 with fees, taxes, multiple phones, extra minutes, and phone company whims, you'll be off by $500 at the end of the year (assuming you can keep the story going that long). And yes, the whole denial thing does include, but is not limited to, any incidental cash you spend on your favorite hobbies. Your need to justify a very real expense by acting as though it doesn't exist is counterproductive to say the least. Just cut yourself some slack and write down realistic numbers in your plan.

TO RECOVER FROM BUDGET BINGES, ADMIT YOU BLEW IT

It may be a stretch for us to assume you've read this far because you are actually following the steps to better budgeting. But we're just that optimistic. You have recorded your spending, tallied your net income, and begun creating a plan. What to do, then, if the wheels come off? Even the most loyal budget devotees experience budget binges from time to time. If only we knew any of those people firsthand, we'd get a testimonial. Let's just say we have a "friend" who has followed the steps to better budgeting. Betty recorded her spending on our handy worksheet that helps her see just where her hard-earned dollars are going. Then she tallied her net income to gauge the difference between her take-home pay and her takeaway. Just when Betty was getting comfortable with the numbers in the subsequent spending plan, her sister had a baby, which led to cash flow problems for Auntie Betty. Her cash flowed for airfare, flowers delivered to the maternity ward, baby gifts, a digital camera, and a brag book for photos. When she returned from welcoming her nephew into the world, Betty feared her budget would never bounce back and she gave up on the project. If you've tumbled off the budget wagon, don't give up. The worst thing you can do when you slip and spend money on a shopping spree that's been designated for regular bills is walk away from your budget altogether. Research shows that could lead to subsequent trips to the shopping mall. Just take a deep breath and move forward. It may take you a month or two (maybe nine) to get back on track, but you will be glad you did.

PAY YOURSELF FIRST AND OTHER CLICHÉS

One of the main objectives of budgeting is to achieve the nirvana that comes with having more income than outgo each month. What you do

Spending Plan Worksheet

Your Spending Plan	Monthly	Yearly	Your Spending Plan	Monthly	Yearly
HOUSING (Probably your biggest outlay)			**CHARITY**		
Mortgage/rent			Donations		
Real estate taxes			**MEDICAL/DENTAL**		
Gas			Premiums		
Electric			Copays		
Water/sewer			Prescriptions		
Phone/Internet			Vitamins		
Cable/satellite			**INSURANCE**		
Trash collection			Auto		
Home repairs/maintenance			Life		
AUTO (usually a close second)			Health		
Car loan			Home		
Gasoline			Disability		
License plates			Long-term care		
Repairs/maintenance			**PERSONAL**		
OTHER WHEELS			Haircuts, etc.		
Bus			Dry cleaning/laundry		

Train

FOOD

Groceries

Eating out

Work lunch

CLOTHES

Adult(s)

Kid(s)

ENTERTAINMENT

Movies/sporting events

Recreation

Other

KID'S ACTIVITIES (if you've got 'em)

School

School lunch

Lessons

Camp

Sports

Gifts

Subscriptions

SAVINGS

Retirement savings

Vacations

Emergency account

DEBT PAYMENTS

Student loans

Home equity loans

Credit card

Credit card

Credit card

Credit card

OTHER

TOTAL

with the extra cash is your business, but we highly recommend that you save some. Put that money to work for your future, and only then will you appreciate true nirvana, O wise one. The most important regular payment you should be making is to yourself. No matter what your age or stage in life, saving for retirement should be a priority, but you also should take steps to be prepared for those unexpected expenses that so readily knock your budget out of whack. (We're going to tackle the topic of saving for retirement in Chapter 7.)

If you don't have an active savings account, open one. There are all sorts of online banking options available if you have an aversion to bricks and mortar. Or save the old-fashioned way at a bank in your neighborhood, although we're fairly sure you won't be able to convince the tellers to manually type your deposits in a passbook like they did when you were a kid. Squeeze whatever amount you can out of your spending plan and put some of the money in your savings account every payday. Better yet, set up direct deposit so you don't need to think about it with each paycheck. Then, don't touch the money until at least a half dozen monthly interest payments have been added to your account. You might actually enjoy watching your money grow, if only a little at a time, and skip the part where you can withdraw money from your account.

The point of this exercise is that you'll end up with money you didn't know you had for times you didn't know you'd need it. Some call it emergency savings and advise that you keep three to six months' salary in the account. Our experience is that if you pressure yourself into saving an exact amount equal to half the year's pay, you might be overwhelmed and give up before you even get started. We strongly discourage that sort of behavior, so all we ask is that you diligently add money to your account, give it time to grow, and replenish the funds if you need to withdraw cash. That way you're prepared for life's little emergencies—including the budget binge we mentioned earlier. What's important is that you put the money away consistently, and then tap it when you absolutely must. Ergo, what puts the "emergency" in emergency savings account. The success of any long-range savings plan depends less on the rate of return than on consistently putting money away and leaving it there.

We sure make it sound easy, don't we? If you're having one of those "why didn't I think of that?" moments in which you want to knock us upside the head, just remember what got you this far in the first place. You know you need to do something about your money situation. You should be commended for at least giving a glance to your spending habits and how they'll shape your future spending plans. We're just reinforcing the positive steps you've already made by giving a plug to our favorite activity: saving.

EVEN YOU CAN FOLLOW THESE STEPS

We understand if you have successfully resisted the budgeting process so far. It isn't fun to work on a budget, and what's the payoff? Seeing in black and white that you're spending more than you have? Not much reward in that. If you're determined to skip the exercises in this chapter that have you creating a spending record and converting it into a spending plan, that's fine by us. Just do yourself a favor and follow even a few of these steps. But be warned that you could end up making progress in your daily financial life.

1. Change your due date. It might be easier to create some semblance of a budget if your bills are due near payday. Most utility companies and banks honor your request to change a due date as long as you're a customer in good standing. The key is to make the request, which involves some effort on your part.
2. Create an occasion. Pick the same day each month to pay your bills and review your expenses. But don't make budgeting worse than it already is by trying to balance your checkbook the same day all your other chores are hanging in the balance.
3. Reduce your debt. If you can't pay for current purchases with current spending, you'll never gain control of your finances. Subtract credit card purchases from your checking account, so the money's there when the bill arrives. We've got a whole chapter on debt because it's so vital to your financial health.
4. Put saving on the top of your spending list. Your assets will grow faster if you view savings as an expense just like the phone bill. You wouldn't even consider not having a telephone, and it

should be the same for a savings account. Start saving regularly—even a few dollars each paycheck—and it will become an expense you take for granted.

5. It doesn't need to be boring. Plan for something you want, like a toy or a weekend getaway. That way you'll have something to look forward to—and cash to pay for it.

6. Follow the money trail. Track your spending and expenses for one measly month. How hard can it be to write down what you spend in a small notebook? Once you get the hang of it, you might just find yourself writing those numbers in categories. Nobody's gonna know what you're doing, so nobody's gonna care that you've changed your mind about a budget.

7. Make a list and check it twice. Shop with a list and buy only what's on the list. You probably don't have time for browsing anyway; so focus on your list and leave those impulse buys on the shelf.

8. Cut costs wherever you can. For example, use a prepaid calling card. You'll avoid hefty surcharges and still be in touch with friends and family. Be sure to read the fine print, though, and only use prepaid cards that don't charge connection fees.

9. Involve everyone in your household in the budget. Money is worth discussing, and it pays if all the people who spend it know where it's going, going, gone.

10. Stay ahead of the holidays. Keep your eye open all year round for items on sale, instead of full price during the height of the holiday shopping season. Avoid last-minute overspending. Plus, limit how much you are going to spend and stick to it.

11. You'll be pleasantly surprised how important your budget will become if you just give it a chance. But if the "B" word gets stuck in your throat, think of it as "optimal spending."

Budgeting isn't a test you pass or fail. It's simply the best tool you can use to gain control of your money situation. A working budget is essential to your fiscal well-being. It's a "working" budget because it's going to take time to see the results. And those results will be as fluid as your life, which means you're working with a moving target. If you did the homework, you may have the numbers to support your theory that you spend more than you make. We'll let that be our little secret. On the other hand, if you jumped through our spending and net income worksheet hoops with money to spare, that will stay between us too. This budget stuff is personal, after all. And annoying. And, oh yes, quite helpful as you set out to make your way in your own financial world. That's our way of begging you to turn the page and keep moving ahead.

3

The Good, the Bad, and the Ugly

Technically, debt is neither good nor bad. It's merely a financial tool. Like any tool, when it's used properly debt can be powerful, but when it's abused, it can be destructive. If you've ever sliced your finger while cutting a bagel with the wrong knife, you know what we mean. There are types of debt that can be advantageous to your long-term financial situation, but there are also types of debt that can have an outrageous effect on your life. Some debt starts out seeming harmless enough, but pretty soon it's wreaking havoc on your emotions, relationships, and general effectiveness on the job. The job of living.

In this chapter we're going to cover which sorts of debt may work with you and which could work against you. Plus we've got a nifty exercise you can use to figure your debt-to-income ratio, a number that won't impress anyone in your social circle, but you can use it to gauge your current situation and where to go from here. Let this be a warning that said debt-to-income ratio can only result if and when you solve a math problem. Don't worry, we'll walk you through it. And we'll walk you through some steps you can take to regain control of your debt if it's already wreaking the havoc we mentioned in the previous paragraph.

GOOD DEBT WORKS FOR YOU

There are certain times when buying on credit is not only reasonable but potentially quite smart. That sort of debt includes debt used for an investment where your gain is greater than the interest you pay, tax-efficient debt, and debt used to make investments in equipment or materials that can help you make gains economically, say, to build your small business.

Let's take a look at debt used to purchase an appreciating asset. What we're talking about here is using leverage to purchase, say, a home. Another form of good debt is loans for higher education, still one of the best investments you can make. Many families can't afford the cost of sending their kids to college—Ivy League or bush league. To borrow money for tuition, room, board, and pizza delivery is completely acceptable. And depending on what kind of pizza, a great source for new college friends.

USING CREDIT CARDS WISELY

Believe it or not, credit cards can fall on the good side of the debt coin. They can provide flexibility and convenience in money management and can make it possible to have emergency funds to cover the unexpected (car repairs, medical expenses, emergency shoe sales) when your cash supply is razor thin. OK, the part about the shoe sale is a joke. It's convenient to use credit cards to purchase stuff, either in person, over the phone, or online. It's so nice and easy. But there's the rub, or should we say the swipe. It's too easy for some. The trick is to see the forest (your needs) for the trees (your wants) and then manage the debt smartly.

You probably have at least a few credit cards, and you may even pay them off every month, although that would put you in the minority. When used wisely, credit cards can be a convenient financial tool. If you doubt us, just try booking an airline ticket or renting a car without one. And rumor has it that organized individuals use their credit card statements as a handy chronological record of purchases, both big and small. We wouldn't know about that firsthand. Alas, credit cards are a fact of life, but they don't need to control yours. Just keep these tips in mind the next time you receive a colorful letter exclaiming that you've been preapproved for a fixed-rate card with no credit limit offering cash rebates on every purchase:

- A fixed interest rate only stays fixed until the credit card issuer changes it, which could be today. So beware.
- Credit cards with rebates and other perks may have high annual percentage rates (APR) and annual fees. If you carry a balance and therefore incur interest charges, the rebate may not be worth the cost to you. Also, be sure to read the fine print. Credit card companies love it when you forget to play by their rules.
- Try deducting each transaction from your checkbook balance, so the money is there when the credit card bill arrives and you can pay it in full.
- If you carry a balance, new purchases aren't given a grace period. Interest begins to grow the minute you make the purchase.
- If you're only paying part of your balance, check how the interest is calculated and what the cost will be in dollars. Call the issuer if you need help. And then call us when you figure out how to escape those nasty phone trees.
- Make a credit card payment even if you get an offer to skip a month. Finance charges will continue to accrue even in that skipped month.
- When you make a balance transfer, usually to a card with lower interest, you may need to make a payment to the old account to keep it current until the new account is set up. This is just a reminder to check your due date on the old account.
- Speaking of due dates, you can ask your creditors to change your due date to correspond with payday, or when you normally pay bills, or any other day that makes paying your credit card bill more convenient. We tried requesting February 29 in non-leap years, but our creditors didn't bite.
- Ask your credit union if it offers credit cards. The interest rate may be lower and it may be easier to qualify.
- Check your statement as soon as it arrives against receipts. In other words, keep your receipts. Contact the credit card issuer immediately with any errors.
- When canceling a credit card account, follow directions exactly as the issuer requires. It may save a headache or two down the road.

COPY YOUR CARDS

Everyone always warns you to cancel your credit cards immediately after they have been lost or stolen, but how are you supposed to do that if you don't have the cards with the toll-free numbers on the back? Here's a simple task even you can handle. Make photocopies of everything in your wallet. Don't bother copying the cash, if you're carrying any. But copy the front and back of your driver's license, credit cards, calling cards and so on. That way if your wallet does a disappearing act, you'll have quick access to the toll-free numbers you need to report it to creditors and cancel your accounts. Assuming that you keep the photocopy in a safe place. We've got more on identity protection in Chapter 11.

HOME EQUITY LOANS ARE SOMEWHERE IN THE MIDDLE

Think of a home equity loan as a fence in the middle of a region called Debt Territory. It's the sort of loan that could be considered "good debt" or "bad debt," depending on which side of the fence you're standing. In the good debt category, home equity loans are available at lower interest rates than most credit cards, depending on your credit record (see Chapter 4 for way more than you care to know about this). The interest you pay on a home equity loan also may be deductible from your income taxes if you itemize your deductions. It's the tax-efficient debt we mentioned a few pages ago.

How, then, can a home equity loan possibly be considered bad debt? Well, people inclined to spend more than they can afford to pay tend to be slow learners. Say you get a home equity loan and use it to pay off credit card debt, after which, you charge up all your credit cards again and end up losing your house when creditors come calling for payment.

Now, that's what we call bad debt. Also, the lending industry may tempt you with borrowing more than your home is actually worth. This could work against you should you need to sell your house for any reason. If you are considering a home equity loan, we would simply caution you to take it seriously. You may need to change your spending behavior if you want the loan to remain in the good debt category.

BAD DEBT WORKS AGAINST YOU

Now let's think about the flip side of the debt coin. Even the word "debt" has a letter in it you don't need, just like half the stuff you buy on credit. And therein lies just one of the aspects of debt that is bad for us. You know it's bad debt when it's not a matter of *if* you've maxed out your credit cards, but *how many*. You know it's bad debt when you ask the department store to increase your credit limit so you can buy all

---

FINANCIAL JARGON MADE EASY

This talk about home equity loans brings us to a vocabulary lesson. What's the difference between a home equity loan and a home equity line of credit? Good question. A *home equity loan* is a lump sum with a fixed interest rate that's paid off over a set period of time in equal monthly payments. Once you've got the loan, you can't add to it. A *home equity line of credit* (bankers like to refer to HELOCs when talking to customers) works more like a credit card, in that after you have been approved for it, you can borrow up to a set limit for the life of the loan. Or you can borrow nothing at all. It's just a line of credit against your home that you can use if and when you need to.

Flip to the back of the book for more jargon.

---

new appliances before you've paid for the riding lawn mower you bought last year. And yes, it's bad debt when you buy something for instant gratification even if it will be months before you're able to pay it off. "The long weekend to Mazatlan was just what I needed. I'll worry about the airfare and hotel bill later."

CASH ADVANCES ONLY PROPEL YOUR DEBT

We already talked about ways to use credit cards wisely, but there are several ways to use them unwisely too. For instance, cash advances. It's tempting and convenient to take a cash advance on your credit card when money is tight and the loose change in your pocket won't cover cab fare or a night on the town, much less both. We're here to advise you to resist the temptation. Cash advances are accompanied by fees and ridiculously high interest rates. We're talking rates that are several points higher than you're already paying. Furthermore, there's no grace period on cash advances, so you're paying interest before the cab driver gets you home.

Any "checks" you receive from your credit card company are usually handled as cash advances. It seems these credit card checks arrive in the same pile of mail as the bill from your podiatrist. You may consider it good timing, but rest assured your credit card lender views it as quick income from an unsuspecting customer. The hefty fees and huge interest rates of cash advances will apply to the checks, so don't cash 'em. Believe us, those fees will hurt more than any ingrown toenail.

If you must get a cash advance for whatever reason, avoid using an ATM if possible because the financial institution that owns the machine will undoubtedly charge an additional fee for the middleman convenience of relaying cash from the credit card company to you. The phrase "adding insult to injury" was first expressed by a guy who got stuck owing a huge fee on top of the cash advance he withdrew to pay the bill on another credit card.

PAYDAY LOANS DON'T PAY

One form of debt that's particularly ugly is the payday loan. You may not recognize the name, but these cash-advances are readily available through check-cashing stores, local banks, and online via wire transfers. A payday loan is basically a postdated check or wire transfer. It's easy to obtain and almost impossible to repay due to high interest and transaction fees that multiply like rabbits. Say you're desperate for cash and go to a check-cashing store for a $100 loan. You write a check for $125 and date it with the date of your next paycheck. The lender keeps the $25 fee off the top and gives you a hundred bucks. The fee varies by lender, but it's really interest on a loan at an annual percentage rate of anywhere from 300 percent to 1,000 percent, depending on how much the fee is and how long it takes you to pay back the loan. Assuming you pay it back when you get your next paycheck, you're already behind for the next pay period by that $125. At that rate you'll never catch up.

Unfortunately, payday lenders rely on the fact that many customers return on payday to renew their loan and pay more fees. The Consumer Federation of America tells the sad tale of a man who couldn't pay back his $400 loan and renewed it 24 times in 15 months, eventually paying $1,612. Another borrowed $150 and paid more than $1,000 in fees over

---

Poll

Which word describes your debt situation?

Nonexistent	13%
Smart (home mortgage, college loans)	19%
Incidental (pay off cards every month)	16%
Manageable (making noticeable progress)	30%
Overwhelming	22%

Poll of visitors to ihatefinancialplanning.com

---

a six-month period without paying on the original 150 smacks. When you're short on cash it's tempting to get a quick loan and tell yourself you'll pay it off quickly—as in, as soon as you get paid. But be wary or you could find yourself stuck in a vicious cycle of fees.

BANKRUPTCY BITES

Sheila (fake name, real person) has a winning idea for a business she'd like to start. She's done the research and picked a region of the country where her product would sell. She's written a rock-solid business plan. Trouble is, when she visits a bank about financing, personal bankers run the other way. No matter how many banks she visits, it's always the same result. Sheila's wearing the dreaded "BANKRUPTCY" stamp across her forehead, you see, and banks fear her condition may reoccur.

Nearly seven years ago, Sheila was struggling to settle in a new community. She had a job but she also had sizeable debt. In her words, her debt "totaled $13,000 but it might as well have been $13 million." Sheila was swimming in a pool full of debt collectors and rude creditors. On the advice of a trusted friend, Sheila filed for bankruptcy. And her life has been a financial nightmare ever since. Aside from the business plan she can't pursue, Sheila has to deal with the reality of her decision every day. She was unable to refinance her car loan because the bank wouldn't touch her. Sheila could get credit cards, but the interest rate she'd pay on balances is almost 30 percent. Therefore, she's chosen to pay cash for everything in an effort to minimize the damage to her reputation. Not exactly convenient.

Sheila knows better than most that money problems are hardly ever about the money. It's easy to see that when you consider that the most common reasons for consumer bankruptcy are unemployment, overwhelming medical expenses, seriously overextended credit, marital problems, and other unforeseen expenses. Insurmountable debt is what's left behind after the unimaginable hits too close to home.

If bankruptcy seems like the only solution for you, do yourself a favor and don't reach that conclusion by yourself. Debt has a way of making people withdraw to protect their pride, but don't go through this alone. Consult with a nonprofit credit counseling service before making an appointment with a bankruptcy lawyer. You may also find more information on the Internet. A quick Internet search could uncover various chat rooms and forums full of people who have firsthand knowledge of what bankruptcy has meant to them. Who knows, you might run into Sheila.

FINANCIAL JARGON MADE EASY

There are two types of bankruptcy for individuals. *Chapter 7 bankruptcy* wipes out credit card balances, medical bills, and other debts, with the exception of recent income taxes and student loans. Debtors must give up most of their assets—assuming they have some—which are sold to repay creditors. States laws determine how much property bankrupt citizens can retain, but they can usually keep company-sponsored retirement plans, a car, future earnings, and personal items, except expensive jewelry and other valuables. In most cases, IRA accounts are not protected. Most states limit the amount of home equity that will be protected from creditors in Chapter 7. You might be forced to sell your home if it's worth more than your state's limit. Delaware doesn't protect any home equity, while Florida, Iowa, Kansas, South Dakota, and Texas let you keep your home no matter what. You'll need to check the bankruptcy law in your state.

Instead of forcing you to give up your assets, *Chapter 13 bankruptcy* requires that you submit a plan to the court explaining how you intend to pay off your debts in the next three to five years. If the plan is approved, you pay a bankruptcy trustee a set amount each month for distribution to creditors. This method only works if you have enough income to make the monthly payment. And that payment usually comes out of your paycheck, so your employer will learn of your bankruptcy.

DEBT-TO-INCOME RATIO

Now that we've tackled an overview of the good, bad, and ugly of debt, let's focus on your particular situation. If debt is merely a financial tool, how are you using it? An easy way to get a snapshot of your current financial standing is to calculate your debt-to-income ratio. We understand that "easy" and "calculate" are contradictory words to the math-impaired, and story problems are the worst. Before you break out in a sweat or toss this book aside in disgust, grab a calculator and breathe deeply.

Your debt-to-income ratio is a number that reflects the amount of your debt (excluding mortgage or rent payments) in relation to the amount you take home monthly. Lenders use it when considering your credit status. You may have overheard them in conversations that go something like this: "Should we loan this schmuck money for a new car?" "Well, that depends on how the debt-to-income ratio looks when magnified 29 times under a microscope." There we go throwing science in an already complicated equation. Let's just stick to the basics. Say your monthly take-home pay is $2,400 and you're making loan and credit card payments of $650 per month. You've got a debt-to-income ratio of 27 percent (650 divided by 2,400 equals 0.27).

What Counts as Income?

Depending on your job, figuring your income can be tricky. We're looking for a monthly figure after all deductions for income taxes, employee benefits, and the like. If you're paid every other week, multiply your take-home pay by 26, then divide by 12. If your income is inconsistent, you can get an estimate by dividing last year's annual take-home pay by 12. Remember to also include conservative averages of tips, commissions, and bonuses; earnings from dividends and interest; and regular income from child support and/or alimony.

What Counts as Debt in This Equation?

If you're like us—and we know we are—you're a debt veteran. But just what is classified as debt when you're doing actual math? It's not always cut-and-dried. For example, your house or rent payment, which is probably a big chunk of monthly change, doesn't count. Neither do ordinary monthly bills for utilities and such. Just be sure to count these things:

- Car payments
- Credit card payments (if you carry a balance from month to month)
- Loan payments
- Bank/credit union loans
- Student loan payments
- Other loans/credit accounts
- Payments for past medical care

Now Do the Math

Once you've got all the numbers you need, it's time for a calculation. Please, hold your applause until the numbers have been crunched. Divide your total monthly debt payment by your total monthly take-home pay income. The answer you get will be your debt-to-income ratio percentage. Visual learners may benefit from an example.

Debt-to-Income Ratio

Monthly Debt:	$400
Monthly Take-Home Pay:	$2,000
400/2000 =	.20
Debt-to-Income Ratio:	20%

Just What Number Do I Want?

Basically, the lower your debt-to-income ratio, the better off you are financially. You're in the right ballpark with a debt-to-income ratio below 20 percent. Depending on your particular circumstances, a ratio of 20 percent or higher is usually a sign that you need to take control of your debt. The consequences if your debt-to-income ratio rises above 20 percent include having trouble getting loans and qualifying for low credit terms. What that means is you may get a car loan, but you won't qualify for the best financing being touted in the ads, or it means the rate the mortgage banker offers you won't be the lowest rate available. The only way to solve the problem—not counting an immediate pay raise of several thousand dollars—is to reduce your debt.

MAYBE THESE WARNING SIGNALS RING A BELL

Let's be fair. Sometimes we end up in debt through factors not necessarily within our control. Divorce certainly qualifies, as do health problems of our own or of a loved one, or a sudden change in our household income. Job layoffs have a way of surprising us, and finding another job can be an elusive task. Truth is, financial hardship is a way of life for more and more people. Whatever the cause, financial worries related to debt can make your life interesting in ways you'd rather they didn't.

Many times we don't see the warning signs of a money crisis until it's too late—the light at the end of the tunnel is actually another train coming right at you. But most financial crises don't arrive on your doorstep by express delivery. These warning signals can help you decide if you're headed in the wrong direction:

- You consolidate your debts by borrowing from a high-interest lender.
- You get distracted from your daily work by the pressure of your debts.
- You freak out at the thought of losing your job because of what it would do to you financially, even in the short run.
- You pay the absolute minimum on a monthly bill or miss a charge-account payment altogether.
- You write a check and hold your breath hoping that it won't clear before your next deposit.
- You put off going to the doctor or dentist, not because you hate needles and drills, but because your finances are unhealthy.
- You work a second or part-time job not because you just love to work 16-hour days but because you must in order to cover your bills.
- You find the idea of saving money or being able to quickly withdraw cash from your savings to cover monthly expenses a sick joke.

- You panic just thinking about having to pay for an unexpected expense, such as car repairs.

If you recognized yourself in any of these statements, your debt may have you heading for financial trouble. Whatever the cause of your debt—whether you lost your job in a downsizing, lost your senses at the electronics store, or lost some household income in a divorce—you must pay the piper. But first, repeat three irrefutable facts until you believe them:

1. You are in debt because you spent more than you earned.
2. The only way to pay off your debts is to stop sending out more than you take in, and pay back what you owe.
3. "Irrefutable" is a tough word to say three times fast.

THESE STEPS MIGHT KEEP YOUR SINKING SHIP AFLOAT

No matter what you owe, it's too much if your debt has affected your everyday life. On those days when it feels like your ship is sinking, you'd send up a flare to alert rescuers but your matches are soaked. Or you're already on the bottom of the ocean. Be sure not to open your eyes if you're wearing contacts. We shouldn't make fun of a serious situation, but sometimes that's the only way to maintain your sanity. If you're drowning in debt or on the verge of falling in headfirst, these steps may be just the life raft you need. They won't solve your problems overnight, but they could help you stay afloat while you struggle for more control of your debts.

1. *Admit your debt is a problem.* Whether you're in denial or just procrastinating, it's time to take responsibility for your actions. And remember that you are not alone. Excessive debt is a problem for the rich, famous, poor, infamous, smart, talented, short, tall, haters, lovers, strong, and strong-smelling. The list could go on, but you get the picture. The only way you can make progress is if you dare accept your debt as a problem you need to start solving.
2. *Change one thing now.* As we mentioned, your problems won't go away overnight, but you've got to start somewhere. If credit card

debt has you by the short hairs, stop using plastic. Do something drastic—use the credit cards to tile the bathroom—but at the very least, remove them from your person. Every new purchase will make any progress impossible. If you can live without the adrenaline rush that comes with buying for at least a couple months, you will see real progress in how much you owe. That provides an adrenaline rush all its own.

3. *Add it up to pay it down.* Gather up your credit card bills and other debts. Then list them in order, with the highest interest rate debt on top. Pay the most you can on that specific loan each month, preferably several times the minimum due. Keep the other debts current and pay at least the minimum on them, but focus on the biggest debt first. When the debt on the top of your pile is gone, put all the money you were paying toward it on the second highest debt and so on. It all goes back to what we mentioned about making progress.

4. *Contact creditors.* Whether it's school loans, credit card debt, or other bank loans, make a few calls and plead your case. Creditors want nothing more than to get paid, and they'll meet you in the middle to get their money. They may establish a payment schedule, lower the interest rate you're paying, or offer loan consolidation. Depending on your credit rating and the amount you owe, consolidation or transferring debt onto one credit card may be a solid option. Be sure to ask the creditors to waive any transfer fees, though, because if they aren't, paying fees can be worse than interest.

5. *Change your habits.* A financial plan is part of the solution but so is an abrupt change of course. For starters, switch from a credit card to a debit card, which will subtract purchases from an existing bank balance. Don't borrow on credit cards for things that won't increase in value, such as furniture and vacations. You don't want to still be paying for one trip when the next one comes along.

6. *Family counts.* If you have a family, you owe it to them to keep them informed and involved in financial matters, debt and other-

wise. Financial woes aren't proof that you're a bad person. The fact that you don't take out the garbage is, however. Being straight up about your financial situation with your spouse or partner is the best first step in letting off some financial pressure. Talking to your children about financial stuff now could make their lives better in the future.

7. *Seek professional help.* If following the first six steps won't put a dent in your debt, you may need credit counseling. But avoid quick-fix solutions at all costs. Your debt and credit issues won't disappear just because some late-night television ad promises they will. Remember the saying about if it sounds too good to be true, it probably is. Professional, nonprofit credit counseling agencies can help you negotiate with creditors and advise you on your particular situation. Read more about credit counseling in Chapter 4.

8. *Save some money.* Don't laugh. You may be in debt, but you've got the future to think about too. If you put a few bucks in a savings account every paycheck, you'll slowly build up some funds to fall back on should the car break down or the cat suffer a breakdown. Nothing can beat that smug feeling you'll have when you can pay the veterinarian with cash and not a credit card.

4

You Gotta Play This Numbers Game

If you're like us, there are a bazillion numbers in your head. First, there are important ones like lucky numbers and your garage door code. Then there's the Social Security number, which has come into play more and more. And we need to remember innumerable PIN numbers and passwords. But if we forget, there's a number to call for help. What about the bus routes and cell phone numbers?

One number you really need to know is your credit rating—and not just when you're applying for a loan. These days your credit rating can affect your auto and homeowner's insurance premiums, your ability to rent an apartment, and even your chances of getting a job. Insurers say your credit score helps them predict how likely you are to file claims, and they look at your credit history while determining whether to insure you and how much to charge. People who score better are more likely to pay less or get the insurance policy in the first place. Whether you pay your bills on time every time is a big deal to prospective landlords for reasons that don't need lengthy explanations. And prospective employers do credit checks to verify information you've provided on your application, and in some cases, to see how you handle your finances. Unlike auto insurance companies, they need to get your permission before they do the credit check.

YOUR CREDIT RATING IS A MYSTERY WORTH SOLVING

What if you don't know if your credit rating is bad or good? An even tougher question is, how do they figure out your credit rating in the first place? Most people have no idea where they stand until they're at the car dealership hoping to qualify for a low-interest loan. It's hard to accept the news that your credit isn't good enough, especially if a two-door coupe is calling your name. In exchange for a ride in that car, we'll give you the scoop.

Creditworthiness is scored on a scale from 300 to 850, with average being about 640. The number to shoot for is 720 because it will help you qualify for the best rates. These figures may or may not interest you, but your credit future could depend on you gaining a better understanding of the scoring process. Credit card issuers and other lenders use your score to determine the interest rate and fees they will charge. As we mentioned earlier, it's one of the factors insurance companies use when figuring out how much your premiums will be, and landlords peek at your score to see if you're lease-worthy. Those are the types of numbers it pays to understand.

The most commonly used credit score is the FICO score, so named for Fair Isaac and Co., the research firm that developed the complex formulas used to create them. FICO scores are based on information from consumers' credit reports maintained by credit reporting agencies. The three major ones being Experian, Equifax, and TransUnion. Take a look at the pie chart on the next page and you'll see what factors combine to determine a consumer's score.

The FICO score deals solely with a borrower's financial information to provide an objective measurement of credit risk. It doesn't consider place of residence, employment history, age, race, sex, religion, national origin, or marital status. That means a change in your marital status isn't factored in your credit rating. You and your spouse (or former spouse) have separate credit histories. A common misconception among divorcing couples is that their financial lives will be severed automatically with a divorce decree. In practice, it's the responsibility

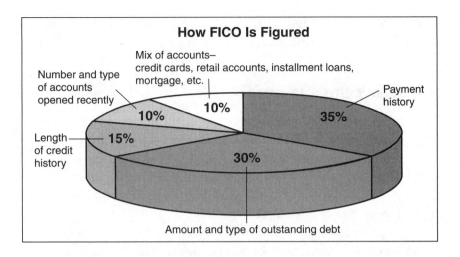

How FICO Is Figured

Mix of accounts–
credit cards, retail accounts, installment loans, mortgage, etc.

Number and type of accounts opened recently

Payment history

Length of credit history

10% 10% 35%

15% 30%

Amount and type of outstanding debt

of the individuals to close joint accounts or remove one person's name from them—or one or both could see their credit reports suffer as a result of missed payments by the other.

It's a good idea to conduct your own credit checkup annually, especially if you're planning a major purchase, such as a home or car. You may want to order a copy of your credit report from the three major credit agencies so you can compare them and get a more complete picture of what is being reported. Just so you know, if you get your FICO score and compare it to your credit rating by the three agencies, you could end up with four different numbers. It's one of the perplexing facts of your financial life, and it happens more often than not. The way lenders and other businesses report information to the credit agencies can lead to different information being in your credit report. Plus, they don't update their records on the same schedule.

Another fact of your financial life is that you'll probably pay for the privilege of getting your credit information. There is typically a charge for the credit report (fee varies by state), but residents of Colorado, Georgia, Massachusetts, Maryland, New Jersey, and Vermont can get an annual credit report for free. No matter where you live, you're entitled to a free copy of your credit report if you've been denied credit, insurance, or employment in the last 60 days because of information supplied by a credit bureau. The company you applied to must provide you with that credit bureau's contact information so you can get to the bottom of it.

BUT WHAT DOES IT MEAN?

It's easy for us to tell you to study your credit report. And it's a snap for you to get a copy. But once you have it, what does the gobbledy-gook mean? We're glad you asked. A credit report contains four basic sections: identifying information, credit history, public records, and inquiries. Some of it is in plain English and some requires serious concentration, but all of it is worth a look-see.

Identifying information is just like it sounds. We're talking name, Social Security number, current and previous addresses, date of birth, telephone numbers, driver's license numbers, employer, spouse's name, and the like. You may find your nicknames listed, but probably not the names you were called as a kid.

Credit history is sometimes called "trade lines." Each account—both existing and closed—will include the creditor's name and the account

GET THE SCORE

You can get your credit rating from three major credit agencies and at myfico.com. We recommend you get copies of all three or a consolidated version. Of course it all comes at a price, so be prepared to pay, unless you're lucky enough to live in one of the states where residents can get a free credit report every year.

Fair Isaac and Co.	www.myfico.com	
Experian International	www.experian.com	1-888-397-3742
TransUnion	www.transunion.com	1-800-888-4213
Equifax Credit Information Services	www.equifax.com	1-800-685-1111

number, which may be scrambled for security reasons. An account may be included more than once if you have moved or if the creditor has more than one type of account assigned to you. You'll also see:

- When you opened the account
- The kind of credit (installment or revolving)
- Whether there are other names on your account, such as your spouse
- Credit limit or highest balance on the account
- How much you still owe
- Minimum monthly payment amount
- Account status (open, inactive, closed, paid)
- How well you've paid the account
- Other comments, such as records of internal collections, charge-off, or default (you don't want these words on your report)

Public records is a section of your credit report you definitely want blank. It's not criminal activity, but financial data, such as bankruptcy, foreclosures, wage attachments, judgments, and tax liens.

Inquiries is the section that lists everyone who has asked to see your credit report. You may have heard that a big number of inquiries can hurt your credit score, but truth is, most of them are ignored when calculating your score. Inquiries within 30 days of you getting a mortgage

---

Poll

How many credit cards are in your wallet?

0 (zero, zilch, nada)	12%
1 (one is plenty)	33%
2–5 (more is better)	49%
6 + (enough for 52-card pickup)	6%

Poll of visitors to ihatefinancialplanning.com

or a car loan are grouped as one inquiry or ignored altogether for scoring purposes.

HOW TO BOOST YOUR CREDIT SCORE

Don't avoid checking your credit report just because you fear the worst. You may be surprised to learn your credit is in stellar shape. Or you could find inaccuracies that need fixing. It's possible, even somewhat likely, that there are black marks on your record that you caused. Whatever the case, it's best to be aware of your full financial picture, and that involves looking at the numbers from time to time. It might be scary to uncover messes you may have caused, but it's important to remember that the boo-boos aren't permanent—and neither is a high score, if you've got one. Adopt these credit-rating enhancement skills, if you haven't done so already. And be patient because it could take some time for your score to soar.

First, get a copy of your credit report and look for glaring mistakes. Are all the accounts listed yours? Is the information out of date? Anything over seven years old, whether correct or not, must be removed, with the exception of tax liens and bankruptcies, which will stick around for 10 years. We've got info on correcting errors a few pages ahead.

Pay your bills on time, but if you have missed payments, get current and stay there. One late notice on your credit report may not be the end of the world. Ask the lender to remove it as a goodwill gesture. Be polite and explain why you slipped up. You'll have trouble with this one if late payments are the norm for you. If you dispute an inaccuracy, it will stay on your report until it's resolved but not factor into your score.

Rather than piling up one type of debt, it's better where your credit report is concerned to have a combination of mortgage, car, school, and credit card loans. Loans from finance companies, though, can drag down your score. This isn't permission to load up on debt, mind you, so don't go getting any ideas. Don't open accounts just to have a better credit mix, because that strategy could backfire and actually lower your score if by doing so you end up having too many open accounts.

Use less of your available credit. Keep balances low or do what you can to lower them by making steady payments. Even if you pay off your balance every month, try to avoid using more than 50 percent of your limit on any one account.

The older your average account, the better your score. If you have too many credit cards (more than three to five), consider closing the newer accounts first, and keep an old card active by using it once a year. Note, though, that closing an account doesn't make it go away. It will still show up on your credit report. And just so we're clear, keeping a credit card active is not the same as keeping a huge balance on it.

Every time you apply for credit, the lender will check your report. Multiple inquiries can have a negative impact on your score unless they're all related to one purchase, such as a home mortgage or car loan. You're allowed to shop around for the best interest rate without it affecting your credit rating. And you can check your own credit report without the inquiry counting against you.

TIME HEALS ALL THINGS—EVEN CREDIT

The good thing about negative information on your credit report is that the older it gets the less important it will be. Sort of like the gossip about you from high school. It doesn't mean much at the 15-year reunion. A 30-day late payment last month will probably hurt your credit rating more than a 90-day late payment from five years ago. People recover to buy homes, get credit cards, and buy new cars, even after they have had to declare bankruptcy. The best thing to do is keep building good credit references by paying your bills on time—all the time. It may take some time to get your credit where you want it to be, but it will happen. Not unlike the dreaded high school reunion.

THEY'RE WRONG, YOU'RE RIGHT, BUT ALWAYS BE POLITE

We have a friend who, while shopping for apartments, got the startling news from a prospective landlord that she was dead. Turns out our living, breathing friend has the same name as someone on the opposite end of the living spectrum, and the wrong information turned up on our friend's credit record. You'd think one quick phone call would clear up

DEBIT OR CREDIT, THAT IS THE QUESTION

One debate financial freaks like us toss around is which is better to use, a debit card or a credit card. Certainly there are pros and cons to each, which makes it possible to debate the issue in the first place, come to think of it. In case you've been stranded in a deserted shopping mall for the past decade, a debit card looks and works much like a credit card but your purchases are immediately deducted from a bank account you designate, usually your checking account. You can also use the card to remove cash from your account at an ATM. Debit cards are a substitute for cash and faster than writing a check, which are rarely accepted anymore except for paying bills. Think of them as a convenient way to spend your own money.

Where your credit rating is concerned, credit cards offer a potential plus that debit cards can't match. If you use credit wisely—and for many people we know that is a huge IF—credit cards can help you build a solid credit history. You use a credit card to borrow money, so every time you pay back that loan in a timely fashion, you're proving credit-worthiness to other potential lenders. Miss a few payments or rack up big balances, though, and your credit report will suffer. Debit cards, on the other hand, don't influence your credit rating positively or negatively because you're not borrowing money when you use them.

the mistake, especially if the person on the other end of the line could hear our friend's frantic voice. Isn't there some sort of an "undo" tool for situations like this? Unfortunately, it isn't that easy. Not when we're talking about credit histories and detailed documentation and the bureaucratic inclination to require proof in triplicate.

Errors in your credit report are fairly common, especially if you have a common name. And those inaccuracies may haunt you if you don't take action—as in, you might find yourself dead when all you really want to do is rent a two-bedroom walk-up. If a situation like this happens to you, be prepared to take action in a way that will generate action by the credit reporting agency. By law, credit agencies must investigate all disputes, and they are expected to initiate the process within 30 days. That doesn't mean your problem will be solved in a month, so don't expect instant results.

You can file a dispute online, by telephone, or by certified letter. We recommend you go the letter route because if our friend's experience is any indication, a phone call from someone who is supposedly dead doesn't necessarily solve anything. With a certified letter, on the other hand, not only will you have proof that the credit agency reporting the erroneous information was contacted, but it will know you have that proof. It's the you-know-I-know-you-know trick and it works.

Get a copy of your credit report and clearly identify any inaccuracies. Return a photocopy of the report (keep the original) to the agency with a letter explaining specifically why you think the highlighted information is wrong (you don't have an account at that store, the address is wrong, you're alive, you name it). Clearly state what action should be taken by the agency (with all due respect, correct the wrong info or remove it from your report). Be sure to include in the letter your complete name, address, date of birth, and Social Security number.

The tone of your letter is important. Stick to simple statement of fact and avoid the temptation to threaten or prattle on about how you wish you had an account at that store because you've heard there are sales all the time. In addition to writing to the credit agency, you may want to write to any company that is reporting incorrect information and include a copy of the credit report. As with most aspects of your credit record, be patient. Diligence will pay off, but you can avoid unnecessary frustration if you give the system time to work.

IS CREDIT COUNSELING FOR YOU?

Maybe you have read Laura Numeroff's book *If You Give a Pig a Pancake*. It's one of a series of children's books exploring the notion

FINANCIAL JARGON MADE EASY

A *charge-off* is the credit industry's way of describing bad debt. A creditor reports a charge-off if the balance is past due (usually by at least six months) and no payments are expected. But a charge-off doesn't mean that the debt no longer exists or that there won't be further attempts to collect it. In fact, the debt is considered due in full thanks to breach of contract, and collection efforts go into high gear. Typically credit companies will sell the bad account to a collection agency, which will pull out the stops with menacing letters and threatening telephone calls. If you've got a charge-off on your credit report, it's a major red flag to potential lenders for up to seven years, and collectors can keep trying to get the money a lot longer than that.

Much like the meaning of "charge-off," financial terms aren't much fun, but that doesn't stop us from trying. Flip to the back of the book for even more jargon.

that "if you give an inch, they'll take a mile." First the pig gets the pancake, then she wants syrup to go with it, then a bath to wash off the sticky syrup, and bubbles for the bath, then a rubber duck, and so on it goes. By the end of the book you're right back at the kitchen table giving that pig another pancake. Incidentally, we have a source who's willing to confirm—off the record—that the book is suitable for children of all ages.

Using credit poorly is sort of like that. It starts with a simple credit application for a shiny rectangle of plastic, and before you know it, you're using the credit card too often just to put pancakes on the table. Or your eyes being bigger than your budget, you add a whirlpool tub in the master bath. A few late payments later, things aren't so simple anymore, and you're forced to cope with consequences you never anticipated. Creditors are calling. Interest rates and fees have caused your balances to balloon beyond recognition. Somebody stop the madness!

A simple fact is that credit is easy to obtain but difficult for some to manage. More and more consumers are struggling with overwhelming debt and its impact on their credit records. Maybe you are one of those consumers. Maybe you're asking the same questions we get asked more frequently than ever:

- Is credit counseling the best way to clean up debt troubles?
- How will it affect my credit rating?

Our answer to both questions is, it depends. We're not being wishy-washy, we're merely telling it like it is. Credit counseling—or debt management, as it's called by the credit industry—involves working with a professional agency that negotiates with creditors to consolidate debt, lower interest rates, or remove fees for late payments. The "counseling," which isn't part of every debt management program, comes in the form of educating consumers in hopes that history won't repeat itself as soon as the debts are paid. For instance, use cash whenever buying pancakes for pigs.

A debt management program may be the best solution for some indebted consumers but not others. It depends on several factors, including how your total debt balances with your potential ability to pay it off in a reasonable length of time based on your current income. One harsh truth about debt is that nobody forced you to assume it, so if you think a debt management program is a quick fix, good luck making it through the screening process. Another reality is that bankruptcy may be the best option, depending on your particular circumstances (we tackled that topic in Chapter 3).

Now for the second question. How will using a credit counseling agency affect your credit rating? In case you read the previous paragraphs in your sleep, the answer is, it depends. On the current status of your credit record, that is. If you have huge debt and are late on payments, your credit has probably already taken a hit. If that's the case, the fact that you are seeking professional help with your debt situation won't matter over the short term. And over the long term in this scenario, the only way is up.

Using a credit counseling program is not going to greatly influence your current credit score. Your credit accounts will be closed and you'll pay the credit counseling agency a predetermined monthly amount, which they will then forward to creditors. Getting that sort of help is not seen as a bad thing. However, if your debt is such that your credit counselor negotiates a lesser amount to be paid back, the lender may report it to the credit bureaus. In other words, if your $500 minimum monthly payment is negotiated down to $300, the creditor could choose to report the account as current or as behind by $200 each month. Either choice is possible—and legal—and there isn't much you can do to influence the decision. Most creditors are reporting accounts in similar situations as up-to-date as a way of letting their customer know they are glad there isn't a bankruptcy on the horizon.

A debt management program will show up on your credit report, and it may affect future applications for credit, but that is up to the individual lender. You may pay a higher interest rate from certain lenders—car loans tend to be the worst where that is concerned. Some creditors, on the other hand, want to see steady improvement with your debt situation, and they view working with a credit counselor as a positive step. Make timely payments while in the debt management program and for several months afterward, and you may be able to get credit at interest rates that are all right.

YOU KNOW YOU NEED HELP, NOW WHAT?

Once you've decided to seek professional help, where do you turn? Is it possible there are more ads on late-night television and the Internet promising instant solutions to debt problems than there are credit card solicitations? Oh yeah. One industry has spawned another, so be cautious when picking a program and start by avoiding those that run obnoxious, big-budget advertising campaigns.

- Talk to a few agencies before deciding, if possible. You want one that spends quality time with you. It's important to get an outline detailing your responsibilities and the agency's services tailored to your specific plan. The firm that offers you a plan in less than 20 minutes hasn't thoroughly studied your financial picture.

- Pick a credit-counseling agency that doesn't promise overnight success. It takes time and effort to eliminate your debt—up to 4 years in most cases. Remember, your debt situation didn't develop in a day, so you shouldn't expect a solution that quickly either. Resist firms that tout their services with unreasonable promises or by appealing to your natural urge to panic. There we go again projecting on your our personal tendency to panic.
- You'll be charged a reasonable fee—usually about $50–$75 to start plus a small monthly fee. Reputable firms allow customers to negotiate the fee based on what they can afford. Avoid outfits that charge big rates or pay their employees by commission.
- Ask about privacy. Make sure the agency doesn't share information on clients without permission.
- Don't fall for programs that tell you to stop paying your bills. They may be looking to pocket your money without helping you one bit.

HELP IS ON THE WAY

Looking for a credible debt management program? Stick with nonprofit firms affiliated with the National Foundation of Credit Counseling. Member agencies are known as Consumer Credit Counseling Services (CCCS) and operate in major communities nationwide. Oh, and "nonprofit" doesn't mean you won't pay. There is usually a small start-up cost and monthly fee.

National Foundation for Credit Counseling	www.nfcc.org	1-800-388-2227
Credit Counselors	www.repaydebt.org	1-888-737-2933

5

The Only Constant Is Change

Change is everywhere. Not exactly a profound statement, but certainly a true one, unless you're looking in our jacket pockets for bus fare, because we've already checked and come up empty. One frustrating thing about the relationship between life and money is that one or the other is always changing. And when your money situation changes in *spite* of your life, well, what that brings is its own set of frustrations. Or opportunities. You can't control the fact that changes will occur. What you can control is how you handle them. Of all the life changes you'll encounter, we have chosen three—job, marriage, and divorce. Just keep reading before you change your mind.

Let's proceed with the type of change that probably occurs most often. The average American changes jobs nine times before the ripe old age of 34, according to the Bureau of Labor Statistics (April 2000). It's probably worth noting that that statistic predates the downsizing, rightsizing, and plain vanilla layoffs that have been so common this century. Just about everyone we know was changing jobs in the past few years, and usually not by choice. Come to think of it, maybe that stat hasn't been updated because the person doing the tallying was laid off. The good news with a number like that is workers don't need to bother dusting off their résumés, because there's been no time for any dust to settle. And what about all the jobs a person has *after* age 34? The point is, if you haven't changed jobs already, you're going to do it sometime, and we can't wait to share our fairly strong opinions on how you should manage the financial aspects of the change.

WHAT COLOR IS YOUR PINK SLIP?

In more touchy-feely times, the book *What Color Is Your Parachute?* by Richard Bolles, was a popular graduation gift. In its pages, readers could uncover their true calling and be inspired to seek out the ideal job. Well, with layoffs so common these days, former employees everywhere are dusting off that book and throwing it in the fire for warmth when money is tight between jobs. Whether you've been given your pink slip or you're dreading its arrival, we've got plenty of suggestions for how you can handle the money end of the situation. They won't lessen the stress of being laid off, but they might help minimize the financial strain.

If you have recently found yourself downsized, put these ideas to work while you're busy mending that parachute:

- First, keep in mind that this is not a reflection on you. It was a business decision by your employer in an effort to keep its ship afloat. Respond by trying to keep your own boat sailing, albeit in rougher waters. Give yourself a break. Let reality set in for a few days before you become irrational about finances and sell your car. Put your initial anxiety to good use, instead, by scrubbing the bathroom tiles with a toothbrush.
- If your employer offers outplacement services, take advantage of them. An outplacement firm may not find you a job, but it can help you with your résumé and interview preparation. Also, it doesn't hurt to commiserate with others in the same boat.
- Make sure you and your dependents have health insurance coverage. It may be least expensive to join your spouse's plan, if that's an option. If not, look into COBRA coverage through your former employer. Refer to Chapter 9 for more insurance info than you can stomach.
- Prioritize your bills, with mortgage and utilities on the top of the pile. You've lost your job; do what you can to not lose your house.

- Assuming you have credit card debt, you may need to make just the minimum payments on the plastic until you get back to work. If your debt is significant or you are having trouble making even the minimum payments, try to negotiate a payment plan with your creditors. Contact them while your payments are still current and ask to work out a plan that won't hurt your credit record.
- File for unemployment, because you have a right to receive those benefits. Unemployment is not welfare, so don't let pride get in the way. We've got more tips on this phase of your adventure coming right up.
- Resist the urge to dip into retirement savings. We know it will be quite tempting as it may seem like easy money, but spending that money now could haunt you down the road. Forget about down the road, you'll pay income taxes and an early withdrawal penalty now. Well, at tax time anyway.
- Avoid canceling your life insurance (if you've got it). If you try to resume coverage on a lapsed policy at a later date, you'll pay more and you may have to prove insurability with a medical exam.

If you're still working but fear the proverbial "end date," these tips can cushion the blow if your parachute suddenly crashes:

- Save some cash. Every penny you put away now will make it easier to adjust to not getting a steady paycheck. But that's just our two cents.
- Apply for a home equity line of credit if you're a homeowner. You don't have to use it, but it's hard to get approved once you're unemployed.
- Consolidate credit card debt at a lower interest rate if your credit rating allows for such a financial move. Chapter 4, on credit, can help you sort that out.
- Pay off any outstanding 401(k) loans. Once you're laid off and can't pay back the loan, it will be treated as an early withdrawal with taxes and penalties due.
- If you might need to borrow from family, bring it up now while you are still working. That way they can think about it before you're desperate.

WHAT'S TO KNOW ABOUT UNEMPLOYMENT BENEFITS

Your time in the unemployment benefits line might be shortened a bit (or at least seem more bearable) if you know how to approach the process. All the rules vary by state, so depending on where you live, there may be a waiting period and it may take a while for your claim to be processed. Surprise, surprise. The sooner you file, the sooner you'll start getting unemployment checks. Just a reminder, though, that if you quit or were fired, you usually don't qualify for unemployment.

When applying for benefits, bring proof that you were laid off. Also, you'll need the names and addresses of your most recent employers. And most important, bring pay stubs or other evidence of your earnings because your benefits will be based on your former salary. To qualify for unemployment, you'll need to demonstrate that you're looking for work. Some states require you to visit the unemployment office periodically while others let you contact them by phone.

Don't forget about taxes. Uncle Sam wants his share of your money, no matter how you get the check. That includes unemployment benefits. Some states let you have income taxes withheld from the checks, but you may choose to receive the entire amount. If you get back to work, put some money aside to cover income taxes in April.

NEW JOB, NEW BUDGET

Maybe you've been in this situation before. You get a job offer that you just can't refuse. The pay is better, the commute not as long, and you start out with twice the paid vacation as your current job provides. You toss out all the shirts emblazoned with the old employer's logo and shop for a new wardrobe. Granted, this is our workaday fantasy world, but it could happen. Then you get your first paycheck. Were your eyes bigger than your pay? You must have forgotten that a bigger paycheck means more taxes going to Uncle Sam. And though the drive to work is shorter, you pay to use the employee parking lot, and that amount is taken out of your check too. Welcome to the real world.

Don't let new job euphoria take control. The most important thing you can do with a pay raise is NOT spend it before you assess its impact on your bottom line. When negotiating a raise, keep in mind that the dollar figure is your gross pay, not your net pay. It sounds obvious but it's so easy to forget that taxes, health coverage, retirement contributions, and other benefits will be taken out of the paycheck. Just don't be shocked when the take-home pay isn't that much more.

Now may be the ideal time to get a handle on your current spending and make plans for how your income increase will affect your budget. Don't let that word scare you. You'll enjoy your pay raise more if you control it rather than letting it control you. We think you'll find our spending record and spending plan worksheets to be quite nifty. You can find them in Chapter 2, on budgeting. We don't blame you if you get tired of us chiding you about budgets, but we're going to keep making the point for two reasons. One, budgets are the cornerstone necessary for keeping your financial house in order. And two, we get a cash bonus every time anyone actually creates one. As you can imagine, it's an administrative nightmare proving that people actually track their spending and plan for future expenses. Lucky for us so few people follow our suggestion that we don't have that much paperwork—or bonus money either, come to think of it.

Poll

Which job would you NOT take, despite the money?

High-profile politician	44%
Reality TV "winner"	38%
Corporate CEO	9%
TV/movie star	5%
Young sports prodigy	4%

Poll conducted by ihatefinancialplanning.com

TAKE IT OR LEAVE IT (YOUR RETIREMENT PLAN, THAT IS)

We've devoted all of Chapter 7 to saving for retirement, but since we know what an exciting topic it is, we're going to give you a preview here with these tidbits on how you might handle your retirement savings when switching employers. When you leave your job, you may be able take your employer-sponsored retirement account with you—the money is yours and so is any matching contribution by your employer, if you are fully vested. When you switch employers, you may also choose to leave your funds where they are, depending on the company's plan, or to roll your investments into an individual retirement account. You may also choose to cash out your retirement account, but that's a poor decision except in the most dire of financial circumstances.

By rolling your retirement account into your new employer's plan, you maintain the account's income tax–deferred status and won't have to pay taxes on the account until you withdraw money from the plan. You'll also avoid penalty fees, and the account's potential for growth won't be interrupted. Those are some pretty significant advantages. If you want to take your investments with you, the first thing to do— probably before you even start the new job—is find out if your new employer allows rollovers. And we don't mean find out if they have tumbling classes. Most do but some don't, and you'll want to know early to help streamline the process.

Be aware that if the rollover check is written to you, your previous employer will be required to withhold 20 percent of the amount you've got coming for income taxes. Say your account is worth $50,000. Your employer will withhold $10,000 or 20 percent, and you'll end up with $40,000. If you haven't yet turned 59 1/2, you'll also get slapped with a 10 percent early withdrawal penalty. You can avoid this by arranging for an "institution-to-institution" transfer. The check will not be in your name and things will go swimmingly. Talk to your former employer to avoid these expensive tax consequences.

You can also roll the money in your retirement account into a traditional individual retirement account (IRA), where it will remain tax-deferred and have potential to continue earning returns, depending on the investments you choose (stocks, bonds, mutual funds, annuities, etc.) With an IRA, you'll gain some flexibility with the investments you can choose, but the annual limit for new contributions is fairly small when compared to employer-sponsored retirement plan contribution limits. Withdrawals from your IRA before you hit age 59 1/2 are treated much like employer-sponsored retirement plans in that they are subject to income taxes and a 10 percent penalty. The penalty will be waived to pay for college costs or a down payment on a first-time home purchase. If you want to use your new employer's retirement plan but you're not yet eligible, you may consider opening a new IRA for that money. If you don't make any new contributions to the IRA, you can then transfer the money once you're eligible for your new employer's plan.

When you change jobs, you may decide to leave your retirement account right where it is—if your plans allows it and your vested balance is more than $5,000 and you're under age 65. Government regulations ensure that you'll continue to get regular statements about your account, and the funds may continue to grow until you retire. And no

MAKE SURE YOU'RE TAKING IT WITH YOU

If you are planning to leave your job, find out when your employer's matching contributions are deposited into employees' retirement accounts. Some employers deposit matching contributions every pay period, but others only make the deposits quarterly or even once a year. In such a case, if you were to leave your job before the contribution for the most recent year were deposited, you could lose a whole year's worth of matching contributions. Of course, you've got to consider the job market and your willingness to stay at a job you can't stand just for the employer match, but it's worth thinking about.

matter how much bad blood may exist between you and your former employer, your money will be managed as if you were still employed at the company. (Did you really tell your boss to take this job and ??) If you're satisfied with the performance of the funds in your plan or you're just not in the mood to make a quick decision about your retirement account, just let it be. You'll probably have numerous jobs over time, though, and it may become a hassle over the years to keep track of all the plans you've left behind.

DON'T TAKE THE MONEY AND RUN

We'll make this short but not-so sweet. Unless you are completely desperate for a quick buck, don't close out your retirement account and take the cash just because you're switching jobs. Younger employees with relatively small balances in their accounts are especially tempted to choose this option, viewing the cash as a sudden windfall that will make life easier. What they're forgetting is that over the course of their working lives, that balance has the potential to multiply many times over—if it's left and allowed to grow. Any money you take now may be subject to income taxes and a 10-percent early withdrawal penalty as well, assuming you aren't yet 59 1/2. Keep the investment and someday you'll be glad you did. We usually don't make firm recommendations because that is counter to our mantra that you take personal responsibility for your financial life. But we feel pretty strongly about this one, so we're breaking our own rule.

FINANCIAL JARGON MADE EASY

As far as the government is concerned, a 401(k) plan is an incentive to save for retirement. But as far as your employer is concerned, it can also be an incentive to join the company or stay there, an incentive that might be seeded with profit-sharing money or a company match on top of any money you contribute.

Employees who have met all the loyalty requirements (one to five years is typical) are considered fully *vested*, as in "having a vested interest." From that point on, when you leave the company you can take 100 percent of the money the company contributed to your fund with you. Rest assured that any of your own money that you contribute to your 401(k) plan will remain yours, regardless of whether you're vested, not vested, or wearing a bright red blazer. If you leave before you've been working for your employer a year, you may not be vested at all. You might not be invited to the company picnic, either. After a year, you could be 20 percent vested. The schedule varies from company to company subject to government regulations, but once you're there, you remain fully vested as long as you stay.

If you have a vested interest in expanding your vocabulary, flip to the back of the book for more financial jargon.

WHEN A JOB CHANGE INVOLVES A MOVE

Sometimes changing jobs means you've got to move to another location. Relocating is an adventure some job seekers openly seek. Sometimes it's a necessary, but unwelcome part of finding a job. We'll leave it up to you to decide where you fit in the spectrum. But one thing is true, no matter how you feel about relocating: You're gonna pay to do it. The biggest costs are associated with buying and selling a home, packing up and transporting your household, and costs to travel to your new home. Let's not forget the random start-up costs, such as telephone installation and utility fees, which can knock your budget out of whack if you aren't prepared. If you're lucky enough to have a relocation package paid by your employer, you'll get reimbursed for most everything. If you're not so lucky, be prepared to dole out some serious cash.

Fortunately, many moving expenses are income-tax deductible if you meet certain qualifications, and because moving expenses are above-the-line deductions, you don't even need to itemize your deductions to claim them. Thank you, Uncle Sam, for making moving costs more affordable. You can deduct moving expenses if you move to a different home due to a change in job locations or if you've started a new job. And both self-employed individuals and employees are eligible for the tax deduction. To figure your net deduction, simply add up any qualifying moving expenses and subtract any reimbursements you may receive from your employer. But first you must pass both distance and time tests as administered by Uncle Sam himself, so bring plenty of number two pencils.

Don't stay up too late studying for the distance test because it's pretty basic. Your new workplace must be at least 50 miles from your old, but if there's no former job in your past, your new workplace has to be at least 50 miles from your old home. Let's say your old job was six miles from your old home. Your new job has to be at least 56 miles from that home. There are two time tests, but you only have to pass one depending on whether you're an employee or self-employed. Employees must work full-time for at least 39 weeks during the 12 months following your arrival in the general location of your new job, which means you can switch employers during that time. The self-employed must work full time for at least 39 weeks during the first year and a total of 78 weeks during the 24 months after you've moved. These are general guidelines, so if you think you qualify for the deduction, consult with a tax professional about your particular situation or read the rules in IRS Publication 521.

Assuming you've passed both tests, what expenses qualify for the deduction? We're glad you asked. You may deduct the actual costs to pack and move your household goods and personal belongings. You may also deduct costs to store and insure that stuff for up to 30 days after the move from your old home but before delivery to your new home. Actual travel costs—transportation and lodging—from your old home to your new are also tax deductible. If you use your own car, you may deduct either the actual cost of gas and oil or mileage at a per-mile rate determined by the IRS each year. Whichever route you choose, add parking fees and tolls. Incidentally, you *cannot* deduct house-hunting trips, temporary living expenses, or any costs associated with selling the old homestead.

START YOUR MARRIAGE ON TRACK

Let's switch gears from switching jobs to making the switch from single to married. Money and finances are a big part of the equation when

SOCIAL SECURITY TAX IS NO FAIRY TALE

If you hold more than one job in any given year, it's up to you—not your employer—to be sure you haven't overpaid Social Security taxes. The maximum amount of wages subject to Social Security tax is $87,900 in tax year 2004. Because the Social Security tax rate is 6.2 percent, the maximum that should have been withheld by all your employers combined is $5,449.80 (87,900 x .062). Take a look at the W-2s you got from all employers, and if you paid more than that, you can claim a credit when filling out your tax return. For a handy worksheet see IRS Publication 17 at irs.gov. Married couples filing a joint return must compute any excess Social Security withholding separately. If you had only one employer but by some strange fluke paid too much Social Security tax, you need to go through your employer—not the IRS—to get the money back.

We've got more than you care to know about Social Security tax in Chapter 7 on retirement planning.

two people say "I do." Uttering those two words is more than a pact to love and cherish one another. Read between the lines and your partner may be saying, "I do have a lot of debt I'm bringing to this marriage, dear heart." Or how about, "Sweetie, I do not give a rip how much it costs, I want a full orchestra at our wedding reception."

In a perfect world, you could plan a wedding without regard to how much you'll spend on the orchestra. But that world only exists in bridal magazines, which boldly tempt the typical bride and groom with expensive ideas while ignoring the price tag. If there's a wedding in your near future, we suggest you watch that price tag carefully or be prepared for the financial consequences. (If you're already married or have a partner in life, skip this short section on wedding budgets and pass directly to the remainder of the chapter.) Starting out with a lot of wedding debt can put a damper on a whole lot more than the honeymoon stage of a marriage. That's why we're starting this part of the life changes chapter with a short sales pitch for wedding budgets. Having one can help you learn important money lessons now that just might make the financial part of your marriage easier as time goes on.

It used to be that the bride's family was responsible for most wedding costs, but with couples getting married later in life and more second marriages taking place, it's not so clear-cut anymore. There's really no such thing as tradition when it comes to who is going to pay for a wedding. What's becoming more common is pooling funds from the bridal couple, her parents and his parents. No matter who is paying, wedding costs will add up faster than you can throw rice on the big day. But keep in mind that actually throwing rice will add a line to your wedding budget for cleanup costs because you'll probably have to pay someone to pick up the rice off the sidewalk.

No matter who is footing the wedding bill, you need to know what you can realistically afford before you do much planning and dreaming. Using the handy worksheet on pages 86 and 87 to handle the task is the easy part, but committing to following it is harder than it sounds. The worksheet may not be perfect, but it's got the basic wedding categories and space for miscellaneous expenses you may have. Be sure to use a pencil, because the numbers are going to change as your dreams meet reality. Skip this process now if you must, but mark the page for future reference. Or go directly to the financial compatibility quiz later in the chapter. It can help couples understand how they handle money, and an exercise like that could eliminate the need for a wedding budget altogether, if you know what we mean.

TILL DEBT DO US PART

Debt is something you want to come clean on right away. We understand if you're carrying some debt that you'd rather keep to yourself, but we don't encourage you to keep that information from your spouse. Likewise, if you've partnered with someone who's got something to hide, you'll never know it unless you push for full disclosure. Presumably, this is the perfect time in your relationship to be completely honest, because presumably, this is the time in your relationship when you are especially looking out for each other's interests. And believe us when we say that debt usually brings with it a lot of interest.

If your partner has been financially irresponsible, it will affect you whether you believe it or not. Love is blind, but that doesn't protect you from an unsightly credit record. Your spouse's debt will effectively reduce your combined income, making it harder to afford homes or qualify for consumer loans. If you don't know how to track down your credit report, find out in Chapter 4. Once you have your credit report in hand, it might be the ideal conversation starter for you and the love of your life. We're not saying you shouldn't trust your partner, but don't be fooled either. You owe it to the integrity of your relationship to be honest and expect honesty in return. If that's not enough to persuade you, imagine putting off the discussion until you end up having it in front of a loan officer at the bank.

BE ACCOUNTABLE TO ONE ANOTHER

Whether you're preparing to walk down the aisle or are already hitched, we recommend you open up to your spouse. Open up your checkbook, bank statements, and bills, that is. It's time to share the intimate details of your financial life. You may be thinking that's harder than putting the cap back on the toothpaste, but it has to be done or the state of your marital union may end up clogged like a tube of toothpaste. Open communication is important to a healthy relationship. There are few topics—besides sex and some nasty medical procedures—that have greater capacity to induce lockjaw than the subject of money. Get in the habit of making money talks a regular part of your communication routine, and you'll be richer in the end. And we're not talking money.

You may want to begin with conversations at least monthly to check in on your new financial partnership. The point of your money talks should be to keep your finances on track by reviewing income, bills, expenses, spending, saving, or investing. It's a time to clear the air about any financial concerns either of you may have and also a chance

Wedding Budget Worksheet

Expense	Budget	Actual
Stationery (invitations, announcements, wedding programs, thank-you notes, postage)		
Attire (wedding gown, veil, shoes, and alterations; tuxedo or suit for groom)		
Rehearsal Dinner (per-plate charges or catering fee)		
Rings		
Ceremony (fee for officiant; church, synagogue, or mosque rental; guest book)		
Reception (hall rental, per-plate charges or catering fee)		
Cake		
Flowers (for church, wedding party, parents, grandparents, reception)		
Music (for ceremony and reception)		

Photography		
Videographer		
Gifts (for wedding party)		
Honeymoon (transportation and accommodations)		
Limousine		
Marriage License Fee		
Other		
Miscellaneous (Why didn't you think of that?)		
Incidentals (Oh yeah, that too)		
By-the-way costs (this stuff adds up)		
TOTAL		

to dream together. Call it "strategic thinking" if you want to stay in a business mode. Money talks can easily lead to deeper discussions about career goals, division of responsibilities in the home, and larger financial goals, so listen carefully. It's best to set aside your emotions when talking about this stuff, by the way, but that doesn't mean you shouldn't take your feelings into account. Let's face it, money is a personal topic.

When you got married, you promised to love one another. Now make some additional promises that will help you openly and honestly manage your money. Promise one another that you will:

- Consult before making a major purchase.
- Use credit responsibly.
- Be a smart shopper, comparing prices and quality, before buying.
- Be responsible yet generous with your money.
- Discuss and agree on gift purchases for family and friends.
- Work together to build a financially stable future for the both of you and any children you may be responsible for.

DUAL OR DUELING BANK BALANCES?

Some couples prefer to maintain separate bank accounts simply because it's easier than sharing an actual checkbook. If you have participated in circular conversations about who has the checkbook, you know what we mean. The more accounts you have, however, the more bank and check fees you will likely incur, so consider consolidating. At the very least, be sure you're both listed on any separate accounts so one would have access to accounts left by the other if some unforeseen tragedy should occur. Whether you maintain one or more accounts, you'll want to agree on how much is allocated to monthly household expenses and savings, and how to manage any leftovers if there is such a thing. Some couples give themselves an allowance for incidental expenses, others prefer a more freestyle approach. You can guess which ones may be likely to come up short at the end of the month. For a cheap date, you can sit down together and balance the checkbook. Come to think of it, maybe a task like that is best assigned to one person at a time.

THE NAMES HAVE BEEN CHANGED TO PROTECT THE INNOCENT

Whether you're changing your name on your wedding day or marrying someone who is, read on. There are three good reasons to inform the government that your name has changed and they are I, R, S. It's only recently that the Internal Revenue Service has put its computers to work screening tax returns for name discrepancies in an effort to prevent tax fraud. The crackdown is probably a good idea to stop crooks, but in most cases the culprits end up being women who failed to notify the government of their name change. If you don't comply before filing your first income tax return as a married couple, it will mess up the number of exemptions you'll be allowed to declare.

You're required by law to get a new Social Security identification card whenever you change your name. It doesn't cost anything and your number stays the same, so don't fear more memorization. Some jurisdictions give couples the form when issuing the marriage license, but others don't. It's your responsibility to follow through, or it will be pie on your face when your tax returns are rejected. (Get more info at ssa.gov.) If you use two names—your married name socially and your maiden name professionally—make sure the name you use when you sign your tax returns matches the one on file with the Social Security Administration.

Name Change Contact List

- Social Security Administration (So Uncle Sam believes you on April 15)
- Employers (To avoid errors in tracking retirement benefits)
- Banks and Other Financial Institutions (So overdrafts are credited properly)

- Schools (To ensure continued requests for money from your alma mater)
- Department of Motor Vehicles (for proper ID on traffic tickets)
- Creditors and Debtors (As tempting as it is not to)
- Insurance, Telephone, and Utility Companies (For obvious reasons)
- Estate Planning Documents (Wills, Power of Attorney, Trusts)
- Voter Registration (It's your civic duty to vote using the correct name)
- Post Office (Unless you want to limit the junk mail)

LET'S SEE IF 1 + 1 = TRUE LOVE

To help you better understand where you stand as a couple, we've developed a financial compatibility quiz you can use to facilitate a discussion about money. Both of you should take the quiz and then compare your scores. If they seem way off, take some time to talk things over. If big problems surface, some time with a marriage counselor or an experienced financial professional may help you and your honey see eye to eye.

1. We talk about money regularly.
   - ☐ Yes
   - ☐ No

2. We have decided who will handle the bills after we marry.
   - ☐ Yes
   - ☐ No

3. I feel my spouse manages his/her own money well.
   - ☐ Yes
   - ☐ No

4. I would feel comfortable if my future spouse made a purchase of $250 without telling me.
   - ☐ Yes
   - ☐ No

5. I feel my spouse knows what my retirement dreams are.

☐ Yes

☐ No

6. I know how much debt and savings (including investments) my spouse is bringing into our marriage.

☐ Yes

☐ No

7. Between us, we have more than five credit cards.

☐ Yes

☐ No

8. I know how much my spouse makes and what percentage he/she is contributing to his/her 401(k) plan at work.

☐ Yes

☐ No

9. I feel my spouse avoids sitting down and talking about money with me.

☐ Yes

☐ No

10. We have the same financial dreams.

☐ Yes

☐ No

11. I feel like my spouse treats his/her money as if it is his/her own.

☐ Yes

☐ No

12. I never talked about money with my parents.

☐ Yes

☐ No

13. I know how my spouse would feel if I wanted to quit my job and start a business.
    - ☐ Yes
    - ☐ No

14. We agree about how much income we need to live comfortably.
    - ☐ Yes
    - ☐ No

15. When we talk about money, my spouse never dismisses my point of view.
    - ☐ Yes
    - ☐ No

16. I feel my spouse is a cheapskate.
    - ☐ Yes
    - ☐ No

17. We have a financial plan.
    - ☐ Yes
    - ☐ No

18. We've talked to a financial professional.
    - ☐ Yes
    - ☐ No

Scoring:
You'll score one point if you answered Yes to questions 1, 2, 3, 4, 5, 6, 8, 10, 13, 14, 15, 17 and 18, and one point if you answered No to 7, 9, 11, 12 and 16.

Red Flag (0 to 6 points)

The proverbial marriage referee is throwing red flags left and right. Make sure your spouse takes this quiz and compare scores. If you see a significant difference in your scores, or you both have low scores, that means you may need some big-time help. Run, don't walk, to a marriage counselor or financial professional to discuss these issues and see if you can work toward a better understanding of each other's perspectives on money.

Fork in the Road (7 to 12 points)

You and your spouse seem to have a few things to work out, but for the most part each of you understands where the other is coming from. Use the results of this quiz to talk about those areas where you don't see eye to eye. Maybe you won't see everything the same, but at least you've got enough in common that you can make it work.

Peas in a Pod (13 to 18 points)

It was love at first sight, right? You're probably the kind of couple that finish each other's sentences. Well, this shows that you're on the right track financially too. Your sense of responsibility shows that you know that financial planning is important.

PRENUPS AREN'T JUST FOR THE RICH AND FAMOUS

Whether you're old or young, getting hitched for the first or umpteenth time, a prenuptial agreement is something to at least think about. It's merely a legal document that limits a spouse's claim to any assets, such as a business or a home, brought to a marriage or introduced through inheritance. As more individuals enter into second and third marriages replete with kids and homes and accumulated assets, the more a prenup makes sense. Even younger and previously unmarried couples might want to consider some additional ink before inking their union. Younger couples who don't own businesses or have children might want to discuss things like how to divide assets brought into the marriage versus those accumulated during the marriage. Or how to differentiate between assets that were a result of the marriage, such as the house, and those that weren't, such as a trust fund (or yes, that precious baseball card collection of yours).

Despite its bad reputation, the prenuptial agreement may be a commonsense tool for many entering a marriage. Getting married has many financial implications, and a prenup provides an opportunity to talk through the issues and come to a mutual understanding. The biggie is to

FINANCIAL JARGON MADE EASY

The "marriage penalty" comes up occasionally in conversation—mainly when friends are presenting reasons why you shouldn't get hitched. And during election years. Politicians have been making campaign promises to eliminate the marriage penalty ever since it was created in 1969. A consequence of the tax system, the so-called penalty results in many two-income married couples paying more in income taxes than they would if they were single, whether they file jointly or separately. Couples who bring similar incomes to their union are hit the hardest. When shown as a simple math problem, it's plain to see why some married people pay more income taxes:

1 income + 1 income = 2 taxpayers

Lawmakers have attempted to minimize the marriage penalty over the years, most recently with the passage of the Jobs and Growth Tax Relief Reconciliation Act of 2003. Among many changes having absolutely nothing to do with penalizing married couples, the law increased the standard deduction for married couples filing jointly to exactly double what's allowed for single taxpayers. It also expanded the 15 percent tax bracket for married couples to twice that of single taxpayers, which prevents part of a couple's income from being pushed into a higher bracket simply because they get married. However, both changes are temporary and in effect only for the 2003 and 2004 tax years, when they are scheduled to begin a slow phase-out that will last until 2010. At that time the law is supposed to revert to its 2001 version, which we simply cannot explain in the space provided. Confusing, isn't it? All of this gives the government several years to evaluate, negotiate, and pass other laws that could affect the marriage penalty one way or the other.

Basically what you need to know about the marriage penalty is that your income tax liability could be affected by your marital status. For the next few years that impact will be less than it's been but not as much as it could be. The thing about laws affecting the federal tax code is they could be filed under the same heading as the name of this chapter, "The Only Constant Is Change."

We've got more financial jargon for you, whether you're married or single, in the glossary in the back of the book.

figure out, hypothetically speaking of course, how you would divide treasure brought to the marriage and accumulated during your years together, in the unfortunate event of a divorce. If you're stumbling over initial conversations about assets and whatnot, you're likely to encounter more difficulties once the knot is tied, so proceed with caution.

HOW TO NOT COME UNGLUED DURING THE GREAT DIVIDE

There's no such thing as a smooth transition from marital money management to our next topic of discussion, so we'll skip that banter. When a marriage doesn't work, and one or both partners are ready to split, the solution may be divorce. Divorce can mean heartache and disappointment, and a serious case of financial upset. It's important to understand how your financial picture will be altered by divorce, since the terms you agree to during the dissolution of your marriage will have an impact on your finances for the rest of your life. We know it's easier said than done, but try to look at your divorce as the end of a partnership rather than the end of a romance. You'll come out slightly more intact if you can treat the settlement like a business transaction. Keep your emotions in check, and you will be better equipped to handle all the messy details.

We've got stuff here to help you get through the divorce from a financial standpoint. It might be stuff you haven't thought about. It is probably stuff you don't *want* to think about. You can take it or leave it, but then don't blame us when your divorce is final and you realize you should have found out what a QDRO is. Because we can help you with that.

HERE'S A TO-DO LIST WHEN YOU HAVEN'T GOT A CLUE

You may have decided that divorce is the best option for you. It may be the only option. But what's next? We're not here to counsel you on anything but the financial issues relating to your divorce, but we're well aware that those issues can be overwhelming. Just take a look at this list to get an idea what you'll need to do in the coming weeks and months. Don't let the tasks freak you out. If you take things one step at a time, you may be surprised how much progress you've made in a few months. And, you can rely on your attorney and financial professional for advice, unless of course, hiring either or both has yet to be crossed off your to-do list.

- If you haven't yet hired lawyers to duke it out, consider hiring a mediator. One of them to negotiate your settlement instead of two lawyers is bound to cost less money. Mediators are able to deal with the inevitable emotional aspects as well as the financial side of the transaction.
- You will need to open new bank and credit card accounts in your name only. If you had credit in your spouse's name, you can start working on building your own good credit history by establishing an account and paying it off every month.
- Get copies of your credit report from the three major credit bureaus (find out how in Chapter 4). Check for errors and make sure that any preexisting debts of your former spouse don't show up on your report. You may need protection from your ex's business liabilities or potential bankruptcies. In other words, both assets *and* liabilities are split in a divorce.
- Read Chapter 11, on identity protection, to ensure that you are doing everything possible to maintain the integrity of your identity on your drive through Splitsville.
- Review the beneficiary designations on all your insurance policies. Your dissolution agreement can require your ex to purchase life insurance with your children as beneficiaries.

- If you don't have access to health insurance at your work, you might want to negotiate funds for health insurance coverage until you find new insurance.
- Find out about your ex's employer-sponsored retirement plan and consult your attorney about just what a Qualified Domestic Relations Order (QDRO) can mean to your financial future. A QDRO has to do with splitting the value of your respective retirement plans, and we get into specifics in just a few pages.
- You'll want to remove your ex-spouse from your will and cancel any power-of-attorney agreements the two of you may have. It's hard to remove a name from a will that doesn't exist, so let this be a clue to the procrastinator in you that it will be more important than ever to have these types of legal documents.
- If you have kids, make arrangements for your ex to leave part of his or her estate to your children, especially if he or she remarries and starts a new family. And you might want to require that your ex contribute to educational trusts for your children.
- If you are keeping the house, consider refinancing under your name only. If the home is sold, you must divide the proceeds with your spouse, unless the two of you agree to do otherwise. If your ex retains ownership and you move out, remove your name from the mortgage. Generally, property transfers resulting from a divorce are not taxed.

WHO GETS YOURS, MINE, AND OURS

It's always tricky to decide who gets what during the great divide. For many, the most challenging aspect of splitting households is to determine who gets what. The bitter feelings that often accompany divorce can make it even harder to part with what you may feel is rightfully yours. Sometimes the financial implications of ownership are not immediately obvious. Take time to think through what you need, versus what you want, versus what you just can't stand the idea of your ex getting. Try not to let emotions dictate your decisions, or you may regret your actions later. The best defense is to arm yourself with information, and you just may avoid a property war. First, take an inventory of all that you own, jointly and separately. Here's a checklist to help you consider all types of assets.

Documents

Federal and state tax returns for the past five years
Pre- and post-wedding agreements
Previous divorce settlements
Wills and trust documents
Pay stubs for the past six months

Account Statements

Savings, bank, and credit union accounts
Certificate of deposit and checking accounts
Mutual funds
Investment and brokerage accounts
Credit card accounts
Other loan statements

Retirement Plans

All company plans, such as 401(k) and 403(b)
Individual Retirement Accounts
Defined benefit plans or pensions
Previous employer plan statements

Employee Benefits

Cafeteria plans
Stock options
Health and other insurance benefits
Bonuses

Real Estate Records

Titles, deeds, and other ownership records
Purchase, rent, or lease documentation for your current residence
Mortgages
Home equity loans
Cemetery deeds

Insurance Policy Documents

Life
Disability Income
Homeowners
Umbrella liability
Medical
Automobile
Long-term care

Appraised List

Valuables
Collectibles
Antiques
Artwork
Jewelry

KNOW HOW PROPERTY IS DEFINED IN YOUR STATE

First of all, there are legal definitions of ownership that will affect
how your property is divided between you and your spouse. And the
laws regulating division of property vary by state. For example, nine
states (Arizona, California, Idaho, Louisiana, Nevada, New Mexico,
Texas, Washington, and Wisconsin) currently follow rules of community property that require a 50/50 split of all marital property.
Other states generally follow some process of equitable distribution,
meaning a fair, though not necessarily equal, distribution of assets

obtained during the course of a marriage. In general, property is classified as either separate or marital property. Separate property includes all that baggage you each bring into the marriage, inheritances received individually during the marriage, and gifts received individually during the marriage. Marital property includes any property (from land to knickknacks) you acquire during the marriage and property owned by both spouses or registered jointly. You should consult a qualified expert or attorney in your state for more information.

WHO PAYS WHEN YOU BOTH OWE?

Paying off old debts, which may have been the source of marital strife to begin with, can be particularly irksome and downright depressing. But if you face the issue head-on, you can make sure you don't get stuck with more than your share. With debt, somebody's gotta pay. If your name is on a bill—even if your spouse's name is too—you are generally obligated to fork it over. Consider everything you owe as you enter divorce proceedings. Think about secured debt like mortgages and car loans; unsecured debt like credit cards, bank loans, lines of credit, and personal loans; tax debt including interest and penalties; and finally, divorce expenses, including what you may owe for court fees, legal or financial help, mediation, and so forth.

Be proactive to avoid a situation where a former spouse fails to pay a debt and you get socked with the bill. Try to use existing assets to satisfy mutual debts, and close accounts you own together. It's worth the expense to gain the peace of mind. Chapter 3, on debt, has all sorts of ideas you can use to help yourself reduce and eliminate debt, before the two of you eliminate each other from your lives.

THE HOUSE MAY NO LONGER BE HOME, SWEET HOME

Face it. If somebody doesn't move, you won't have a divorce. You'll have a really bad roommate. Who's it going to be? Maybe both of you will pull up stakes and move. If you plan to sell, you might want to sell prior to the divorce to get full tax benefit through the capital gains exclusion. It currently allows the exclusion of up to $250,000 individually or $500,000 jointly from the sale or exchange of a principal residence if you've owned the home at least two years.

Before you can make a decision, consider whether you can afford to stay. If kids are involved, it's especially tempting to do so because you may not want to uproot them from the neighborhood and schools. Just don't let your heart be your only guide in the debate. You've also got to take a serious look at expenses. Homeownership is not cheap, and those little pencil marks on the wall noting a child's growth spurts won't pay the mortgage—or the property taxes, utilities, and general maintenance costs. If for some reason you don't have a handle on what your household has been spending to live in the house, do yourself a favor and review the checkbook register before you decide. We're not telling you it's out of the question to stay in your home, we're just prodding you to look at the numbers.

You can choose not to sell. One option is to agree to rent-free occupancy. In this situation, the custodial parent may live in the house while the other parent pays the house payment. The downside for the paying spouse is that the house payment is usually not income tax–deductible. Another option is to agree to sell the house at a future date, for example, when the kids leave for college.

WHO GETS THE RETIREMENT SAVINGS?

In a divorce proceeding, your soon-to-be-former spouse may be given a right to receive a portion of your employer-sponsored retirement plan. The court order giving one spouse rights in the other spouse's retirement plan is called a Qualified Domestic Relations Order (QDRO). It may allow the receiving spouse to roll over the benefit he or she receives into an income tax–deferred account without incurring any early withdrawal penalties or paying taxes on the funds until distribution later on. If you have a QDRO spelling out how the benefits are to be assigned to each party in the divorce, the retirement plan sponsor must recognize it.

The IRS makes certain provisions to help divorcing couples split retirement savings without penalty. We'll give you a quick overview of the most popular retirement plans, because the type of plan you have will influence how you can go about dividing the assets. *Defined contribution plans* are 401(k) or 403(b) plans. The value of the account will depend on who contributes (the employee, employer, or both) and the length of employment. At the time of your settlement, you can withdraw funds from the transferred account without paying the 10 percent early withdrawal penalty tax, but you will get hit with current income taxes on the amount withdrawn.

Other employer-sponsored plans include *defined benefit plans*, which guarantee a certain amount per month after retirement. There are two common ways to handle a split for this type of benefit. The first is a buyout, where one spouse gets a lump-sum settlement to offset the future benefit to the working spouse. Another option allows that each spouse is awarded a share of the benefits if and when they are paid. The share is calculated based on the number of years of marriage. In this arrangement, it is wise for the nonemployee spouse to specify how the benefit will be handled if the employee spouse does not retire and does not take the benefit when expected.

DON'T FORGET SOCIAL SECURITY

There are all sorts of theories about whether Social Security will be available and for how long. You might even get some twisted pleasure out of blaming your former spouse for Social Security's demise. But before you do, keep reading. If you were married for 10 or more years and the divorce is at least two years old, you may be entitled to Social Security benefits based on your spouse's earnings and entitlement. Of course, you'd only want to pursue this route if the amount from your spouse's benefits exceeds the amount you'd receive based on your own contributions. If you remarry, you may lose the right to claim any portion of your former spouse's benefits. Consult an attorney or tax professional for more information.

UNCLE SAM DOESN'T CARE ABOUT YOUR MARITAL STATUS

When you split from your spouse, there will be all sorts of nagging reminders that you are no longer hitched. One will happen at income tax time when you are trying to figure out your filing status. If you're divorced by the last day of the year, Uncle Sam will consider you unmarried for the whole year. Same goes if on the last day of the year you're legally separated from your spouse. In either case, you can choose to file your income tax return as single or head of household. Head of household filers receive a higher standard deduction than either single or married, filing separately taxpayers. And there's a different tax rate schedule too, which means you'll probably pay less income taxes overall. To qualify as head of household, however, you must be able to answer "yes" to all three of these questions:

1. Are you unmarried or considered unmarried (legally separated) on the last day of the year?
2. Did you pay more than half the cost of keeping up a home for the year?
3. Does a qualifying person (a kid) live with you for more than half the year, not including temporary absences for things like school? (If you have a dependent parent, he or she doesn't have to live with you in order to qualify for head of household status.)

If you share children, both you and your former spouse can legally file as head of household if you manage the process properly. You'll need to cooperate with each other—and probably with an income tax advisor or certified public accountant—to ensure that everything is in order to make that possible. Who knows? You may both be a little happier at tax time.

THERE'S A BIG DIFFERENCE BETWEEN ALIMONY AND CHILD SUPPORT

It may seem as though maintenance, formerly called alimony, and child support play similar roles, but the IRS sees it differently. Child support isn't considered income to the recipient and it can't be listed as a deduction for the noncustodial parent. But if you are paying maintenance, you can deduct it from your income taxes, and the recipient has to pay income taxes on it. Make sure the divorce decree specifies which is which, because otherwise it may all be considered child support for income tax purposes. If you are required to make house payments on a jointly owned home, you can deduct half the total payment as maintenance. Plus, when you itemize your income tax deductions, you can claim half the interest and property tax. As we have mentioned more than once, you may want to consult an attorney or tax professional for more information.

MONEY CAN'T BUY THEIR LOVE

If you've got kids, your trip to divorce court is more complicated in many ways. You know that already. What you may not realize is that divorcing parents tend to overspend on their children during the course of the separation and divorce in some bizarre attempt to substitute money for emotional support. During this difficult time, we caution you to be aware that finances and emotions are two very different things. We're not going to pretend to offer parenting tips in a personal finance book, but we do have a few suggestions you can choose to read or ignore.

- Maintaining two households for your kids is going to cost both parents in ways it's hard to plan for. If you overspend on the kids when setting up those households, how will you handle their reaction when you run out of cash? Don't set yourself up to incur the added stress that big debts can bring.
- For the good of the kids, try to maintain a civil attitude when discussing financial issues with your ex, either in front of the kids or in private. Money messages stick on kids like lollipops. Chapter 12, on money and values, has more insights on this.
- Finally, avoid shopping sprees to compensate for guilt feelings you may have. Your kids would probably rather spend the afternoon with you than spend your money at the mall.

6

Home, Sweet Investment

Of his house, Yogi Berra, the famous baseball icon and infamous quote-meister, supposedly said, "It's nothing but rooms." If you subscribe to that theory of homeownership, you can probably skip right over this chapter because we happen to think your house is much more than that. Whether you've been a homeowner for years or you're still squirreling away pennies for that first down payment, your house could very well be the largest asset you'll ever own. Hardly "nothing but rooms," if you ask us. It's rare that anybody actually *asks us*, however, which is probably why we'll never be sought out for quips and quotes like the legendary New York Yankee.

If you're still reading, we'll assume your home means more to you than a block of square footage. Maybe it's your castle. Maybe it's a money pit. Maybe with its size and location it's not quite your idea of the American dream but you can see it from there. Are you looking to buy? To sell? Ready to switch from an adjustable-rate mortgage to one that's fixed? Have you put off a call to the refi guy long enough? What was it your coworker said the other day about how making an extra payment every year could cut your mortgage term by years? How can you find out if you should put that mortgage in reverse? Do you know anything more about your homeowners insurance policy than that the premiums keep climbing? Which is better, a new kitchen or a paint job? In this chapter we've got answers to some fairly big questions about your fairly huge investment. We've got to warn you that as with most aspects of home ownership, the answers all depend on your unique situation, so this chapter might generate more questions than it answers.

MYRIAD MORTGAGES DEMYSTIFIED

We'll take care of the dull stuff right away. Mortgages are a mystery most of us don't understand, but thankfully that doesn't stop us from buying and selling houses with reckless abandon. You've probably been the proud owner of at least one mortgage, according to Census 2000 results revealing that 66 percent of Americans own their homes. But have you got any clue what a mortgage is all about? We certainly don't want to add to the confusion, but with mortgages being a fact in two out of three American lives, we must fulfill our obligation to inform and educate. Local libraries have stacks of books about mortgages, so we'll leave the heavy lifting to someone else. We merely want to provide a brief overview of the various types of financing you'll encounter (have encountered?) in the home lending market. There are other types than we mention here, but these are the main mortgages and mortgage programs available. A professional lender can help you decide which is best for you.

Conventional Loan

You may have heard it called by its other name, the fixed-rate mortgage, which aptly describes what a conventional loan offers—a fixed rate for the life of the loan. This type of loan is most typically appropriate for individuals with good credit and a down payment. It's not guaranteed or insured by the government, however, so don't go thinking you can count on Uncle Sam to make your payments for you.

Adjustable Rate Mortgage (ARM)

From the outset, an ARM is going to offer a lower interest rate than a fixed-rate mortgage. But as the name implies, after a certain number of years, the rate on such a loan will adjust up or down based on some specific benchmark, often U.S. Treasury securities. If you are consider-ing an ARM, compare the maximum variation allowable in the interest rate (up or down) between ARMs you are considering before signing on the dotted line. An ARM is an especially useful financing tool if you don't plan to own your home for a long time.

Federal Housing Authority (FHA)

This type of loan generally requires a low down payment and allows the borrower to borrow more money. It's one way the government encour-ages home ownership and is designed to help moderate- and low-income individuals find affordable housing. A mortgage insurance premium (MIP) is added to an FHA loan, usually at closing, to protect against default. It's different than private mortgage insurance, which we discuss ad nauseam later in the chapter.

Veterans Administration (VA)

United States veterans are eligible for this home loan based on the length of service. A down payment is generally not required, but the same goes for VA loans as FHA loans where MIP is concerned.

Balloon Loan

This loan has a fixed rate with low monthly payment, but there's a large lump sum that is due at the end of the term. Borrowers must be sure they can handle the final payment at the end of the loan because it tends to surprise them, much like a balloon popping in a quiet room. A balloon loan is usually borrowed by people who intend to refinance or sell before it pops.

Contract for Deed

This is a seller-financed arrangement, which can help a buyer get into a home when other lending options fall short. The buyer and seller agree to the terms of the contract. A contract for deed usually spans a shorter time frame for repayment than a mortgage (less than 5 years versus 15 to 30). Payments are made by installments with a balloon payment at the end of the loan period.

Jumbo Mortgage

The name says it all. It's basically a conventional loan for homes priced above about $333,000 (higher in Alaska and Hawaii). Jumbo mortgages generally have a slightly higher interest rate than smaller mortgages, and not just because everything about them seems bigger. The higher rate no doubt has to do with higher potential risk.

Reverse Mortgage

If you're 62 or older you may want to know more about the reverse mortgage, but we're not going to bore you with too much here because there's an entire section on this sort of mortgage later in this chapter.

BE SURE YOU GET WHAT YOU PAY FOR

The mortgage business has its own language, but you can master it if you do your homework. Points, rates, and fees are certainly important numbers when you are making home loan decisions, but they aren't the only considerations you have when selecting a lender. You have to be able to effectively compare those numbers and understand that some lenders use different names when describing them. One lender might offer to waive one fee and then add another one. Another lender might quote one interest rate, then add or subtract some discount points that could make the loan cheaper or more expensive than another lender's loan at the same interest rate. Have we confused you sufficiently? Welcome to the world of mortgage madness. The key is to keep asking questions until you get all the answers you need.

When shopping mortgages, you'll want to request a standard good-faith estimate from prospective lenders. It lists all the things you can be charged for or what will affect the actual cost of the loan. Not every deal will involve fees for all of the services, but keep them in mind so you're prepared in the end. The estimate includes discount points and fees for the appraisal, loan origination, lender's inspection, underwriting review, administration, and application processing. There is also the cost of a credit report, a tax service contract, the title search and insurance, the notary, recording fee and tax stamps, and courier services. Can you believe that after all of those fees, they will charge you for courier services too? At least the lender can't charge you for a good-faith estimate, and requesting one doesn't commit you to that lender either.

WHEN A LOCK ISN'T SECURE

Securing an interest rate on your mortgage is a critical step in the mortgage application process—whether you're getting a new mortgage or refinancing. Depending on how low interest rates are when you're shopping for a mortgage, consider either signing a written rate-lock agreement or floating the rate until just before closing. A formal rate-lock document is essential if rates are dropping because if mortgage business picks up, the closing could get delayed, and you might end up getting stuck with a higher rate if rates climb during the delay. Floating the rate is smart during fluctuating periods in the mortgage market because the rate could go down, but if you're locked in you might need to jump through hoops to secure a lower rate. Oral agreements are usually binding if they're made within 10 days of closing. Laws on locking mortgage rates vary by state, but one universal truth is that unless you have proof you've been quoted a specific interest rate, there's no guarantee that rate will still be available on closing day. Pay attention because even small changes in the interest rate can be worth thousands of dollars over the life of your mortgage.

MORTGAGE MISTAKES HOMEBUYERS MAKE

Whether you're shopping for your first home or plotting the purchase of a vacation home at the lake, learn what *not* to do by reading these common mortgage miscues. You can find out the hard way, but it's more fun to read how other people mess up. Whether you learn from them or make the same mistakes yourself is up to you.

1. *Not fixing your credit.* The number of buyers who use the cross-your-fingers approach when applying for credit is astounding. Long before you start looking at homes, look at your credit report to gain a better understanding of your credit history. Nicks on that report could cost you dearly when you're negotiating with a mortgage lender. Give yourself six months to challenge errors and improve the factors that are hurting your score, such as paying down credit card debt and canceling some department store accounts. See Chapter 4 to find out how to get your credit reports and how your credit rating affects your ability to get good rates.

2. *Not getting preapproved for a loan.* The main thing here is knowing the difference between being "prequalified" and "preapproved" for a loan. You're prequalified when a lender tells you how much you can probably borrow based on your income, debt, and cash available for a down payment. Getting preapproved, on the other hand, is a process whereby you actually apply for a loan and provide documents proving your income, debt, and available cash. The lender will verify your information and agree in writing to make the loan. It's basically the difference between looking at the home section of the Sunday paper and being able to make an offer on your dream home. Most sellers look favorably on an offer from a preapproved buyer because they can be confident the individual will be able to obtain a mortgage to seal the sale. Keep in mind that most preapproval commitments do not lock in the interest rate, so if you dillydally for six months while interest rates take a hike, you may be looking at altogether different terms from your lender.

3. *Making changes before you close.* Say you get preapproved, find the perfect dwelling and the seller accepts your offer. Now don't

do anything wacky. Home buyers who experience "material changes" between the time they sign the purchase agreement and sign their lives away at closing just may end up without a mortgage. Lenders look carefully at job changes and credit purchases, especially. Don't go financing a new car to drive to the closing, for example. And if you must switch jobs during this crucial time period, be sure to keep your lender in the loop. A job change in the same field or salary ballpark won't have much of an impact, but if you quit your job to start your own business, you'll have a lot of explaining to do. Especially if you plan to run your business out of the trunk of that new car.

4. *Borrowing too much money.* We all have friends who are house poor. Perhaps all you need to do to find someone in that situation is look in the mirror. Lenders will loan you as much as you qualify for, with no regard to what you can actually afford to spend each month. Instead of stretching yourself too thin, consider limiting your housing costs—mortgage payments, property taxes, and homeowners insurance—to 25 percent of your gross income, versus the nearly 35 percent lenders may be willing to hand you. Be warned that calculating this percentage will involve actual math, and then you'll need to be disciplined too. Sort of a double whammy.

5. *Taking the first rate that's offered.* Many buyers will search tirelessly for an abode with just the right bathroom fixtures, but they'll take the first loan that's offered. In an effort to boost profits, mortgage brokers may ask for a higher interest rate than your credit standing would qualify for. Be sure to shop around and do some research before you walk blindly into an interest rate that's too high or mortgage restrictions that could stifle. And be sure to read the fine print.

6. *Same goes for fees.* Most of the closing costs on a mortgage loan are legitimate, but brokers have been known to pad their take on the deal by inflating fees for document preparation and the like. Don't be afraid to challenge every line on the good-faith estimate of closing costs, or at the very least, ask for a thorough explanation of every fee. Compare anticipated closing costs when shop-

ping for a lender, and let them know you're doing it. You may still end up paying some questionable fees, because frankly, they're hard to decipher and lenders are good at disguising them.

7. *Skipping an inspection.* You might be sorry if you fail to make your purchase contingent on a home inspection. Professional home inspectors cost less than $500, and they're bound to uncover potential problems with their trained eye that you can't see. Stuff like a leaky roof or basement, outdated mechanical systems and faulty appliances. It could cost you dearly if you don't pay someone to case the joint before it's yours.

8. *Not planning for closing costs.* Many home buyers are so excited to move into their new place and spend money decorating it that they forget to plan for a pretty sizeable expense called closing costs. The day of closing on your home, you'll probably need to pay somewhere between 2 percent and 7 percent of the cost of the house for attorney's fees, taxes, title insurance, points, and other fees. They should be detailed in the good-faith estimate, but keep in mind that the operative word there is "estimate." You're probably also paying for any refreshments you're offered at closing, so enjoy that "free" cup of coffee.

9. *Misplacing mandatory paperwork.* Most of our readers won't be affected by this one because it involves advance preparation—something procrastinators shy away from. Any home purchase requires that you turn over stacks of financial documentation to the lender—pay stubs, bank statements, and whatnot. If you're inclined to pack up your existing household in anticipation of your move, just be sure to keep that paperwork off the moving truck. It's a common occurrence, especially if there's a short period of time between purchase and closing, and can lead buyers to make frantic calls to their employers and banks for duplicate documents. But as we mentioned, most of our loyal readers haven't a clue what it means to plan ahead.

10. *Blowing off the banker.* Let's hope this one never comes into play, but should you ever find yourself in dire financial circumstances and unable to make your mortgage payment, don't hide from the lender. Your bank wants you to be a successful customer, but you

have to stay in touch. The worst thing you can do is ignore phone calls and letters, yet fearful homeowners often take this route. There are several options if you can't stay current on your mortgage, but you need to work with your lender to find the one that's right for you.

FALLING FINANCING RATES FUEL REFINANCING FRENZY

Hype-filled headlines like that—packed with allure and alliteration in equal amounts—were used repeatedly by news editors in recent years as mortgage rates dropped so low they could win the local limbo contest. Just when it seemed they could fall no more, rates would lose another quarter percent, luring another quarter million eager mortgage brokers into the business chasing what must have seemed like more than a quarter billion dollars in fees. You know things are out of hand when it's not a fad merely to refinance. Homeowners had to do so multiple times in one year to achieve mood-ring status at parties.

Low interest rates that translate into lower monthly payments are certainly a motivating factor, but there are several other reasons why refi-

---

Poll

What are you doing with your home to boost its value?

Remodeling a room	29%
Nothing at this time	28%
Making extra payments to increase equity	24%
Landscaping	13%
Replacing the roof	6%

Poll of visitors to ihatefinancialplanning.com

---

nancing your mortgage could make your home an even better investment than it already is. If you have an adjustable rate mortgage (ARM), you can refinance to a fixed rate that may not be as low, but at least it will no longer fluctuate up and down. You might also be able to eliminate private mortgage insurance (PMI) from your monthly payment during the refinance process. If the value of your home has increased to a level that gives you at least 20 percent equity, say hello to extra cash previously wrapped up in PMI each month. (Look for more on PMI later in this chapter.) Yet another reason to refinance is that you may be able to change the term of your loan. Imagine owning your home free and clear in 15 years instead of 30. Your payment will be higher, but the light at the end of the tunnel will be a lot closer.

There are some fairly steep fees associated with any refinance, so it may not be such a good idea if you're planning to move soon. You want to remain at your address long enough to justify the cost of the transaction. Should your mortgage happen to be small, refinancing may not be for you unless there's a big difference between your current mortgage interest rate and the one you'll pay following the refinance. That's simply because you'll pay a lot to get the deal done. You may be better off prepaying your current mortgage, which we discuss at length on the very next page.

Your lender may be willing to work with you on a low-cost refinance or modification to your existing mortgage, perhaps without an appraisal. It's worth asking, especially if you don't want to shop around for the absolutely lowest rate. Speaking of, your ability to qualify for rock-bottom interest rates will depend on your credit rating, which will also have an impact on your lender's willingness to cut out some of the paperwork and fees. Chapter 4, on credit, can help you crack the code on credit ratings.

A cash-out refinance is one of the more common transactions—and potentially most ill-advised. In a cash-out refinance, the new mortgage is larger than the existing one, with the extra money resulting from the fact that the equity in the home is worth more than what is owed on the mortgage. Borrowers oftentimes use the cash to finance home improvements, debt consolidation, a new car, or whatever else. Depending on interest rates, a cash-out refinance can be a wise money management tool, but allow us to remind you to refrain from refinancing your home solely to use the equity as cash and spend it like there's no tomorrow. Because tomorrow tends to show up and ask for payment due. You'll be sorry if your home ends up going to the bank in foreclosure.

SHAVE YEARS OFF YOUR MORTGAGE

Owning a home gives you many options. You can replace the water heater or you can adjust to cold showers. You can plant a garden or plant an idea in your neighbor's head to trim her weeping willow that droops on your power lines. You can pay your mortgage according to schedule, or you can save interest dollars by putting extra cash on your loan.

Any additional money you pay on your mortgage is applied to the principal, which will reduce your total interest costs over the life of your loan and shorten the length of your loan. But since mortgage interest is deductible from your income taxes, you also reduce potential tax breaks. It's important to weigh that in the balance when deciding what to do. There's usually no penalty for paying off your mortgage early, but it's wise to confirm that with your lender nevertheless.

Prepaying a mortgage isn't for everyone, but it could be smart for homeowners who pay the private mortgage insurance we discussed earlier. You may be paying PMI if you have less than 20 percent equity in your home. Making extra payments could put you over the top and subsequently eliminate your need for that pesky PMI. Prepaying also works well for homeowners who don't deduct mortgage interest from their income at tax time. We encourage you to take advantage of every tax break you qualify for, so if you're not deducting mortgage interest simply because you're too lazy to itemize, you're wasting your own money. If, however, your mortgage is small and your interest doesn't exceed the standard deduction, paying off the loan early could be something you want to consider.

There are a variety of ways to pay off your mortgage early. The easiest method is to add an extra amount to your regular payment. Even $25 or $50 a month could really add up. Here's an idea of what you could save in interest if you pad your house payment every month.

These figures are based on a 30-year mortgage for $150,000 at a fixed rate of 6.5 percent. This example is purely hypothetical and doesn't factor in property taxes and homeowners insurance, which are real costs that would affect any potential savings.

Potential Savings with Extra Payment on a 30-Year Mortgage

Prepay	Interest Paid	Interest Saved	Pay Off
0	$191,317	0	30 yrs.
$25	$174,526	$16,791	27 yrs., 10 mo.
$50	$160,819	$30,498	26 yrs.
$100	$139,592	$51,725	23 yrs., 1 mo.
$200	$111,401	$79,916	19 yrs.

Another strategy for prepaying your mortgage is the biweekly payment plan. Instead of making 12 monthly mortgage payments each year, you make a payment every two weeks, which translates into 13 payments a year. (52 weeks in the year = 26 half payments = 13 full payments.) The biweekly plan works well if your monthly cash flow would benefit from two smaller house payments instead of one big one. But if you're paid once a month or self-employed, it may be difficult to make a mortgage payment every 15 days. Take a look at the potential savings on these hypothetical mortgage amounts, which again, don't include property taxes or insurance.

Potential Savings with Biweekly Payment Schedule on a 30-Year Mortgage

Mortgage	4.5% Interest	5.5% Interest	6.5% Interest	7.5% Interest
$100,000	$14,520	$21,464	$30,329	$41,324
$200,000	$29,040	$42,928	$60,659	$82,648
$300,000	$43,560	$64,391	$90,988	$123,972
$400,000	$58,080	$85,885	$121,317	$165,297

You can establish an official biweekly plan with your lender or a third-party organization that will handle the paperwork, but you'll pay an initiation fee and also a monthly service charge for the convenience. An easy alternative is to make any extra payment yourself, either by adding 1/12 to each monthly house payment or forcing yourself to save money until you have accumulated enough for a full extra payment. Depending on how disciplined you are, you may decide it's worth it to pay someone else to manage the process, but those fees may not be worth it if you don't intend to live in your house long enough to make the expense worthwhile.

Whatever your strategy, your prepayment plan will only work if you keep it up over the long term. A one-time, lump-sum payment certainly can't hurt, but you won't see the benefits until the end of the mortgage. If you think paying an extra $100 here or there is the same as consistently adding $50 to your monthly payment, all those remarks your math teacher made about your skills in school are probably true. We're compelled to caution you against becoming so consumed with paying off your mortgage early that you neglect other financial goals, such as paying off those high-interest credit cards, saving cash for normal upkeep on your home, and maximizing income tax–deferred retirement accounts. Don't pay extra on your home if you don't have the rest of your financial house in order.

PROPERTY TAX GOING THROUGH THE ROOF?

If you're tired of watching your property taxes climb into the rafters, go to your local assessor's office and find out what property taxes your neighbors are paying. If you're paying more for a similar house, challenge your tax bill. Also, read the fine print because errors in square footage or the number of bathrooms in the assessor's description of your home could result in your being charged too much. You may have to file an appeal, which the assessor's office or local board of tax review can help you with. Don't say we didn't warn you that all of this will take some effort on your part.

IMAGINE GETTING PAID TO LIVE IN YOUR OWN HOUSE

If you're a homeowner who's older than 62 or you know someone who is, you might want to know more about something called a reverse mortgage. It's a tool that is becoming more popular as older folks look for ways to maintain their lifestyle in retirement. Basically you draw cash out of what might be your biggest asset—your house—and you don't need to pay it back until you move or die.

Homeowners age 62 or older are eligible for reverse mortgages. There's no credit rating or income requirement and you can use the money for whatever reason you want. Depending on which type of loan you choose, you can receive a fixed monthly payment either for a specified period or for as long as you (or your spouse) live, a lump sum, or a line of credit you can access as the need arises. Most people choose the line of credit option, so the money is there if and when they need it, but they aren't forced to take a monthly check just to satisfy the terms of the loan. The amount of money available depends on the value of your home, your age (or your spouse's, if you have one who is younger), and the interest rate. The older you are the more you can get, presumably because you won't be around as long, but that's a thought we'd rather avoid.

When the last homeowner on the mortgage moves or passes away, the amount that must be paid back is the total principal and interest, plus any fees financed as part of the loan. The fees can be steep and usually include mortgage insurance, but they'll be subtracted from the amount you receive, so you won't have to pay them out of pocket. If you move or die soon after the transaction, you won't get the same return you would if you were to live a long time, but that goes without saying.

Reverse mortgages are mainly for people who don't want to pull up stakes and move. If you are in a position to sell your home and buy or rent something cheaper, you may want to consider it before committing to a complicated reverse mortgage. And believe us when we say these things are complicated. One more thing, federal law requires that people who want a reverse mortgage undergo financial counseling. Who knows why, but it's true. The counseling is free and provided by federally approved agencies. Maybe they're looking for people with skeletons in their closets, but that's unlikely considering that those people have to stay in their house to make a reverse mortgage work (and they probably need the closet space).

The Federal Housing Authority (FHA) has a program called a home equity conversion mortgage, which is the only reverse mortgage insured by the federal government. Interest and fees are consistent from lender to lender on this one, so you don't have to worry about getting taken by an ambitious mortgage broker. There are some fees on the FHA conversion mortgage that vary, including an origination fee and a monthly servicing fee. Learn more about the FHA home equity conversion mortgage at the National Center for Home Equity Conversion (reverse.org). The AARP (aarp.org) has a guide—including a nifty calculator—that can help you figure out if a reverse mortgage is right for you.

HERE'S A FLOOD OF INSURANCE INFORMATION

Burglaries. Fire. Floods. A broken back from hauling that mattress up the stairs. These are some of the things you can protect yourself from financially when you own a home. There are several types of insurance that cover these unfortunate occurrences, and it's important to investigate each one further to ensure you'll have the right types and amounts of coverage. You may also need other types of coverage, such as private mortgage insurance. The following list should pretty well cover you for the coverage you should consider covering yourself with.

Homeowners Insurance

This is standard stuff if you own a home, and it protects you (and in some cases, your lender) from financial setbacks that can occur from unfriendly hazards to your home or belongings. What we're talking about is stuff such as burglary, fire, lightning, hail, windstorms, explosions, civil riots, and comets arriving uninvited for dinner. Technically we're not sure whether that last one is covered; it probably depends on what you're serving for the main course. We get into more detail on this essential coverage in a few pages.

Umbrella Liability Insurance

Most standard homeowners policies include personal liability protection that usually covers bodily injury to non–family members and property damage resulting from personal activity or conditions on your property. However, the limits may be fairly small ($1,000 per person for injuries and $100,000 for liability is common), so you may want to consider an umbrella or excess liability policy for broader coverage. Most policies like that cost less than $300 for $1 million of protection, and the umbrella pops up when you use up standard coverage from your home or automobile policy.

Flood Insurance

Nope, it's not typically covered under your standard homeowners policy. Don't ask us why. But thanks to Federal Emergency Management Agency (FEMA) you can purchase flood insurance (anything's available for a buck, right?) through most property/casualty insurance companies and agents. And if you live in a flood-prone zone, you may be required by your lender to get flood insurance. If you live in the desert, beware of the flood insurance salesperson knocking on your door.

Mortgage Life, Disability, or Unemployment Insurance

People often confuse this with private mortgage insurance. Silly people. Actually, it's easily confused. Mortgage life insurance pays the outstanding balance on your mortgage if you die before it's paid off. This coverage pretty much amounts to term life insurance with a face amount that shrinks each year as you pay off the mortgage, so it may or may not be a good value for you. Mortgage disability and unemployment insurance cover you for a set number of payments (usually up to about a year's worth) if you get hurt or get canned, respectively.

Title Insurance

"Mr.," "Ms.," "Sir," or "Hey You" are not the kind of titles we're talking about. The title is this case is a document that determines the claim to ownership in a home, and it's usually one of the multiple documents you pay for when you buy a house. Title insurance covers you in cases of unanticipated claims to an ownership interest in your home. As if anyone would buy a home *anticipating* that someone else would claim ownership of it.

Personal Property Insurance

You've got your real estate. And you've got the stuff that's inside—your household goods. Personal property insurance covers homeowners and renters, not to mention people just moving stuff around from place to place or storing it in those mysterious self-storage facilities, in the event of loss or damage to all that precious, semiprecious, and flat-out junky stuff you've acquired in life.

Private Mortgage Insurance

If you make a down payment of less than 20 percent when you purchase your home, you are probably going to pay for private mortgage insurance (PMI), an extra monthly payment that is about as much fun as any of the other "extra" payments you've got to pay in life. Lenders typically require PMI to protect themselves should borrowers who don't make a 20 percent down payment default on their conventional mortgages. But did you know that PMI may help you afford more house?

When a home buyer buys a PMI policy, lenders may choose to increase their loan-to-value ratios because the risk they are assuming is lessened. What that means to the home buyer is that he or she can purchase a PMI policy, make a smaller down payment, and afford more house, perhaps even as much as 95 percent of the home's value. As with other types of insurance, you must qualify (i.e., meet certain requirements such as income and credit ratings) to obtain a policy. And we insist you also be cautious when stretching to get into a house you can't afford. Being house poor can be a frustrating existence.

Another important thing to keep in mind about PMI is that it's not forever. Once your equity exceeds 20 percent of your loan value as you make payments over time and/or property values increase, you may be able to petition your lender to remove the PMI. You'll be asked to show that your house has not lost its value and that you've made regular payments. Keep reading for more info on eliminating the PMI payment from your budget.

MAKE A CLEAN SWEEP OF PRIVATE MORTGAGE INSURANCE

After discussing the potential benefits of PMI, we'll tell you that once you accrue 20 percent equity in your home, PMI should no longer be required. At anywhere from $30 to $200 or more every month, it's worth sweeping PMI off your mortgage as soon as possible.

GIVE YOURSELF A PIGGYBACK RIDE

The piggyback mortgage is a clever way to maneuver into a home loan without too much pork. And for the record, the loan has nothing to do with pigs. What it is, though, is a method of avoiding private mortgage insurance by stringing together first and second mortgages at the same time. The buyer makes a down payment of say 5 percent and borrows the remaining 95 percent in two loans split into 80 percent and 15 percent. The combination of down payment and 15 percent loan allows for the 20 percent equity threshold a buyer needs to eliminate PMI from the equation. The piggyback payments are usually lower than one payment with PMI added would be. Plus, the interest on the second mortgage may be income tax–deductible but a PMI payment certainly wouldn't be. You'll pay a slightly higher interest rate on the second mortgage than the first and may have a shorter term on it—maybe 15 years instead of 30. Ask your lender to help you crunch the numbers next time you're mortgage shopping to see if it'll put you in hog heaven.

Rising property values mean that making monthly payments isn't the only way to reach the 20 percent threshold. Say you put down $20,000 on a $200,000 home three years ago and borrowed the rest at 7 percent. What you owe now wouldn't put you over the 20 percent mark, but the house is worth $220,000 in your market and that additional $20,000 in equity gives you the bump you need.

A federal law established rules for automatic cancellation of PMI on most home mortgages issued after July 29, 1999, when the loan-to-value drops below 78 percent (FHA or VA loans are not included). If your mortgage predates this law, find out whether you're paying PMI and ask your lender how and when it can be terminated. You may have to pay for an appraisal. Some states have laws that apply to early cancellation of PMI. Call your state consumer protection agency. Also, low interest rates in recent years motivated homeowners to refinance their mortgages in droves. If interest rates still favor a refinance, see if you can eliminate PMI during that process without incurring extra costs.

IT'S GOOD POLICY TO UNDERSTAND HOMEOWNERS INSURANCE

Whether you're a seasoned homeowner or shopping for a starter home, it's smart to get a grip on homeowners insurance. It's usually something homeowners buy when they're about to close on their house and then never think about again. When was the last time you read your homeowners policy? Do you even know where it is? We dare you to find it.

Take a look at the policy you're about to buy, or dig up the one you've had for a while, and find out if it includes guaranteed replacement cost protection. That is optional coverage, but with property values and construction costs constantly on the rise, it may be an option you want now. You could be underinsured if you live in a hot housing market or you've made changes to your home that have added to its replacement value—and we don't mean putting a slipcover on the couch you've had since college.

You want enough insurance to cover 100 percent of the cost of rebuilding your house, but don't confuse what you paid for your house with rebuilding costs. The land isn't at risk from theft, fire, windstorms, and other calamities covered by your policy, so don't include its value when you're deciding how much insurance you need. Premiums are high enough without insuring what doesn't need protecting. A good way to estimate replacement cost is by multiplying the square footage of your house by the local square-foot construction cost, which you can get from a real estate appraiser in your area or the local builders association. Say your house is 2,000 square feet and building costs are $120 per square foot in your area. It would cost $240,000 to replace the home.

While we're talking homeowners insurance, let's review the basics of your policy. It's probably pretty standard, meaning it covers your house and possessions from damage caused by fire, smoke, lightning, windstorms, hail, explosion, rioting, vehicles, theft, and building collapse. Generally, it should offer combo coverage:

- protection if the house is destroyed by fire or robbed, etc.;
- protection against a lawsuit if someone slips on your front steps;
- protection if some natural catastrophe hits home (excluding floods or earthquakes, which require an additional insurance purchase); and
- protection that will cover living expenses and/or the cost of making your home livable while it's being repaired after disaster hits (and by this we don't mean a visit by your in-laws).

Your policy won't cover damage caused by procrastination, neglect, or boredom. Or stuff like mold or termite or other pest infestation. If you have a lot of jewelry, computer equipment, collectibles, or other valuable items, you'll pay extra to protect them because a standard homeowners policy won't cut it. We'll leave it up to you to decide whether that's money well spent. All we know is that reviewing your policy now is time well spent.

WHAT WE CLAIM TO KNOW ABOUT CLAIMS

How an insurance company handles its claims can be an important factor in your homeowners insurance purchasing decision. Just take a look at two policies from a couple of different companies and you'll know what we mean. They may seem virtually identical in terms of coverage but be completely different when it comes time to pay a claim after you've had a loss. Find out if you receive the entire claim or just a fraction of it up front. Does the company pay for everything you've lost or just the things you replace? How long do you have to replace your things? A time limit may be a hindrance if you need to stuff your entire family into a motel room while your home is being rebuilt after a fire. Also, find out about any exclusions or limitations on the policy and consider how they may affect possible claims. If a tree falls on your house, repairs to the structure may be covered, but will the policy pay to remove the tree from your property? Just something to think about.

IT MAY BE TIME TO GET A CLUE

One perturbing fact about homeowners insurance is that it can count against you to contact your insurance company and inquire about filing a claim, even if you don't end up doing so. Yes, you read that right the first time. Let's say an electrical storm in your neighborhood fries your computer. We'll skip the infuriating part of such an incident and head right to what many homeowners would do—pick up the phone and ask their insurance agent if their insurance policy has replacement coverage for the PC. Your agent says no, sorry, and you search the ads for a computer sale. What you don't know is that your insurance agent may be required to log in your simple Q and A as an unpaid loss in a database called the Comprehensive Loss Underwriting Exchange, or CLUE. Paid claims are recorded in the CLUE report as well, and everything stays for five years. Insurers can check the database for the five-year claims history of both homeowners and particular properties. CLUE data alerts insurance companies of problem properties and homeowners with a habit of filing claims.

The rules vary by state, so informal inquiries may not be required on CLUE reports where you live, but you might as well assume they are just to be safe. Keep your CLUE history clean by reviewing your homeowners policy so you don't need to rely on your insurance agent for basic questions about coverage and deductibles. It shouldn't be necessary for you to contact the insurance company unless you intend to file a claim for damage you know is covered. Also, refrain from reporting minor damage or losses to avoid having unnecessary claims end up in your CLUE file.

CLUE reports aren't new, but it's only recently that homeowners have been able see theirs. In fact, now it's a report you can buy or get for free depending on where you live. A handful of states (Colorado, Georgia, Maryland, Massachusetts, New Jersey, and Vermont) allow homeowners to receive a free CLUE report every year. Under the Fair Credit Reporting Act, you're entitled to a free copy of your claims report if you've been denied insurance in the past 60 days, no matter where you live. It's smart to get a copy to glimpse your home's claims history, especially if you're selling your home or shopping for a different homeowners policy and want to see your home as prospective buyers and insurers see it. If you're buying a house and want to see its CLUE history, you'll need to request it from the seller because you aren't authorized to request a report on property you don't currently own.

LET'S TAKE INVENTORY

When you file a claim on your homeowners insurance, you've got to prove you own stuff and verify what that stuff is worth. That's tough to do when you no longer have your stuff! Therefore, it's important to take inventory of everything you've got. Use a video camera to shoot quick tape of all your possessions. Or write a list and snap a few photos. Do whatever works for you. Just do it. Then stash the evidence and your insurance policy in a safe place—preferably not on the premises, if you know what we mean. One more thing: update your inventory periodically as you acquire more stuff. Avoid the urge to listen to your inner procrastinator.

You can order your CLUE report from either of two companies that create and maintain claims history databases. Contact ChoicePoint for a CLUE report at www.choicetrust.com or by calling toll-free 1-866-527-2600. Call Insurance Services for an A-PLUS report at 1-800-709-8842.

HOME IMPROVEMENTS: BEFORE THE PAYOFF YOU GOTTA PAY UP

Homeowners have used low interest rates to fuel their home improvement desires for a couple of years now. You can buy a house that needs fixing up and borrow the money to do the work, or you can get a home equity loan fairly easily for a quick—and costly—kitchen makeover. Banks are throwing loans at creditworthy homeowners, and in turn, they are landscaping and tiling and painting and adding on two-story decks with built-in hot tubs.

But hey, somebody's gotta pay for all the renovation. Even if the bank wants to loan you the money, you've got to take responsibility for paying it back. There are financial ramifications to every project you undertake, and we're here to caution you against building an in-ground swimming pool if you can't afford the water to fill an inflatable kiddie pool. Whether you're plotting minor repairs or a major renovation, it's important to maintain control over the project, i.e., create a budget and stick to it.

If you're like us, you've resisted budgeting your everyday expenses, but don't risk it with your home improvement project. Do-it-yourselfers often delude themselves into believing that saving labor costs means the project doesn't cost anything. Nothing could be further from the truth. In addition to materials and labor, remember to include incidentals such as equipment rental, delivery charges, and disposal fees. And put a line item in your budget for unexpected expenses, because home improvements tend to have a lot of those. Also, it's an unsolved mystery how a simple new vanity in the bathroom can morph into skylights and updated plumbing. Know your limitations and/or keep the contractor's suggestions at arm's length until you price them. Does your budget allow for it, or are your eyes bigger than your pocketbook?

Know your limits and strive for quality craftsmanship. Some projects require an expert—electrical work and plumbing come to mind. Unless you really know your stuff, you might just be creating a mess you'll need to pay a professional to clean up anyway. Your remodeled family room may lose some of its luster if you can't turn on all the lights without blowing a fuse. Ask friends, family, and coworkers for referrals. Then get bids, and be sure any contractors you hire are licensed, bonded, and insured.

Consider low-cost alternatives. Maybe your kitchen doesn't need new cabinets and a butcher-block counter. Maybe all it really needs is a new coat of paint. Be sure to understand every line on your contractor's bid. Are you paying for top-of-the-line tiles when linoleum will do? Forget peer pressure and pay attention to your own bottom line. Just because your neighbor took out a wall to expand her kitchen doesn't mean you need to.

Finally, can you go without? Sure, that home improvement project may increase the value of your home, but is it really necessary? Consider how long you'll stay in your home and alternatives for the money you're budgeting for the project. There we go mentioning the "B" word again. In case we haven't made it clear enough that we're keen on budgeting, a quick look at Chapter 2 may do the trick.

CONDUCT A HOME-IMPROVEMENT APPRAISAL

Which home improvements create the biggest bang for your buck? It depends. The answer varies depending on three questions:

1. What is the project? The thing about answering this question is that value is often in the eye of the beholder. Boosting curb appeal with landscaping or a fresh coat of paint is always a good idea, especially if your intent is to sell the property in the near future. Some renovation projects are smarter than others, based purely on the percentage of the total cost you'll recoup if you sell your home. The estimates of recouped costs below are based on national averages, so who knows if you'll get 88 cents on the dollar if you remodel your bathroom in your neighborhood in your neck of the woods and then turn around and sell the place. But it's worth a shot.

2. How long are you going to live there? Every project needs an answer to this one. If you're considering a square-footage expan-

WHICH HOME IMPROVEMENTS PAY OFF?

Project	Recouped Costs
Bathroom Remodel	88%
Finished Basement	79%
Family Room Addition	79%
New Siding	79%
Window Replacement	74%
Kitchen Remodel	67%
Swimming Pool	*

* Negligible value added based on personal preferences
Source: *Remodeling Magazine* (November 2002)

sion or a landscaping project because you plan to live at your address for the foreseeable future, it's hard to put a price tag on your desires. On the other hand, if you're just sprucing things up so you can sell the place, you may want to leave big projects for the next owner. The longer you live in your home after completing a project, the less you'll recoup of those costs when you finally sell.

3. Where do you live? Certain geographic locations demand certain projects. How real estate is selling in different markets—even specific neighborhoods in those markets—has an impact on which home improvements pay off. The key is to do research in your area.

FIXING TO MOVE

What's that saying about you don't get a second chance to make a first impression? It's never truer than when you're primping your humble abode for suitors. If your primary goal is to get your house ready for resale, there are several inexpensive home improvements you can do to make the place shiny and happy for prospective buyers. You want to set your house apart from others on the market in the same price range, and you can find dollars in the details. We mean details such as cleaning the carpet or refinishing hardwood floors. Just a little elbow grease could go a long way.

Outdoors, consider a fresh coat of paint all around. Fix any broken windows, light fixtures, and door locks. You may not mind jiggling the handle so the key will turn, but what message does that send to a buyer about the home's safety? Make sure your gutters are cleaned and weeds in the sidewalks are pulled. Caulk windows where there's a draft. This stuff sounds basic, but homeowners tend to overlook quirky details.

Indoors, leave complete overhauls to the new owner and focus on—you guessed it—the details. In the kitchen, for example, forget your dream of new cabinets and simply install updated hardware. Which rooms need painting? Regrout the shower and tub and fix cracked tiles in the kitchen and bath. Repair every leaky faucet or toilet and unclog every slow drain within in a 50-yard radius of your house. Technically, you're only obligated to make those fixes on your own home, but you get the idea.

After considering all this information on mortgages and insurance and home improvements, it kind of makes us wonder why they say home is where your heart is when a more appropriate adage might be home is where your headache is. There's so much to think about and so many decisions to make. Not to mention so much work to do. On the other hand, there's so much to gain with home ownership and so many valuable lessons to learn. Maybe it's most appropriate to say home is a heartwarming headache. Let's see if we can get Yogi Berra to make that quote stick.

7

Saving for Retirement—And Other Never-Ending Jobs

If you believe all the hype, retirement is something you pay cash for on your sixty-fifth birthday, and if you don't have money stockpiled by that time, forget about it. There are a few flaws with this thinking, most notably that 65 isn't such a magic retirement number anymore (see what we've got to say about full retirement age a little later on). Plus, there's no switch that gets flipped when you retire to reverse the flow of money from income to outgo only. You can still earn it from a variety of sources, but whether you need to—or choose to—is an entirely different matter. And where does it say that *quantity* means the same thing as *quality*? There's simply a lot more to retirement than hoping you have enough money saved at the start to live through it.

Don't take that the wrong way. We do encourage you to save as much money as you can and take personal responsibility for managing your assets. But we don't believe there's a certain figure you need to obtain or a deadline to meet before retirement can happen. The key is to plan your vision of retirement and set out to make it happen. There's that awful word again, "plan." Can't we include one chapter in this book that doesn't force you to think ahead, make some effort, plan? We probably could, but then we would risk not ticking you off, and sometimes what you need to take action is a little motivator we affectionately call irritation. Getting mad at us for pushing you off Procrastination Peak just might enrich your retirement. And we're not just talking about money.

The point is, you are responsible for making your future happen. Forget about everything else and focus on that. The stage you should be at in your retirement planning depends a lot on your age right now. So take a breath, find the paragraph below that applies to you, and continue at your own pace. That's the point anyway. Things we mention in these age-related blurbs are covered throughout the book, so forget about blaming us when you don't follow through. And dare to make mistakes. Chances are that not every choice you've made in life has turned to gold. As long as you're flexible and willing to learn, you can turn mistakes you make—financial or otherwise—into opportunities you didn't expect to have. Let's stop with the pyschobabble already and get busy.

YOU'RE NEVER TOO YOUNG FOR BAD HABITS

In your twenties retirement is an especially foreign concept. But we'd be remiss if we didn't give you a push in the right direction. Save just a little money on a regular basis—preferably in an income tax–deferred retirement plan sponsored by your employer—and it could add up to any goal you dare set for yourself. If you establish a budget, it will be easier to find the money for saving. Be responsible when paying off your school loans and be cautious when using credit cards. Oh yeah, be sure you've got health insurance. A medical calamity now could jeopardize your finances for years to come.

THIRTYSOMETHINGS SHOULD DO SOMETHING

Take to heart what we said to those whippersnappers in the previous paragraph. In your thirties your biggest asset isn't a portfolio but your ability to earn a future income. An essential at this stage includes disability income insurance and possibly life insurance. Are you participating in an employer-sponsored retirement plan? Start by saving at least what your employer will match and increase the amount every year you're thirtysomething. At the very least establish a traditional or Roth IRA. If you're self-employed, there are tax-efficient plans you shouldn't overlook.

FORTIES AREN'T FATAL

Ditto on what's listed above, plus you should be saving at least 10 percent of your earnings every year (emphasis on "at least"). Keep paying off the plastic. Hint: it's easier if you don't keep charging. If you have kids, college funding may be on your mind, but don't let it crowd out thoughts of retirement. Students can borrow money to go to school, but you can't take out a retirement loan.

"FIFTY" IS JUST ANOTHER "F" WORD

There's a never-ending debate about the future of Social Security and whether it will disappear. Thanks to your age bracket, you will most certainly have access to those government retirement benefits. Who cares about the younger set? But Social Security won't pay your entire way. You should be saving about 20 percent of your salary every year. Get rid of your consumer debt and prepay your mortgage if possible. For a good time, read what we've got to say about early retirement at the end of the chapter.

Poll

What color will your retirement be?

ORANGE you glad I maxed out my retirement savings	42%
BLUE that I won't be prepared	28%
RED because I'll have too much debt	18%
GREEN with envy I can't keep up with the Joneses	12%

Poll of ihatefinancialplanning.com visitors

TOO BAD IT'S NOT AS EASY AS ABC

If you are determined to ignore the planning process, you may discover that you have no choice down the road but to ignore the fact that all your friends are retired and enjoying themselves. It's your privilege to make that choice. We respect your desire to skip having a plan, but the least you can do is start putting some money in an account that may earn more than a traditional savings account. Especially over time. Don't put it off another day. These ABCs should help you frame the beginning of a retirement plan based on your personal circumstances.

A. Imagine Your Future

Before asking the following questions, rest assured there is no right or wrong answer to any of them. How old will you be when you retire? How old will you be when you quit working? Same job, fewer hours? Different job, more hours? Before you retire, do you aspire to earn a much larger income than you're taking home now? Where will you live? Will your retirement be full of exotic travel to all parts of the world, or do you plan to stay close to home and spend time with your grandchildren? Or will you still be raising your children? What children?

B. Define Your Goals

Now that you've let your imagination run wild, put some shape around your dreams by thinking of them in terms of your future goals. If you want to retire early, say when you reach 55, you'll have to save far more aggressively than if you plan to wait until you reach what the Social Security Administration calls your "full retirement age." How important is that goal when you consider how much you have already saved, what your risk tolerance is, how much you will earn between now and age 55? And if you plan to make a lot more money before you retire, how do you plan to make that dream a reality? Why do we keep asking questions? There are usually more questions than answers when it comes to retirement planning. That's because everyone's plan is different, based on needs, expectations, family obligations, life expectancy, and a host of other variables that are just plain complicated. This is work. But it's work that you can do.

C. Determine Your Income Requirements

Use the spending record and spending plan worksheets in Chapter 2 to document how much you are spending today. They will help you project anticipated spending throughout your working life and then into retirement. Estimate anticipated Social Security benefits using the benefits statement you receive from the Social Security Administration every year or the tools at ssa.gov. Make conservative estimates for return on investments. If you want to assume your savings will earn 12 percent, go ahead, but you run the risk—and it's a BIG risk—of ending up with far less money than your assumptions may indicate. Consider, too, that normal volatility will result in some up years and some down years. Over the long haul, those ups and downs are more likely to balance each other out. But that's only if you have a "long haul."

D. Plan Your Investment Strategy

Even if the "D" didn't make it into the ABC headline above, it may be the most important step. It all goes back to personal responsibility. The more you know about how much you've got, where you're investing it, and why, the more you'll be able to relax during your earning years knowing you're doing the best you can to accumulate money. And the more you'll be able to relax during retirement knowing you've got the money to live comfortably, however you define that term. At the very least, pay attention to your retirement accounts. And pay attention to your own ability to stomach the risks involved in investing while keeping in mind that more risk doesn't always translate into more money. If you know you can handle more risk, what do you need to do to diversify your investments accordingly? On the other hand, how much money will you need to save to compensate for the lower long-term returns available on more conservative investments? Turn to Chapter 8 to figure out more about investing.

THESE PITFALLS COULD BE YOUR DOWNFALL

In order to take steps to achieve your retirement goals, you need a plan that will work for you. Our goal is not to alienate you, but to encourage you to take positive steps. We'll start by outlining a handful of

IT'S NOT ONE-SIZE-FITS-ALL

Retirement means different things to different people. And different income expectations are had by all. Consider these scenarios when trying to decide how much income you'll need in retirement.

You may need about 80 to 100 percent of your current income if you:

- Will retire early and therefore need money over a longer period of time.
- Want to enhance your current lifestyle with travel, a second home, or other perks.
- Will still be supporting children or other dependents when you retire.
- Expect to have significant medical needs and/or not have access to health insurance paid by your former employer.
- Will have a sizeable mortgage payment or rent to pay in retirement.

You may need about 60 to 80 percent of your current income depending on whether you:

- Have contributed the maximum to your retirement accounts over time (presumably you won't make those same contributions in retirement, which will free up that cash).
- Will own your home free and clear by retirement (60 percent).
- Expect to simplify your lifestyle in retirement (60 percent).
- Will still have some mortgage debt or modest rent to pay when you retire (80 percent).
- Have assets you plan to sell in retirement, such as a second home or business.

- Will wait until "full retirement age" to retire and qualify for the maximum Social Security retirement benefits you are eligible to receive (the jury is still out on Social Security, but we're betting it won't completely disappear).
- Want to maintain your current lifestyle throughout retirement (80 percent).

common retirement-planning errors that people make. If you see the typical foibles spelled out, you may be able to stop a bad habit before it gets started—or before it causes too much damage to your dreams.

Planning Too Late

It's common for people to wait to save for retirement until they have established their career, got married, had children, or any other of a myriad excuses. Start now, no matter if you are 24, 34, or 44. Don't give up if you're already 54. The magic of compounding interest, or earning interest on interest, will work wonders over time on whatever small amount you are able to systematically invest.

Ignoring Employer-Sponsored Plans

Have you ever seen a glacier move? Well, glaciers move about as slowly as employees enroll in their company-sponsored retirement plans. If they aren't eligible the day they start their jobs, employees tend to forget to enroll when they do become eligible. Also, most people feel inadequate when faced with making investment decisions, so they put it off. Still others are unaware that the tax advantages and long-term growth potential of company-sponsored plans outweigh their "I can't afford it" rationale or other procrastination techniques. Whether it's a 401(k), 403(b), 457(b), Thrift Savings Plan, or another option that your employer offers, participate as soon as you are eligible and contribute as much as you can. We get into retirement savings vehicles later in this chapter, and believe us when we say there's something for everyone, whether you're employed by yourself or someone else.

Miscalculating How Much Is Enough

Is there such a thing as too much? Probably not where retirement saving is concerned, unfortunately. Nobody wants to outlive their money. How much you save depends on so many factors, and whether that amount is enough depends on even more factors. It's a tough nut to crack, because inflation, taxes, the uncertainty of Social Security, life expectancy, and debt all play a significant role.

Investing Too Conservatively

If you're building a retirement portfolio, treat it as an investment account, not a savings account. Spending too much effort (and too much cash) trying to preserve principal in guaranteed accounts or conservative investments presents risks you may not be prepared for. We're not saying every investment has to be as risky as parachute jumping, but don't settle for a slow walk on a well-lit street either. Do you follow? You may think you're playing it safe, but the result may leave you unprepared to experience life to the fullest. The earlier you start investing, the more time you have to recoup any potential losses from normal market downturns. And the more time you'll have to figure out that just because you've assumed some risk doesn't mean you'll come out ahead. You may end up deciding to find a financial professional you can trust to help you with your investment decisions.

Forgetting Uncle Sam

After you retire, April 15 will keep coming once a year. If you moonlight in the workforce after you are retired, the resulting income will not be free like refills on coffee. You will be taxed on it. You'll also pay income taxes on Social Security retirement benefits above certain thresholds as well as distributions from retirement vehicles (excluding Roth IRAs, which accumulate income tax-free because the contributions are made

HOW LONG WILL YOU BE AROUND?

When calculating what you need for retirement, consider how much you'll spend but also how long you'll be spending it. Based on statistics gathered by people who make their living predicting how long we all will live, these life expectancy estimates may help when figuring how many years you'll need an income after you stop earning one. Consider, though, that genes and lifestyle choices have a huge impact on what these numbers may or may not mean for you.

Life Expectancy by Age and Gender

Current Age	Male	Female
25	75.4	80.4
35	76.1	80.7
45	77	81.3
55	78.5	82.3
65	81.1	84.1
75	85	87.1

Source: National Center for Health Statistics, 1999

with after-tax dollars). There aren't any easy formulas we can provide that will help you solve the equation, but our best guesstimate is that close to one-third of the money you've got stockpiled will end up in Uncle Sam's pockets. Plan to save additional money to prepare for the inevitable or search for the most income tax–efficient investments to make. Or both.

Too Much Debt

You probably use more than one credit card. Maybe a home equity credit line. Perhaps a car loan or two. You pay interest on the money you borrow, which basically means you're paying extra for everything you buy. When you borrow, you trade away your future, and your future is what retirement planning is all about. As we stated in the debt chapter, there are smart ways to incur debt, but be careful as you approach retirement not to have too much—even of the good type of debt. The best thing you can do for your retirement is to get out of the habit of borrowing and into the habit of investing. Continuing to borrow money is like putting the car in reverse when you mean to go forward. It gets you further and further away from your goal.

Overlooking Inflation Could Cost You

Inflation poses the biggest threat to your retirement goals—or other financial goals, come to think of it. Inflation is the increase in the cost of living, expressed as a percentage increase over last year's prices. You may not pay much attention to it while you're working, in part because wages tend to rise along with it. But when you stop working, your income will probably be more or less fixed, making inflation a major issue. Even small changes in the inflation rate will make a huge difference in the amount of money you need throughout retirement. Oh, sure, you'll still have the same number of dollars in your pocket, but they may not buy as much. It's easy to justify purchasing a movie ticket for 10 bucks, but not so easy if the price climbs to $20 (especially if you add popcorn and Junior Mints).

The key is knowing how a normal level of inflation will affect your retirement planning. And all we can say about that is "it depends." Inflation may have little or no effect on Social Security, pensions, or other defined benefit plans because their benefits typically increase with the cost of living, but other types of retirement accounts aren't so lucky. (Pessimists should ignore the fact that we used "Social Security" and "lucky" in the same sentence.) Inflation will erode any return you get on 401(k), IRA, and other retirement investments. Let's say your investments produce an 8 percent return. After factoring in a 4 percent inflation rate, your actual return is cut in half.

Failing to Protect Your Assets

You've worked hard for any assets you have, and it would be ridiculous not to preserve them. Adequate protection may involve insurance that would cover both your financial and physical well-being. Life insurance may be an important consideration, but disability income insurance is often overlooked, yet even more essential. People believe they are invincible and will work until they retire, no questions asked. Statistics show otherwise, unfortunately. For more encouraging words like this, read Chapter 9, "Sickness, Disaster, Death, and Other Fun Topics."

All of those pitfalls considered, wouldn't it be great if you could step into a time machine containing really powerful calculators and step out with a failsafe retirement plan? Truth is, nothing in life is that easy. But don't get discouraged. You can take steps to help ensure a secure financial future, if you are open to establishing a plan and changing your plan when your life changes. And it will change.

SOCIAL SECURITY DOESN'T HAVE TO BE A MYSTERY

Since its creation early in the twentieth century, during the Great Depression, Social Security has been a sort of security blanket Americans count on for financial protection when they need it—while disabled, after a loved one (who is also a breadwinner) dies, and throughout retirement. Some self-proclaimed experts argue that it's time to fold up the security blanket and put it in the linen closet because it's going to go bankrupt, and—presumably—you are all grown up and need to take responsibility for yourself. Not so fast, other experts claim. Social Security isn't going anywhere. No matter whom you believe about the future of Social Security, it makes sense to understand that comfy old blanket and not rely on it at the same time.

Perhaps this brief explanation of how the money accumulates on your behalf during your working years will answer a few of your questions, assuming you have actual questions about it. A big assumption, we know. Starting with the end in mind, we'll say that the Social Security benefit you'll eventually receive depends on how much you earn during your working life. The more you earn, the higher your benefit will be, up to a certain maximum Uncle Sam has put in place to put the rich in their place.

Every year you and your employer pay taxes for Social Security and Medicare hospital insurance. Your employer pays half the cost, and you get all the benefits. That fact sounds good and it is. Two separate payroll taxes are withheld from employee wages, 6.2 percent for Social Security and 1.45 percent for Medicare. Most of the time the two are added together (7.65 percent) and treated as one amount called FICA payroll taxes, a familiar acronym meaning Federal Insurance Contributions Act. For those of you who are self-employed, you pay the combined employee-employer rate. The good news for self-employed individuals is that half of your Social Security and Medicare taxes are federal income tax deductible each year.

You should receive an annual Personal Earnings and Benefits statement from the Social Security Administration that estimates retirement, disability, and survivor benefits that you and your family may be eligible for. It's wise to study your statement when it arrives so you have a better idea how much supplemental saving you'll need to do to prepare for retirement. Don't be alarmed that the report shows your earnings to be less than what you have actually made. That's because you and your employer pay Social Security taxes on just part of your earnings (that FICA tax thing we talked about). Most important, remember that the annual statement is only an estimate. If you don't receive yours by your birthday each year, request one at www.socialsecurity.gov/mystatement.

TEST-DRIVE THESE RETIREMENT VEHICLES

All this talk about the common pitfalls and what Social Security may end up *not* being has probably blurred your vision of that ideal retirement we've encouraged you to visualize. And that's just fine because we've come to the part of the retirement chapter where we back up

WHEN WILL YOU REACH FULL RETIREMENT AGE?

Year of Birth	Full Retirement Age
1960 and after	67
1959	66 and 10 months
1958	66 and 8 months
1957	66 and 6 months
1956	66 and 4 months
1955	66 and 2 months
1943-1954	66
1942	65 and 10 months
1941	65 and 8 months
1940	65 and 6 months
1939	65 and 4 months
1938	65 and 2 months
1937 and before	65

what we said about taking personal responsibility for making your future happen. Skip this section if you're standing in line to blame inflation or income taxes for preventing you from getting there. Or maybe you jumped over to where people are lining up to charge the government with conspiracy for pulling the rug out from under workers who want Social Security to fund a cushy retirement lifestyle. Could be you're just sick and tired of wondering what the corporate scandals and market collapse that happened earlier in this decade will mean to your retirement in decades to come. Perhaps you've thrown your hat in the it's-too-late-why-bother ring, although there's barely room for even another bonnet in that one.

We'll let you in on a secret. It's not too late. You're not too tired. It's not that far. You can take steps to make it to retirement and thrive. You're halfway there if you can accept that only you can make it happen. And that's the longest half of the trip. There are a range of retirement vehicles you can use to get you the rest of the way, whether you are self-employed, work for a large corporation or small company, are a federal employee, serve in the military, or have just about any other job there is. These long-term plans get you into the habit of investing money, and they'll give you some income tax breaks to boot. Depending on the plan you pick, you may deduct your contributions from current income, and any earnings grow income tax–deferred until withdrawn from the plan. But you've got to start now and invest often, no matter who signs your paycheck.

The sophistication of retirement plans has evolved as a result of technological advances and a changing job market. It used to be that you weren't eligible to participate in your employer's plan until you had worked there at least a year, and then you had to call someone in Human Resources to see what your balance was. It's become more common for employees to be eligible immediately upon joining a company. Also, more and more employers now offer their employees online access to their plans, making fund rebalancing, loans, beneficiary changes, and much more available at the click of a mouse.

THE MOST POPULAR RETIREMENT PLANS ARE THE 401(K) AND THE 403(B)

Personal financial responsibility got started in the late 1950s with a defined contribution plan called the 403(b), which is a retirement plan for employees of certain nonprofit organizations, hospitals, public schools, and universities. The 401(k) plan was introduced about 20 years later primarily for employees of for-profit organizations. In both plans, participants direct their employer to deduct a portion of pretax dollars from their paycheck and put it into investment accounts.

FINANCIAL JARGON MADE EASY

Traditional pension plans, also called *defined benefit plans,* are becoming a dying breed in the workaday world, much like corporate loyalty, gold watches, and retirement parties. Most employers have switched to *defined contribution plans,* and you know them by their numbers and letters: 401(k), 403(b), 457(b), and the TSP (Thrift Savings Plan). The key difference between the two is that with defined benefit plans, the employer bears responsibility for funding them and then paying a specified benefit based on your years of service, your final average income, and other factors explained in the plan. In other words, the plan's *benefits* are clearly defined, as opposed to the *contributions* being clearly defined in the more common defined contribution plans, which have participants bearing the investment risk of their individual accounts.

Now that you know about these defined plans, flip to the back of the book for more defined financial jargon.

When an employer offers a 401(k) plan, it establishes a trust to hold the plan assets. Generally, employees may choose among a range of investment options, usually mutual funds, fixed accounts, and company stock. Most 403(b) plans are voluntary, meaning that the employer (hospital, school district, etc.) lets a third party offer its plan investment vehicles directly to participants. This makes the plan much easier for employers to administer. Also called tax-sheltered annuities, 403(b) plans have investment options that include fixed and variable annuities and mutual funds (no company stock is available for Hometown High School).

Many employers match all or part of your contributions to your 401(k) or 403(b) plan. If this is the case where you work, it's all the more reason to take advantage by contributing at least what the boss will match. Failing to do so is like passing up a raise in pay. Also, federal income taxes will be deferred on any contributions to your plan—from you or your employer—as well as any earnings. It won't count as taxable income until you start taking the money out in retirement. If that's not enough, both 401(k) and 403(b) plans are portable, which means you can take the funds with you when you leave your job. These plans are so cool, there is just no reason not to take advantage of them. But any questions you may have as to why parentheses are used around the "k" and the "b" instead of, say, dashes or slashes should be directed to the IRS.

One key difference between 401(k) plans and their nonprofit counterpart is the catch-up provision. Many 403(b) plans allow participants who have the same employer for at least 15 years to make additional contributions to their plan in order to catch up on time they lost in earlier years by not participating. The annual catch-up limit on 401(k) plans, on the other hand, is only for participants who are older than 50. If you're participating in a 403(b) but haven't had the same employer for 15 years and you're over 50, you can benefit from the same catch-up provision as with a 401(k). The provision doesn't make up for all the years of lost compounding, but it does help boost the balance.

A simple fact to be aware of is that some employers do not offer eligible employees the catch-up provision. It's an optional perk they can choose not to administer, and they're given that leeway, even though the plans are regulated by federal law. Smaller employers, especially, sometimes can't afford the expense of administering this complex aspect of their retirement plans. If you're 50 or approaching that age, find out if your employer offers the catch-up provision, and if not, ask them why. Maybe you can help make it happen.

PLAN LOANS: SPEND NOW AND YOU'LL PAY LATER

Have you ever gotten your quarterly plan statement the same day all the bald tires on your car went flat? Many employer-sponsored retirement plans have loan provisions to tantalize participants. Even the Solo 401(k) allows self-employed types to borrow from themselves when they're strapped for cash. It's easy to think your cares will be solved if you just borrow some of the money in your retirement account to pay off untimely expenses. What good is it doing stuck away for 20 years or more anyway? Allow us to remind you all the good it's doing.

If you take out a loan on your retirement plan, the compound interest those contributions may earn will cease to compound. All that means is that your account will be much smaller when you retire, which could lead to a much smaller retirement. This problem is compounded, if you will, when you also stop making contributions while you're paying off the loan. If you quit your job or are fired, you probably will be required to pay back the entire loan immediately. Talk about bad timing! What's more, if you fail to pay back the loan right away, it may be considered in default and be treated as an early distribution from your plan. Guess what that means? A hefty income tax bill on the outstanding loan and a 10 percent penalty fee for extra measure if you don't meet the requirements for an exception, which include, but are not limited to, a secret handshake.

Speaking of if you quit your job or are fired, you'll have some entirely different decisions to make regarding your retirement account. Do you leave your money where it is? Do you take it with you? How fast can you spend it? It won't surprise you to learn we have some pretty strong opinions on the subject, which we cover in the section on changing jobs in Chapter 5.

JUST LOAN ME THE MONEY

All that being said, the first step in borrowing from your account is to make sure your plan offers a loan provision. Some plans have strict rules about how the money can be used (just for home purchases or college costs, for example). Contact someone in Human Resources or the benefits department to find out the restrictions on your plan, including how much you may borrow. Actually getting through the voicemail system to speak with a live body may be the most difficult step in the entire process. If you have online access to your account, you may be able to skip the human contact altogether. Once you've received the loan, there are a few standard procedures you'll need to follow to pay it back. Loan principal and interest may be deducted directly from your paycheck after taxes and deposited in your retirement account. Also, in most cases you'll have just five years to pay it back, unless you've used the money to buy a home, in which case you may have longer.

THIS MAY PUT YOU INTO WITHDRAWALS

Your 401(k) or 403(b) plan may allow what the IRS calls "hardship withdrawals" from your retirement account, but you'll be taxed and may be penalized the standard 10 percent. Not to mention the personal penalty you'll experience in retirement when your account balance is lower than it could have been. The IRS defines acceptable hardship in most cases as the need to withdraw money to pay college tuition that's due in the next 12 months; to make a down payment on a primary residence; to pay medical expenses for you or your dependents; to prevent foreclosure or eviction from your home; or some other factors based on personal circumstances.

GOVERNMENT EMPLOYEES GET THEIR VERY OWN PLAN

The 457(b) plan is a tax-exempt deferred compensation retirement program for employees of local, state, and federal governments and tax-exempt agencies. This includes school districts, county governments, and political organizations. Deferred compensation is a fancy way of stating that an organization makes a promise to defer the compensation of the employee to some future date for services currently performed by the employee. A 457(b) plan is similar to 401(k) and 403(b) plans in that earnings grow on an income tax–deferred basis and contributions are not taxed, but you'll pay income taxes on distributions at retirement. With those similarities accounted for, the 457(b) plan takes a fork in the road, however, and goes its own way from other employer-sponsored plans. There is a catch-up provision for participants 50 and older, but what sets the 457(b) plan apart from other plans is that in the three years prior to full retirement age the catch-up bursts to two times the annual contribution limit.

Annual Plan Contribution Limits and Catch-Up Provisions

Contribution Limits	401(k) and 403(b)*	457(b)†	Thrift Savings Plan‡	SIMPLE IRA	Solo 401(k)§	SEP IRA¶	IRA and Roth IRA
2004	$13,000	$13,000	$13,000	$9,000	combo of salary & profit sharing	20% of income if self-employed	$3,000
2005	$14,000	$14,000	$14,000	$10,000			$4,000
2006	$15,000	$15,000	$15,000	Indexed			$4,000
2007	Indexed	Indexed	$15,000	Indexed			$4,000
2008–2010	Indexed	Indexed	Indexed	Indexed			$5,000
Catch-Up Provision (Age 50+)							
2004	$3,000	$3,000	$3,000	$1,500	$3,000	N/A	$500
2005	$4,000	$4,000	$4,000	$2,000	$4,000		$500
2006	$5,000	$5,000	$5,000	$2,500	$5,000		$1,000
2007	Indexed	Indexed	Indexed	Indexed	Indexed		$1,000
2008–2010	Indexed	Indexed	Indexed	Indexed	Indexed		$1,000

Contribution limits and catch-up provisions are scheduled to revert to 2001 levels in 2011.

Indexed limits may increase to reflect a cost-of-living adjustment.

* Certain 403(b) participants with at least 15 years of service may be eligible for an additional catch-up contribution.

† There is more than one type of 457(b) plan and each has its own rules, regulations, and technical difficulties. See detailed information about the catch-up provision in "Government Employees Get Their Very Own Plan."

‡ There are different Thrift Savings Plans for federal employees and active military. The contribution limit for active military includes incentive, special and bonus pay.

§ Contribution limits for Solo 401(k) is based on combination of deferred salary and profit sharing, depending on how the business is established.

¶ Contribution limit for SEP IRA is 25% of salary if you're an employee of your own corporation.

Distributions from your 457(b) plan are generally allowed in the case of retirement, separation from service, unforeseeable emergency, or death of the participant. Leave it to the government not to pull any punches on that one. When leaving your current place of employment, you may roll over your governmental 457(b) plan assets to an IRA or to a new employer's plan, such as a 401(k), 403(b), or even another 457(b) plan that accepts such transfers. It used to be that if you worked for a company and also moonlighted for the government, your contributions to one retirement plan limited your participation in the other. But that is no longer the case. Now you can make a maximum contribution to both plans, assuming you've got the cash to do so. If you have that kind of dough, maybe you could loan us some money for our retirement?

THRIFT SAVINGS PLAN FOR CIVILIANS AND MILITARY PERSONNEL

The Thrift Savings Plan is an optional retirement plan for members of the military and civilians employed by the federal government. Civilians have had their TSP since 1987, while active military personnel have only been eligible to participate in their TSP since 2001. The plans are similar yet different, but both offer participants the same type of income tax–deferred investments that 401(k) and other plans do. TSP participants may invest in other qualified employer plans or the 457(b) plan, but total annual contributions to all plans may not exceed the limit in any given year. In 2004, for example, no matter how many plans you qualify for, your total contributions are limited to $13,000, plus any applicable catch-up contributions. If we haven't confused you too much, keep reading.

Loans and financial hardship withdrawals are available from TSP accounts with most of the same basic rules and regulations we detailed a few pages ago, including possible IRS penalties for early withdrawals. One variation with the TSP is that any contributions you are making to your account will be stopped for six months after each hardship withdrawal. That may seem like no time, but think of the potential earnings you'll miss out on. We probably sound like a broken record when it comes to harping about the impact of reducing the principal in your

TSP, but all we're really asking you to do is evaluate all your options before withdrawing money from your account.

Career military types may wonder why they should save their own money when they'll qualify for military retired pay soon enough. We're here to tell you that things change, and even the most loyal soldier may not make it to 20 years. Military retired pay is based on your years of service and the rank you hold at the time of your retirement, rather than on the amount of your contributions and any earnings. Besides, TSP is yours to keep even if you don't serve the 20 years ordinarily necessary to receive military retired pay. If this isn't enough information to get you to enlist, learn more at www.tsp.gov.

RETIREMENT PLANS FOR EVERY SMALL BUSINESS

If you own a small business or are self-employed, you have a range of tax-deferred retirement plan options too. The government has created several plans, but you'll have to do some thorough research because there's no such thing as one size fits all. Come to think of it, that may be the reason you're in business for yourself in the first place. One similar feature of most of these plans is that contributions don't have to be made every year. If your business has a bad year, you can decide to temporarily discontinue contributions to some plans.

The first thing you need to do while choosing a retirement savings plan is to define the status of your business. Are you self-employed or a small business owner? An amateur may think it's an obvious distinction, but it isn't. A self-employed individual may or may not have employees while small-business owners may have no employees or up to 100 employees, and they may or may not be incorporated. Huh? Leave it to us to drop the messy business status figuring in your lap, but all we really care about is that no matter what sort of operation you're running, you're saving for retirement.

The 401(k) Goes Solo

The newest do-it-yourself retirement plan is the Individual 401(k), which is basically a traditional 401(k) but with a much higher annual contribution limit. Technically it's been available for many years but was too expensive to administer before tax laws were modified in 2001. Income tax–deductible contributions may be a combination of salary deferral and an employer profit-sharing amount, depending on whether the business is incorporated. In 2004, you can contribute the first $13,000 of your income plus 25 percent of additional income up to a maximum of $41,000. That's a lot of cash.

Much like its corporate counterpart, the Solo 401(k) has a catch-up provision for owners 50 and older. Plus, the plan has a loan feature that allows owners to borrow from their account without paying income taxes or penalties on the loan amount. Eligibility is limited to business owners with no employees, or only a spouse as employee. Fees for establishing and maintaining Solo 401(k) accounts vary by plan administrator.

The SIMPLE Plan Is Easy Too

We never thought we'd use both "IRS" and "minimal paperwork" in the same sentence, but the SIMPLE Plan makes it possible to do so because there are no annual tax forms to file. The Savings Incentive Match Plan for Employees (SIMPLE) is designed for self-employed workers and companies with fewer than 100 employees. The SIMPLE IRA offers income tax–deferred savings and employer-matching flexibility, plus the catch-up provision for participants over 50. With this plan the employer chooses the financial institution (bank, brokerage firm, or mutual fund company) to maintain the plan and accept contributions, and the employee chooses how to invest the contributions. In many cases those decision makers happen to be the same person, but if there are other employees, the employer is required to contribute to the plan on their behalf even if they don't kick in money themselves.

What the Heck Is a SEP?

A Simplified Employee Pension (SEP) is a type of employer-sponsored IRA for smaller companies and self-employed individuals. With a SEP, the employer makes all the contributions and all eligible employees must be included in the plan. Employees aren't permitted to contribute unless they are the sole employee. As with traditional IRAs, employees are not taxed when contributions are made but later, when distributions are taken. The employer gets an income tax deduction for contributions made on behalf of employees, but the SEP is portable so employees leaving the company can take the plan with them. Roth IRAs aren't eligible for SEPs, although IRAs that contain SEP contributions may be converted to a Roth IRA.

Keogh May Be the Way to Go

The Keogh plan was created in the early 1960s to give small business owners and their employees access to tax-efficient retirement plans similar to qualified pension plans offered by corporate employers. Contributions and earnings are income tax–deferred until withdrawn. Of all the plans for small business, it's probably the most complicated plan to set up and maintain. The three different types of Keogh plans are the profit sharing plan, the money purchase plan, and the defined benefit plan. Profit sharing contributions can change every year, but with a money purchase plan, you must make the same percentage contribution every year, whether the company has profits or not. For that reason it's become less popular as more plans for small business have been introduced. The defined benefit plan is the most complex of the three Keoghs, and it isn't for do-it-yourselfers.

IRAs ARE THE ALTERNATIVE RETIREMENT NEST EGG

Individual Retirement Accounts were authorized by the federal government 20-some-odd years ago as an incentive for individuals to save for retirement. That's why they used "individual" in the name. The IRA encourages regular, long-term savings, and it also offers income tax advantages as well. Because of the fairly low contribution limits, however, the IRA isn't designed to be the only route you take for retirement savings, but rather to be combined with other retirement savings options.

Many people think an IRA is an investment product, but it's simply a tax-favored individual retirement arrangement. Think of it as a folder marked "IRA." In this folder, you put all the stocks, bonds, mutual funds, and other investments you choose to make, up to your allowable annual IRA amount. One exception is anything ever featured on *Antiques Roadshow*. You can move your IRA money from one type of investment product to another (buy and sell stocks, etc.), as long as you continue to keep those investments in your IRA folder. Talk about flexible. Annual contributions may be tax deductible unless you (or your spouse) participate in an employer-sponsored retirement plan, in which case the amount you may deduct could be phased out depending on your adjusted gross income.

You will generally need to leave your IRA investments untouched until age 59 1/2 or pay a 10 percent withdrawal penalty (unless you qualify for an exception), so don't think of your IRA investments as ready money until you reach retirement age. One important exception: If you cash out in regular installments before age 59 1/2, there is no penalty, but those payments must continue until you are 59 1/2 or for five years, whichever is longer. Also, you'll need to begin taking the minimum required distribution on your IRA by April 1 of the year after you turn 70 1/2. We've tried to figure out the half-year requirement on all these rules, but we can't find an explanation that translates into plain English.

You can open an IRA through banks, brokerage firms, insurance companies, mutual fund companies, or other financial services companies. As with most things these days, you can also open an IRA on the Internet. So many options, so little money. Whichever route you go, there will be forms to fill out and decisions to make. For instance, you can either make your annual contribution in one lump sum or in regular installments. To receive any income tax deduction you may qualify for in the current year, money must be deposited in the account by April 15 of the following year.

WHAT ABOUT A ROTH IRA?

If you want to invest more money than your employer-sponsored plan allows, a Roth IRA can be a good way to do it. Contributions to a Roth

IRA are made with after-tax dollars and are nondeductible, so you can't subtract your contribution from this year's income. The annual contribution limit for a Roth IRA is small, but you can continue adding to the account after turning 70 1/2, and you can leave the money in the account as long as you live. We wonder what's the point of that? Distributions from a Roth IRA are tax-free (as in "no taxes") if made after age 59 1/2, assuming you've held it for five years. You paid taxes on the money before adding it to your Roth account (and earnings are tax-free), so it only seems fair that you won't be taxed again. Did we just use the word "fair" when referring to taxes?

CHEAT SHEET FOR EARLY RETIREMENT

If you've gotten to the end of this chapter and are still actually reading, we're impressed. Planning for retirement is a daunting task, but you are up to the challenge. Maybe you're even pondering an early exit from the workaday world as part of your game plan. Look around and you'll see retirees have come up with all sorts of crazy ways to make it happen, and as more baby boomers retire, their solutions are only going to get better. It won't be long before we quit using phrases like "early retirement" because they will no longer be relevant. As the voice of reason, we're compelled to provide some pointers to follow, should you be plotting an early out.

- Think early and often about retirement and what it could mean for you. If you plan to relocate, for example, find out which states impose an income tax on residents and which do not. Then decide if that will affect your dream for a destination, and keep in mind there will be other taxes to pay, no matter where you live. Do your dreams of world travel correspond with your bank balance? Either way, there's still time to manage those expectations. The more you plan now, the better your future can be.
- Be sure to think about health insurance because the costs could derail your plan. One myth is that these expenses will decrease once you retire, but the truth is health insurance (and prescription drugs) may cost several hundred dollars a month. Depending on

where you work just before retiring, you may be able to take advantage of COBRA benefits, which allow you to continue group coverage for 18 months. However, you pay for the coverage plus administrative charges. Some employers offer health-care benefits to retirees, but probably not those who retire early.

- Many homeowners are living in their biggest asset. Consider selling yours and buying or renting a home that costs less. Federal law allows you to pocket up to $250,000 in tax-free profit ($500,000 for married couples) on the sale of your home—a tidy sum to add to your nest egg. If you want to stay in your house, consider a reverse mortgage, the loan homeowners 62 and older can use to borrow on home equity with no payment due until you leave the house for good. We tackle this strategy in Chapter 6.

- Seriously consider the price tag of the first few years of early retirement. Dream vacations, a cabin in the woods, trips to the outer reaches of the world, and any number of other expectations cost money. If you haven't prepared for these types of expenses, you could be forced to draw on investments too soon, which could jeopardize your long-term financial picture.

- Don't assume that your investments will stop working just because you do. If you plan ahead, you can draw on other money first and leave income tax–deferred accounts alone until you're required to start withdrawing funds, usually about age 70 1/2. Under current law there are options, such as the Roth IRA, that don't have withdrawal deadlines.

- Phasing into retirement is also a viable option. Get a part-time job, open your dream business, or become a consultant. What would it take to turn your hobby into a money maker? Perhaps you'll make enough to avoid drawing on your retirement investments too early. It's a way to stay in the rat race but run on a different track.

- Be sure to factor in things you can't control—taxes and inflation— when considering your retirement aspirations. They can be overcome, by the way, but you need to be aware that your dollar may not be worth the entire buck after taxes and inflation take hold of it.

- Assuming everything stays as is with Social Security, you'll pay a price for retiring early, where your benefits are concerned. Not only will you need to make it through the initial retirement years without any help from Social Security (you aren't eligible for benefits until age 62), but once you start getting those monthly checks, they will be smaller than if you work until full retirement age. Back to the first word in this paragraph, "assuming" the best possible scenario for the future of Social Security is a risky proposition.

- There's a lot to know and understand where your financial future is concerned. Perhaps you want to consider consulting with a financial professional to sort out your situation.

8

Past Performance Is No Guarantee of Future Results

If you believe the ads, personal finance is a lot like personal health and fitness. And the headlines promoting them are eerily inter-changeable, oftentimes conflicting:

"For fast results, only buy XYZ Fund!"
"For fast weight loss, only eat protein!"
"Inflation is not good for you!"
"Coffee, wine, dairy [insert beverage here] is not good for you!"

We actually bought an abdominal exercise machine back when they were the latest fad. In exchange for three minutes a day doing what amounted to stretching a big rubber band across our waist, we were going to have tight abs in time for summer. We plunked down our money even though we knew the rippled tummies on the models in the ads had to be the result of some serious sweating. We paid full price for an exercise "machine" despite the fact that we had resisted exercise in most forms for a full decade. And been quite good at it, incidental-ly. We bought that ab flex because we wanted to believe there was an easy way to get in shape, and we were willing to pay money to suspend our disbelief.

And that's another way personal finance seems like personal health and fitness. We put off tasks like investing because we don't know the best way to go about it or it just doesn't seem like that much fun. It's easier and more comfortable somehow just to ignore the concept as a whole rather than figure out what it's about and then actually put away some money. Then we see somebody with a beefy portfolio and we want in on the action. Great returns in just three minutes a day? Where do we sign up? Forget that this stuff takes time and effort—not unlike any serious exercise program. Never mind that the investors who flaunt their financial figures don't usually brag about ones that lost money. There's just no such thing as a guarantee, but that shouldn't stop you from trying.

Investing in its most basic terms is putting your money to work to earn more money. Sounds simple, but you have decisions to make about how much you want to invest, where to invest it, how often, and so on. Those decisions involve all sorts of things you'd probably rather not think about. Hey, we understand that inclination, but we're here to tell you it's not that bad. We're going to summarize it now and then break down the process with more thorough explanations throughout the chapter. We're not going to get too technical or throw a lot of complex terms at you, although be warned there are some phrases that may sound strange. But once you get used to hearing them they're not nearly as intimidating as they sound. You may even catch yourself using them in casual conversation. Just try not to smirk.

Before you invest any money, it's smart to set a goal because that will help you figure out which steps you need to follow and which investments you'll likely want to make. Think of it as a continuum with your goals at the beginning and potential, eventual investment returns at the end. That's when you spend the money, by the way, so try to hang in there that long. Once you've got a goal, it's important to assess both your time horizon and your tolerance for risk. How long you've got to let your money grow could affect how you invest it, but only if you're willing and able to assume the risk necessary to invest it there.

Speaking of risk, there are a bunch of inherent risks where investing is concerned, not the least of which is that you could lose money. We're going to uncover the main ones but also provide several investment strategies you might employ to help minimize those risks. We'll mention them here so they don't sound so foreign in a few pages—asset allocation, dollar-cost averaging, and portfolio rebalancing. Nothing's guaranteed, of course, and you could still lose money no matter how cautious you are or which techniques you use to combat risk. We will be compelled to continue reminding you of that fact throughout the chapter to meet the quota established by our legal team. Let's move on to the actual investments you might make after you understand your goals, time frame, risk tolerance, and ways to minimize risk.

You've no doubt heard of stocks, bonds, and mutual funds. They're three of the basic investment vehicles, and they're anything but fads. *Stocks* are shares in companies that may appreciate in value based on the performance of the companies. Owning stock is like owning a piece of the corporate pie. The extent of your potential for loss or gain—the cherry on top of that pie—is based on how many shares you purchase. *Bonds* generate earnings through what basically amounts to you loaning money to a company or government agency. A bond certifies that the issuer has borrowed your cash and needs to repay it with interest by a certain time. You might include bonds in your portfolio to provide diversification and balance. *Mutual funds* allow a pool of investors to put their money in a portfolio of stocks, bonds, and other assets, which is then run by fund managers who know what they're doing. Investors of all sizes, and we mean net worth, benefit from the diversification mutual funds offer and also from the fact that they can get started with less money than what's required by other investments.

READY, SET, GOALS

Enough already with the summary; let's get down to the nuts and bolts. The first step in deciding what should go in your portfolio is to figure out what your financial goals are and how long you have to achieve them. In theory, you mapped out your goals—or at least *thought* about potential goals—in Chapter 1, "'Plan' Is a Four-Letter Word." Goals pop up all over the place where financial planning is concerned, especially when you're trying to figure out how to invest your money. That's because having something concrete to work toward will help you determine just how aggressive you need to be with savings and investments.

Your time horizon can have a big impact on your subsequent investment decisions. How long you have to let your money work is important because the shorter the time period, the less difference it will make where you put your money. If you want to adopt a child, for example, and are hoping to do so in three years, you may need to be willing to assume more risk with your investment in hopes of achieving your goal, depending on how much money you've got to invest. Time is a variable that can help you solve the other investment variables—or force you to modify your goal.

Take a look at this example showing various purely hypothetical investment time frames and investment returns. It doesn't reflect any specific investment and won't have any material impact on your investments, but it does illustrate how time can influence your investment decisions. When considering your time horizon, you want to think about how long the money has the potential to grow and also how long the money needs to last.

$100 Monthly Investment Over Time				
	Total Invested	**2%**	**8%**	**12%**
5 Years	$6,000	$6,312.33	$7,341.39	$8,110.34
10 Years	$12,000	$13,281.65	$18,128.28	$22,403.62
25 Years	$30,000	$38,851.51	$91,483.80	$170,221.03

Hypothetical values figured using the Save Every Month calculator at ihatefinancialplanning.com. Calculations assume monthly compounding from the beginning of the period and don't take into account any investment fees or expenses.

READ AT YOUR OWN RISK

Most everything you do involves some risk, from talking to the good-looking stranger at the bus stop to deciding between two equally challenging and high-paying job offers. In the interest of full disclosure, we'll admit we have never actually secured a date with anyone at the bus stop, and the thought of two prospective employers fighting over our skills makes us hysterical with laughter. But you get the picture. Risk is just a part of life. And somehow, most of us are able to avoid disaster most of the time.

Risk is integral to investing, and it's important to understand your tolerance for it. Are you a thrill seeker, or does the thought of watching a day trader reach for his mouse make you queasy? Maybe you're somewhere between those two possibilities. The good news is that investments offer a spectrum of risk levels, which allows you to choose the vehicles that best match your psyche. Traditional savings accounts offer the guarantee of being FDIC insured, but you pay for that guarantee with lower returns. Bonds may offer balance to a portfolio, but they also have their share of risk that could mean your investment would lose money. And with mutual funds and stocks, the price per share may go down in value and lose principal, but it may also go up, up, up. In return for increased risk, mutual funds and stocks offer the potential to increase in value. Translation? No pain, no gain.

One aspect of risk is fear of the unknown, and that is why you are here, unless it's because our relatives are paying you to read this book. We can shed some light on the types of risk that affect your financial situation, both positively and negatively. Just remember there are no guarantees in any aspect of your life, so don't expect it to be different where your money is concerned. The key is to find your personal comfort zone by balancing potential risks in hopes of realizing potential reward.

INVESTMENT RISK IS AS REAL AS THE DAY IS LONG

Savers decide how much they are going to save, and that amount will be in their traditional savings account when it's needed, plus interest. Assuming, of course, that their procrastination gene doesn't overpower their inclination to save in the first place. Investors don't enjoy the same guarantee because they can't predict how—or even if—their money will grow. That is what is called investment risk. Changes in market conditions will cause investment principal and earnings to fluctuate over time. The end result is that your money could be worth more or less than the original amount you invested. There's always the chance that an investment won't earn what you expect it to. You could lose money, but you could also enjoy a healthy profit. Generally, the higher potential return on your investments also has a higher potential for loss.

INFLATION CAN BE DEFLATING

One of the most constant risks your investments will face is inflation. Simply put, inflation is the increase in the cost of living, expressed as a percentage increase over last year's prices. Inflation is a simple concept that preys on people who ignore it. But keep in mind that inflation is normal and has been hovering around 2 percent to 4 percent in recent years. What ultimately counts is whether your investments have potential to beat the inflation rate. An investment that's too conservative can actually leave you at risk. If you've got all your cash in an FDIC-insured bank account, it may seem reassuring to know the interest rate is guaranteed, but say that rate is below 3 or 4 percent. It may not keep pace with inflation, and you could end up losing ground. And don't forget, you have to pay income taxes on your earnings too. File that under double whammy in your investment portfolio.

SOME OF WHAT GLITTERS IS FOOL'S GOLD

When you invest your money, it is subject to business risk or the chance that the business behind your investment will lose money. The stock market is a bit like Hollywood, and a hot stock is often fawned over like a starlet. Don't let the glamour fool you. A rush to judgment can lead to a false swell in a stock's price. This happens frequently with initial public offerings (IPOs) whose stock valuations may shoot up and then eventually settle into a more reasonable stratosphere. Of course, IPOs were sent scurrying during the stock market's most recent rocky period earlier this century. Not too many companies wanted to go public during such a volatile time. They need to prove they can sustain themselves and grow over time, instead of just trying to pose for the camera.

OPPORTUNITY KNOCKS ON RISK'S DOOR

One type of risk that drives investors crazy—especially risk takers—is lost opportunity. It's the premise behind most game shows. Do you pick Door Number One, even though what's behind Door Number Two could be worth more? Where your money is concerned, unless you happen to pick the very best option every time you invest, there's going to be something that will outperform it. Unlike loss of capital or loss of

HAVE WE GOT SOME TIPS FOR YOU

Have you ever heard of TIPS, as in Treasury Inflation-Indexed Securities? TIPS don't get much buzz—mainly because they were introduced in 1997 when investors were too busy buying into the stock boom to pay much attention. TIPS is barely a functional acronym for a phrase that doesn't even contain a "P," but it turns out they're called Treasury Inflation-*Protected* Securities by some folks.

TIPS are notes guaranteed by the U.S. government to give a real rate of return during a 10-year maturity period. You buy TIPS in $1,000 increments, and the government adjusts your principal against inflation, based on the consumer price index. Say you invest $1,000 and inflation is 2 percent. Your principal grows to $1,020 and interest is paid on that amount. The return isn't usually huge, but no worries about inflation nicking at your investment's net worth. In the rare case of deflation, your principal will never drop below the amount you originally invested. TIPS investors are protected against inflation but not income taxes. You'll pay Uncle Sam on interest and inflation adjustments to the principal every year, unless you put the TIPS in a tax-advantaged investment such as a Roth IRA. And much like with a bank CD, you may have to pay a penalty to redeem your TIPS early.

The government sells TIPS through its TreasuryDirect program four times each year, in January, April, July, and October. Learn more at www.publicdebt.treas.gov. Or buy TIPS any time of year through brokers and some banks, but you'll pay fees.

purchasing power (inflation), opportunity loss doesn't take anything out of your pocket. That doesn't mean, however, that it isn't real. Just ask anyone who claims they "couldashouldawoulda" earned a lot of money during the stock market glory days in the 1990s. Right or wrong, opportunity risk can be the motivating factor behind many investment decisions.

THE RISK OF NOT MEETING YOUR GOALS

Although this type of risk doesn't get much attention, it's really the most important one. If you set your sights on a new house or a college education but don't achieve the goal, you might feel like a loser. Speaking from personal experience, you can't put a price tag on being a loser. But enough about us. Some investors, in trying to avoid losses or trying to make sure that they own the best bet, end up courting the biggest risk of all—that of not being able to meet their financial goals. We're certainly not saying that investors should be satisfied with sub-par performances from their investments. But don't lose sight of the fact that your primary goal should be to meet your future financial needs. All of that, incidentally, involves actually having goals, which is our cue to send you back to the section devoted to setting goals and keeping them in Chapter 1.

ASSESS YOUR APPETITE FOR RISK

Where your money is concerned, you don't want to take too many risks. Or do you? Does the chance of doubling your money in a short period of time outweigh the anxiety you feel when considering a future with empty pockets? Would you rather be sure your principal is safe and risk ending up with net gains less than zero due to the nasty effects of inflation? Is personal finance this absolute? Absolutely not. Take a look at this quick and somewhat nonsensical assessment of your toler-ance for risk. It may be better suited to your tolerance for fun, but it might also help you in some small way figure out how much risk you're willing to take with your money.

A Short Bit on the Tax Bite

Isn't it funny how we tend to overlook Uncle Sam? The fact is, you will be taxed on any money you may make with your investments, whether Sam's your favorite uncle or not (unless you buy tax-free securities). Dividends are proceeds paid out periodically if the investment is actually posting earnings, which doesn't always happen. Whether you choose to reinvest your dividends or choose to receive them in cash, you will be taxed on them. Capital gains is money you earn whenever shares or holdings are sold for a profit. You will be taxed on any gains at both the federal and state level.

1. A friend invites you to join a fantasy football league to the tune of $40. You could win over $800 if your handpicked fantasy team wins. What do you do?
   A. Say no thanks, and invite your friend to a Gamblers Anonymous meeting.
   B. Ask another friend to go halfsies with you, since a $20 loss hurts a lot less than a $40 one.
   C. Do a quick study of the NFL and join the gang.
   D. Find out if you can purchase two teams, to increase your odds of winning the jackpot.

2. Your brother-in-law tells you about a ground-floor opportunity to invest in a hot new company. He's certain everyone who invests will become a millionaire within the year. What do you do?
   A. Nod politely as you reassure yourself that sis married a fool.
   B. Gingerly write a check for $100, simply as a way to keep peace in the family.

   C. Get more information about the opportunity, and if it looks solid, invest $1,000.

   D. Take the kid's college savings and buy as many shares as possible.

3. Your year-end bonus is a choice of $500 cash or $1,000 in stock options that must be held for at least 12 months, during which time the stock price could go up or down. What do you do?

   A. Take the money and run.

   B. Decline the bonus and promise the boss you'll work even harder next year.

   C. Take the stock options and cross your fingers that you won't be sorry.

   D. Happily take the stock options, confident the stock will increase over time.

4. Your parents decide to give you a gift of $5,000, asking that you invest it wisely. What do you do?

   A. Buy a home theater and invite the folks over for movie night.

   B. Put the cash in a bank certificate of deposit earning 5 percent.

   C. Find a hot start-up company and invest it all for huge potential reward (and risk).

   D. Study the stock market and select several stocks that represent different risk levels.

5. A stock you bought over a year ago has suddenly increased in value by over 30 percent. What do you do?

   A. I bought stock?

   B. Sleep easy, and keep things right where they are.

   C. Buy more stock, certain it will keep going up.

   D. Sell, and stash your dough in a low- or no-risk investment now that you've made a cool profit.

Scoring this is easy. Give yourself 1 point for every "C" answer and 2 points for every "D." Picking "A" or "B" is the same as shooting an air ball—zero points for the home team.

0 points: To say the least, you're a wary investor, one who essentially avoids risk like the plague. You might be most comfortable with saving options that offer some guarantees, like bank savings accounts or under the mattress of your bed. Before you do anything else, check to be sure you have a pulse.

1 to 9 points: You're standing somewhere in the middle of the road when it comes to risk. You're willing to wager a bit for more reward, but you won't wipe out your savings to do so.

10 points: You're probably reading this book while skydiving. Either you've got a lot of money on hand, a lot of years ahead of you, a lot to learn, or you could teach us all something about guts. Does an aggressive investment portfolio sound appealing?

YOU TOO CAN MINIMIZE RISKS

The risk of investing can be reduced by applying certain investment strategies. You can manage business risk to the extent that you make intelligent investment decisions, based on your own or a trusted professional's research. And you still may get a loser. It's important, therefore, to attempt to minimize your risks by putting some tried-and-true techniques to work for you. As we mentioned earlier, they are asset allocation, systematic investing using dollar-cost averaging, and finally, portfolio rebalancing.

The roots of asset allocation may be traced to the 1950s when a University of Chicago graduate student in economics was in search of a dissertation topic. Harry Markowitz ran into a stockbroker who suggested to Harry that he study the stock market. Harry took that advice and developed the theory that became a foundation for financial economics. He later earned, along with Merton Miller and William Sharpe, the 1990 Nobel Prize in Economics, following work they did that pioneered the Modern Portfolio Theory. Today, Modern Portfolio Theory is the basis for asset allocation. This concept could help pad your portfolio, but most likely not win you the Nobel Prize. Asset allocation can be tricky to do and is not a guarantee against loss, so consider consulting someone who makes a living at it, like a stockbroker or financial professional.

Asset allocation is essentially the notion that you can minimize your overall investment risk and increase your potential for gain by spreading your investment dollars across various types of investments, or asset classes (stocks, bonds, real estate, cash). Just how you allocate your investments will depend on a lot of things, most notably your ability to handle risks and how long you plan to hold your investments. Notice any recurring themes here? How much money you're dealing with and your goals play a pretty big role too, incidentally. A general rule of thumb is that the younger you are, the more aggressive you can be with your investment decisions because the longer your investments will have to possibly recover from the normal ups and downs of the market. Of course, if your idea of risk is not putting jelly on a peanut butter and jelly sandwich, your age really doesn't matter.

You might find the following sample asset allocations helpful when deciding how to diversify your portfolio. They aren't meant to tell you exactly what to do. You've got that little voice in your head for that. Rather, they're suggestions that you may consider when making investment decisions. You'll also need to factor in junk like how long you plan to keep your money invested when making actual decisions with real money.

A *conservative investment portfolio* includes investments that seek to produce income or protect the stability of the principal invested. It is usually more appropriate for investors with a timeline of five years or less who need investment income now to supplement their cash flow. These are cautious investors who are willing to accept relatively low returns in exchange for less risk. Less risk is more important to them than outpacing inflation. And they never go to bed without brushing their teeth.

A *moderate portfolio concentrates* on an investment mix that provides some income now and aims for moderate growth while trying to compensate for the possible effects of inflation. It's usually better for investors with a timeline of five years or more who can accept moderate risk and potentially more moderate returns. To save you some time counting, we used the word *moderate* five times in this paragraph, including this sentence.

An *aggressive investment portfolio* concentrates on equity investments, such as stocks or stock mutual funds, that aim for strong growth. It's generally more appropriate for investors with a timeline of 15 years or more or those who have a high threshold for risk and want to see their money potentially grow quickly. It's the ideal portfolio choice for thrill seekers everywhere.

SYSTEMATIC INVESTING IS A SOLID SYSTEM

It may not seem as exciting as buying and selling when the mood strikes you, but consistent investing is considered one of the best strategies for taking advantage of inevitable market fluctuations. A popular systematic investment strategy is dollar-cost averaging, which doesn't guarantee you'll make a profit or prevent a loss, but it can help you invest in a methodical way. With dollar-cost averaging, you invest the same amount at regular intervals, whether the market is up or down.

Poll

What is your best source for the worst investment advice?

Coworker	34%
(Make all your trades on company time)	
Stockbroker	28%
(Trust me, you'll always be broker)	
Brother-in-law	19%
(I'll let you in on a secret)	
Spouse/Partner	13%
(Honey, I shrunk the portfolio)	
Therapist	6%
(How does losing money make you feel?)	

Poll of visitors to ihatefinancialplanning.com

You buy more shares when the prices are lower and fewer shares when prices are higher, with the result being a lower average cost per share as you take advantage of swings in the market. Think of it as a built-in bonus for people who tend to procrastinate or ignore the aforementioned mood if and when it strikes.

You may already be using dollar-cost averaging if you participate in an employer-sponsored retirement plan and contribute to your retirement account through payroll deduction. Or perhaps you buy a set dollar figure of mutual funds each month. It's not recommended if you're concerned about continuing to invest during a prolonged market slump, which is always a possibility. Just be sure to consider your financial ability to continue buying through periods of both low and high price levels. The purely hypothetical example on page 173 shows how buying at regular intervals in a fluctuating market evens out the ride and reduces the average cost per share.

STAY TUNED TO YOUR NEEDS

Portfolio rebalancing is something to consider as time passes because the percentage mix of your investments will change as they increase or decrease in value. The following scenario may help you see why, even though Joe isn't a real person, and his fund choices aren't specific. They're merely intended to show you how periodic rebalancing can help you stay tuned to your investments. Joe invested $12,000 evenly in three mutual funds. In the past year Fund B performed well and Joe's $4,000 has grown to $5,500, while Fund A held its own and Fund C has shrunk to $3,500. Joe determines that according to his original asset allocation, he needs to shift some of his assets from Fund B over to Fund A and Fund C to regain his original allocation. It goes against his emotions to give up some of the gainer to the fund that's lost some value, but he keeps his eye focused on his goals and subsequent asset allocation. Doing so allows Joe to use the gain to purchase more shares of Fund C at a low price. It's a win, win investment situation.

You may have heard the phrase "buy low and sell high." It's easy to sell high because you see your profits piling up, but buying low is another thing altogether. Are you disciplined enough to put money into an

$100 Monthly Investment in Fluctuating Market

Share Price	Shares Purchased In					
	January	February	March	April	May	June
$4						
$5	20					
$6			16			16
$7						
$8				12	12	
$9						
$10		10				
$11						
$12						

Total amount invested: $600
Number of shares purchased: 86

Average cost per share: $6.98 (600/86)
Average market price per share: $7.17
You save: $0.19 per share

investment when it's performing poorly? Portfolio rebalancing may give you the discipline you need to carry out the task. And there are a few ways to do so. You might transfer funds like Joe did, or you can also add a lump sum to the accounts that have gone down. You've probably got a lump sum of cash sitting idle in the pocket of an old pair of jeans just waiting for a situation like this. Or not. You might also decide to modify future allocations so more money goes into some accounts than others so as to maintain balance. Just keep in mind that while rebalancing your portfolio occasionally is a smart thing to do to reduce your risk, it's not necessarily going to increase any investment returns.

Beyond the behavior of your investments, significant changes in any area of your life can have a trickle-down effect on your portfolio. Have you changed jobs? Did you win the lottery? Did you have another child? Have your expenses increased or decreased dramatically? If you suddenly lose a job, you may need to reduce the risk in your portfolio to lessen the overall risk to a future source of income. On the other hand, if your fortunes turn for the better, you may be able to tolerate more risk than you could previously and so it might be in your best interests to put more toward riskier (and potentially more rewarding) investments.

WHERE GOES THE MONEY?

Let's move beyond investment techniques and strategies and concentrate on where you can invest. It's much more fun talking about money than Modern Portfolio Theory anyway. We mentioned the main sorts of investments in the beginning of the chapter—mutual funds, stocks, and bonds. There are other ways to save and invest too, and we'll touch on those. Of course, leaving your money in the change jar is always an option, but you'll never get more out than you put in, especially if someone raids it for laundry money.

Aside from that money jar, some of the safest savings vehicles are cash equivalents or liquid investments, meaning you can turn them into cash with relatively little effort or penalty. They feature relatively stable principal with modest-to-minimal interest rates and risk. Maybe you have a savings account or money market account at the bank or other financial institution. You can get at the money whenever you need to, but in exchange for that convenience, you earn a low interest rate. The difference between the two types of accounts is that money market funds aren't guaranteed and could actually lose value. Bank certificates of deposit (CDs) are another common short-term savings tool that offer a slightly higher interest rate for a fixed period of time. Much like savings accounts, deposits are FDIC insured, but you may pay a penalty if you withdraw the money before maturity.

THE FUND-A-MENTALS OF MUTUAL FUNDS

Mutual funds allow you to buy, with a relatively small investment, shares of a fund that owns securities across a variety of industries and investment objectives. In other words, you can play with the big boys on a modest scale, say with $1,000. Mutual funds offer diversification right off the bat because they hold shares in a greater number of securities than any single investor is likely to buy on his or her own. Just as the shareholders share the costs of buying securities, they also share any proceeds from the fund's growth. Not to mention they share the prospect of overall losses. Makes you wonder if they always share and share alike.

Another benefit of investing in mutual funds is taking advantage of the professional money management. Unless you get your jollies studying the financial statements of hundreds of companies and look forward to spending leisure time monitoring the economic outlook of numerous industries, you'll appreciate the expertise offered by fund managers. They identify securities that may meet the fund objectives and research potential investments. They time purchases and sales within the portfolio. Then they continuously monitor the investments in the fund while you, on the other hand, go skiing, make a soufflé, or complete crossword puzzles. Finally, they assure diversification of assets with the hope of making the ride smooth and even for investors.

A FUND FOR EVERY BOY AND GIRL

No matter what type of investor you are or how much—or how little—money you've got to invest, you will probably be able to find a mutual fund that meets your needs. There are thousands to choose from and just about as many opportunities to buy. To increase your chances for a satisfying mutual fund experience, pick funds that match your investment objectives and tolerance for risk. Because, as you well know from reading this chapter word for word, risk is just a part of the investment landscape. Your reward for reading this far is a brief overview of the basic types of mutual funds.

The largest category of mutual funds is *equity funds*, which invest in stocks of corporations. These funds are usually categorized by the type of stock that is bought—growth stocks, value stocks, or a blend of the two. Growth stocks have a history of strong growth whereas value stocks offer consistent growth over time.

Bond Funds are also called fixed income or income funds, and they're funds that invest mainly in government and corporate debt. The primary objective of these funds is to provide a steady cash flow to investors, which makes them popular with conservative investors or retirees who are looking for current income.

The goal of *balanced funds* is to provide a balanced mix of safety, income, and capital appreciation. They do so by including some stocks and some bonds in the fund. If we were talking coffee, it would be an ideal blend of beans resulting in a flavor that appeals to a wide variety of coffee drinkers. Of course, the main risk associated with coffee is burning your tongue, a claim balanced funds simply can't make.

Index funds are passively managed mutual funds that try to mirror the performance of a specific index, such as the Standard & Poor's 500 Composite Stock Price Index. There are several index funds to choose from if you're not keen on the S&P 500. Since portfolio decisions are automatic and transactions are infrequent, expenses tend to be lower than those of actively managed funds.

Global or international funds invest in companies and industries all over the world (global funds even include the United States in the mix). They can be hot, as in volatile, depending on the state of global affairs, currency fluctuations, and other factors. The world is shrinking, so don't disregard the investment possibilities offered by non-U.S. companies. If you find yourself humming "It's a Small World" after reading this paragraph, we will understand. Maybe we can drown out the music in your head with a reminder that investing in foreign securities may pose risks not associated with staying home, such as changes in exchange rates, as well as different government regulations, economic conditions, and accounting standards.

Sector funds specialize in stocks of a particular industry. Say you can't take your mind off widgets. Surely there's a widget fund that can help you ride the wave of widget-mania for every cent it's worth. But beware that it's a particularly risky investment with the possibility of big gains if widgets really take off, but an equal chance that widgets will go the way of the Chia pet.

CAN'T SEE THE FOREST FOR THE FEES?

One thing to consider when deciding whether mutual funds are the route you want to take is that all of them charge fees that can eat a hole in your profits in no time. Even no-load funds get their money somehow. You want to make money and so do the fund people. The decision you need to make is how much you are willing to pay for research and investment advice because you'll pay more in fees for top-of-the-line service. It's that way in any business, so you're probably used to having to make that choice. The challenge is to determine what you believe to be a reasonable assessment for management services and balance it against the profit you hope to make from a successfully managed fund.

The up-front fee is your basic *front-end load* you may have heard about. It's the sales commission, if you want to know the truth, a sales charge assessed at the time of purchase, ranging from 1 percent to 7 percent of your investment. Sometimes the sales charge is assessed at the time of sale, or as a *back-end load*. We call them the on-the-way-out fees. You may pay a *redemption fee* if you sell the shares in your mutual fund after owning them for a short time—anywhere from 90 days to three years. For the privilege of cashing out you may have to pay about 0.25 percent of the redemption amount. We call the *annual operating expenses* the every-year fees. They include management fees, brokerage commissions, administrative costs, and other costs of being in business. Last but not least, there are *12b-1 fees*, which some funds assess to offset the cost of marketing and advertising the fund.

THE ABCs OF MUTUAL FUND SHARES

Another thing you'll want to be sure to understand is the difference between Class A, Class B, and Class C shares. But only if you care what you'll be charged to buy, own, and sell mutual funds. *Class A shares* usually charge a front-end sales charge. If you've got $1,000 to invest but pay a front-end load of 5 percent, your actual investment is $950. You'll pay other charges and fees while you own the shares, but they tend to be lower than the other share classes. Class A shares are typically for long-term investors or those with a large sum to invest because investment companies may offer discounts for large purchases.

Class B shares usually don't have a sales charge when you buy them, but the ongoing expenses and fees—which may decline over time—could be higher than those that come with Class A shares. And if you sell your shares in the first six years or so, you'll pay a back-end load. B shares are typically purchased by investors who may not have a lot of money to invest but plan to leave it alone for a while. *Class C shares* usually don't charge front-end or back-end sales charges, but the ongoing fees and expenses don't go down over time. You may also pay a back-end load if you sell in the first year. C shares are typically for investors who may not hold their shares for a long time.

Mutual funds are generally considered long-term investments. Most experts would advise you to select mutual funds aligned with your goals and objectives and then hold on to them for the long term. Most experts have never tried to hold on to a runaway roller coaster. If you pay any attention at all to the ups and downs of the market, you may be tempted to sell when the downs last too long. Most experts would advise that before you sell, you should look up the definition of "long term" in the dictionary and write it down 500 times because in many cases, where there are downs, the ups may be soon to follow.

There may be some legitimate reasons to sell your mutual fund shares prematurely, which we'll gladly share with you because we want you to know what we know. If your personal circumstances change, it may be necessary to modify your portfolio to meet your new goals—as you grow older, if you begin to earn a significantly higher income, if you need cash for an emergency. If the fund manager suddenly starts buying trendy investments without regard to the fund's long-term

LOAD VERSUS NO-LOAD: IS THERE A QUESTION?

Actually, this is a valid question. While a less expensive mutual fund (one without "loads") may appear to be an obvious choice, you could get hit with advisory fees or other assessments that take a serious chunk out of your profit margins. By the same token, paying the "load" in a load fund buys you the investment advice, knowledge, and research of the registered representative who sells the fund. Basically, paying a little extra up front—or at the back-end, as the case may be—could save you a lot of time researching mutual funds. Read the fund information carefully, do some calculations, ask good questions, and check with a financial professional, all to help you determine whether the fees you're paying will help you realize greater potential for profit in the long run.

objective or criteria for its holdings, you may want to sell. If you bought shares of a certain fund because you liked the manager, you may want to sell if he or she leaves to manage a different fund. Don't act too fast, though; give the new fund manager a chance. It may be a good time to sell if the fund raises its fees or changes its investment objectives. Finally, sometimes a fund has more assets than it has investment prospects. In this case, if the fund manager doesn't close the fund to new investors, it may be a signal that management standards have lowered, and you may want to sell.

PLAYING THE STOCK MARKET

Stocks, or equities, are investments that represent ownership with the potential to appreciate in value. As we mentioned earlier in the chapter, owning stock is like owning a piece of a corporation. Your ownership, and potential for loss or gain, is based on how many shares you purchase. Sure, there are risks, but there is also the potential for a big payoff. Just keep in mind that investing is meant to be a long-term adventure filled with normal market fluctuations that cause earnings to rise and fall.

Over the years, investing in the stock market has often been a reasonable investment with potential for solid results. However, it's quite possible to lose a great deal—or even all—of your money. Investing in the stock market is a risk-based proposition, with the upside being profit and the downside being loss. The market is simply not a good venue for your money if you plan to impatiently plunk your money in stocks willy-nilly. For those of you scoring at home, in this instance "willy-nilly" is defined as without careful assessment of risk.

HERE'S A TIP THAT COULD PAY DIVIDENDS

If you're looking for a way to buy stocks, DRIPs—or dividend reinvestment plans—allow investors to buy shares of stock slowly (as in, a low minimum investment) and methodically (as in, buy a few shares each month and reinvest any dividends). DRIPs are meant to be a long-term adventure: you can start small, add to your portfolio over time and watch as dividends and gains provide potential growth. You could lose money with DRIPs, much like with most investments.

DRIPs were popular among do-it-yourself investors during the boom, but during the bust that made most investors feel like drips, dividends shrank. Plus, those dividends were taxed at the investor's income tax rate—up to 38.6 percent, depending on income—a lot of dough at tax time. Thanks to a new tax law called the Jobs and Growth Tax Relief Reconciliation Act of 2003, the maximum income tax rate on stock dividends is now 15 percent. Investors in the bottom two income tax brackets (10 percent and 15 percent) pay just 5 percent on their dividends. This break is intended to motivate investors and companies alike—now perhaps more companies will add dividends to their stocks or increase existing dividend payments. As with most of the new tax law, these lower rates are scheduled to disappear like a varmint in a gopher hole unless Congress extends them by 2009.

For a list of companies with DRIPs, go to netstockdirect.com or dripinvestor.com. You can pay a fee to join the National Association of Investors Corp., an organization for investment clubs that helps individual members enroll in DRIPs. ShareBuilder.com and BuyandHold.com are online brokers that offer DRIP investors reasonable charges for trades and purchases. They do so by completing small trades in bundles, which means you can't control your share price.

BONDS MIGHT BRING BALANCE

Most of us have been in the position where we have had to ask someone for money. It's not a fun feeling. Well, how about being on the other side of the coin? Bonds are a form of investing that can generate earnings through what basically amounts to you loaning money to a company or government agency. One of the oldest ways to invest, a bond certifies that the issuer has borrowed a specific sum of money and needs to repay the principal and interest to the bond holder by a certain date.

What makes bonds appealing to some investors is that they tend to be more predictable than other securities because many of the financial variables associated with them are known at the time they are issued. Many investors include bonds in their portfolios, therefore, to provide diversification and balance. The main attraction of bonds is that they can provide a source of fixed income for a defined period of time, assuming a bond is not called, or paid off by the issuer. Certain types of bonds may offer less risk than many stocks. Of course, that generally means they offer lower rates of return.

For the use of your money during the period of the bond—and there are bonds issued for many different lengths of time—the issuer pays interest in the form of coupons or interest payments, usually twice each year. The exception is the zero-coupon bond, which offers no coupons. Instead, the zero-coupon bond is traded at a discount from its "par" price, which varies depending upon interest rates and the bond's maturity, and offers a final lump sum payment to include interest-on-interest as if the coupons had been reinvested. You may be wondering why they're called coupons if you can't redeem them at the grocery store on two-for-one coupon day. Well, bond certificates were originally issued with a sheet of coupons attached. At regular intervals, the bond holder would clip a coupon and present it at the bond issuer's bank for interest payments.

Mortgage-backed bonds are another variation of bond issued by the feds that represent pools of residential mortgages. This type of bond repays the investor a portion of principal plus interest each month, similar to a mortgage payment. This means you can run out of investment if you choose not to reinvest your principal. *Corporate bonds* are issued by private and publicly held companies. You'll find everything from highest quality investment grade bonds to highly speculative junk bonds in this category. *Municipal bonds,* or "muni" bonds as they are affectionately called, are what help local or state governments pay for public projects, such as construction of schools, streets, highways, bridges, hospitals, airports, water systems, and other public works. To encourage taxpayers to invest in these bonds—and therefore help make their communities a better place to live—the federal government (and many state governments too) may offer income tax advantages to certain bond holders, depending on your income bracket. The tradeoff for any income tax breaks is a lower yield than you'd get with a comparable corporate bond. You can't have both high yields and tax advantages, after all.

GUARANTEES AND STEADY INTEREST ARE SUCH A DRAG

Consider yourself warned that this is going to be boring. You'll have to determine just how dull, but on the scale of 1 to yawn, it likely ranks somewhere in the watching-grass-grow range. You probably know the dry details about savings bonds. The government guarantees them, and federal income taxes on the earnings are deferred for up to 30 years (earnings are exempt from state and local taxes). Use the income for qualifying college expenses and you won't ever pay federal tax on it. Savings bonds are meant to be a long-term investment, so you may be penalized about three months of interest earnings if you cash them before five years. The minimum holding period for bonds issued before February 1, 2003, is six months and a year if purchased anytime since then.

Series EE Bonds continue to earn interest for 30 years. Interest earnings are exempt from state and local income taxes, and you defer paying federal income tax until you cash them in, unless you use them to pay for college, in which case you could skip income taxes altogether, depending on your income and other rules. You buy Series EE Bonds for half the original face value, so 25 bucks will get you 50 if you let the sucker mature. In response to the terrorist attacks in 2001, the government introduced the Patriot Bond, which is different than Series EE Bonds in name only. Despite rumors to the contrary, your investment in the Patriot Bond does not fund military spending.

The I Bond is different in that its return is a combination of a fixed amount plus the rate of inflation. That means you don't need to worry that inflation will stink up your investment. The fixed rate is figured twice a year (May and

November) and paid as long as you own the I Bonds, while the inflation-based portion can vary twice a year based on the Consumer Price Index. They're sold at face value in a variety of denominations.

Many employers offer Series EE savings bonds through payroll deduction, but you can also buy and redeem both EE and I bonds easily at banks or online at savingsbond.gov or savingsbonds.com. The preferred way to purchase savings bonds now is via the Internet, so you don't even need to get those colorful paper bonds as proof of ownership. Think of it as one less thing to lose.

THE PROSPECT OF A PROSPECTUS

When considering an investment, the most reliable information can be obtained from the legal documents a public company is required to make available to investors. In light of the corporate accounting scandals in recent years, you're probably skeptical that public companies would actually tell the truth to shareholders. Those scandals represent just a tiny percentage of companies. If we were accountants we could quantify "tiny" for you, but we've never even owned a pocket protector.

A prospectus can be a valuable source of information for potential investors, assuming you can stay awake while reading the document. Don't let the size of the words scare you out of reading it. Most of the truly important stuff is summarized in "plain English" in the first several pages. All bets are off on who gets to decide just how plain the English really is. Although prospectuses are one requirement in a highly regulated industry, the investments you make are neither guaranteed nor insured by any government agency. That means if you lose money, nobody's going to swoop in and make up the difference. Just one more reason to do your research. At the very least, uncover this information in the prospectus before you buy shares of any mutual fund.

- For starters, how long has the fund been around? If it has a track record of at least five years, you will be able to get a decent look at its performance, keeping in mind that past performance doesn't guarantee future results.

- How well has the fund performed in the past? That information is typically illustrated in a line graph comparing it to an index fund. Many prospectuses don't list long-term results, but they provide a chart of returns for each calendar year. You can scan them to detect performance patterns, but again, don't go thinking the past has any bearing on the future where results are concerned. For a quick reminder of that fact, reread the name of this chapter a couple dozen times.
- Consider the manager's tenure with the fund because a record is irrelevant if the current manager didn't compile it. Some prospectuses make it clear as mud by telling you how long the management company has operated the fund but not how long the current manager has been steering the ship.
- How much it will cost you. Mutual fund returns aren't predictable, but expenses are, so find out what you're in for. The expenses section explains if the fund has a sales load and how much it is. It also breaks out management fees and other expenses. Look for a table illustrating how much you pay a year for every $1,000 invested.
- Beware any mention of pending lawsuits or regulatory review, especially in this day of scandals.

READING THE ANNUAL REPORT

Before purchasing stock, it's wise to review the company's annual report, and once you've invested read it every year because it's full of information that can help you become a better investor. All publicly held companies must release an annual report containing both a glowing description of the company and thorough documentation, as dictated by law, of the company's financial performance. These financial statements, which must be audited by an independent entity, can speak volumes about a business. Pay close attention to the income statement, which details net sales, gross profit, net income, and earnings per share. It's the bottom line we're always instructed to look at. Also review the balance sheet that includes assets and liabilities. It's basically a snapshot of a company's financial health at that point in time.

THINK ABOUT HOW THIS MAKES YOU FEEL

You may have taken one of those personality tests that categorize you as either a "thinker" or a "feeler." It's hard to believe that a person can't be both, but the experts who create these sorts of tests have done their research (while presumably not harming any lab rats in the process). We've discovered that most people are, in fact, both thinkers *and* feelers. You may have heard them say, somewhat defensively, "I'll think about getting my finances in order when I feel like it." When it's put that way, perhaps you're a thinker and a feeler too.

It makes no difference whether you use your right brain or your left, you can use the Internet to get answers to questions you didn't even know you had. That's right. Rocket scientists and starving artists alike have access to the same financial tools. Lucky for you—and all sorts of people like you—the Internet is an ideal resource for tons of information about money and investing. If you don't believe us, do a search next time you're on the Web with words like "debt," "financial advice," or "invest." You'll be amazed at what you find (and you won't need to complete a personality test before using the helpful information). It may be intimidating at first, and you may never actually enjoy the task, but you're the only one who can make a difference where your personal financial situation is concerned. We're fairly sure both analytical and creative people agree on that one.

Successful investing doesn't happen overnight. You can begin investing on a small scale, track your results, and then gradually increase your commitment. The important thing is to get started, and be consistent, always keeping in mind that there are pros and cons to most investment decisions. If you want guarantees, you may sacrifice potential earnings. Would you rather defer income taxes or wage a war on inflation? Will you still be content at age 60 that you did nothing at 30? We figure if we throw the pros and cons of a range of money ideas at you, we just might con you into doing something for yourself. Even *not* doing anything is doing something. You can avoid fees, deadlines, inflation, growth, and the rest by doing nothing at all. But then, where will that get you?

9

Sickness, Disaster, Death, and Other Fun Topics

We know a young man who was just three years old when his 32-year-old father died suddenly. When Ted graduated from high school he paid cash for his first car and enrolled at the community college in a neighboring town. Both milestones were possible thanks to the death benefit of a small life insurance policy his father had purchased when Ted was born, which grew in an interest-bearing account until he was 18.

And what about Michelle? After earning her medical degree, she became a family practice physician and spent her vacations offering free medical care in Third World countries. On one such trip, Michelle blew out her knee playing basketball with other volunteers. Nerve damage to the knee left her disabled and unable to practice medicine or stand upright for any length of time. Fortunately, Michelle could rely on the disability income insurance policy she had purchased for the income she'd need.

We tell you these stories to illustrate that insurance can be a good thing. Sure, it requires you to think about all the uncomfortable subjects in the chapter title. Plus, it demands you learn more than you care to about risk protection and the differences between insurance policies and other junk you'd rather ignore. And you may never even need to use it (knock on wood). Oh yes, it can be quite expensive. But it's a good thing just the same, and you often pay money for a good thing.

We know heartwarming stories rarely motivate procrastinators to protect themselves from similar circumstances, unfortunately. Nor do we hold any illusions that we'll sway skeptics into policy-toting insurance spokespeople. After reading this you may hold fast to your belief that insurance is something you can live without. And that's fine. All we ask is that you agree to use this chapter as an instructional tool or sleep aid, whichever you prefer. We'll never know.

HEALTH INSURANCE IS A MUST-HAVE

Health insurance is an especially irritating topic. Everybody knows it's necessary, fewer of us than ever can afford it, and the cost of health care shows no sign of going anywhere but up. Still, our message to you is you probably want to make sure you've got health insurance. The bottom line is you don't want to end up jeopardizing your entire financial future as a result of some unforeseen medical emergency. If your employer doesn't offer it, buy an individual policy. If you're self-employed and can't stomach the premiums, find a policy you can afford. Many professional, alumni, and fraternal organizations give members access to their group rates. And access to group rates means you probably won't need to prove you're healthy or have no preexisting conditions. We'd tell you to call your local chapter of Procrastinators Anonymous, but they never got around to installing a telephone.

At the end of this chapter you'll find several sources for health insurance quotes, but first we prescribe that you read what you're in for with the various types of coverage.

Short-Term Health Insurance Fills a Gap

Short-term health insurance is temporary health insurance if you're between permanent health plans and only need coverage for up to six months. It may be the answer if you're between jobs; waiting for employer group medical coverage to kick in; a recent college graduate (have diploma, need insurance); a dependent losing coverage under your parent's health plan; or a laid-off, striking, terminated, temporary, or seasonal employee. Which pretty much describes everyone we know.

Many short-term policies include coverage for office visits, prescription drugs, intensive care, lab and X ray, and ambulance service. Plus, you usually can choose your own doctors and hospitals. Maternity costs aren't covered, but complications from pregnancy usually are. Preexisting conditions aren't covered, and if you need to extend coverage beyond the initial term, you must apply again. Any illnesses or injuries you may have had during that term are considered preexisting and won't be covered. That's what we call a reverse grandfather clause.

Rates for this type of coverage vary depending on which deductible you choose, and that can range from $200 to $2,000. Once you meet the deductible, the insurance company usually pays 80 percent of the next $5,000 and 100 percent of anything more. Many short-term policies charge the deductible per injury or illness, so the meter starts over every time you need medical attention. Eligibility requirements are pretty stiff as well, and they vary greatly by insurance company.

Having COBRA Doesn't Make You a Snake Handler

The Consolidated Omnibus Budget Reconciliation Act of 1985 (COBRA) guarantees most Americans continued health care coverage when they leave a job. In general, it applies to employers of 20 or more people, as well as government employers, but not the federal government or certain church-related employers. To qualify for COBRA coverage, you must be covered by group health insurance when you leave a job, and you must not be fired for gross misconduct. Full-time and part-time employees are eligible, and self-employed people may be eligible if they're covered by a group health plan.

COBRA coverage is a reassuring option, especially if you have a preexisting health condition that makes it difficult to qualify for other coverage. You have 60 days after you leave to decide whether to continue your group health coverage through COBRA. If you do, coverage will begin retroactively from the day you leave. You can keep your coverage for up to 18 months at your old group rate, but if your employer was paying a portion of your premium, you'll have to pay that portion now, along with a 2 percent administration charge. That's the part of the snake that bites. You may find that individual health insurance is cheaper than COBRA, depending on your deductible amount. The higher the deductible, the lower the premiums you'll pay.

Catastrophic Coverage Is Worst-Case Protection

If you want to be covered for life's nicks and bruises, you don't want catastrophic insurance because it only pays for major medical expenses and hospital stays. We're talking treatment in the intensive-care unit after a car crash, not stitches in the ER. Deductibles are high for this sort of worst-case protection—anywhere from $500 to $15,000—but so is the maximum benefit—up to about $3 million. Catastrophic insurance is appealing to young, healthy individuals who are self-employed or don't have insurance through an employer. They're willing to pay cash for routine office visits, X rays, prescriptions, and so on, but they want protection if disaster strikes. People in the 50 to 65 age group may buy catastrophic insurance coverage to guard against costs for treatment of serious illnesses such as heart attacks or cancer.

Poll

Which employee benefit is most important?

Health Insurance	60%
Steady Employment	23%
Retirement Savings Plan	10%
Flexible Hours	4%
Paid Vacation	3%

Poll conducted by ihatefinancialplanning.com

SCAMS ARE SPREADING LIKE A RASH

Skyrocketing costs for health insurance and medical care have created an environment ripe for unscrupulous business practices. Portraying themselves as insurance companies, thieves sell you a bogus insurance policy and run. Sometimes they pay a few claims to build credibility before disappearing. They prey on small business owners or self-employed individuals who are seeking affordable health coverage but don't have the resources to check out prospective plans.

Since 2001, unauthorized health plans have left thousands of unsuspecting citizens with $85 million in unpaid medical bills and—worse—without health coverage, according to the Commonwealth Fund, a private foundation that supports research on health and social issues. Bringing illegal health care plans to justice is tough because the thieves move quickly and change their business names frequently.

Unfortunately, there's no safety net when this type of fraud occurs, and innocent patients are left holding the bill. Watch for these telltale symptoms:

- Ironically, if you find a policy charging inexpensive premiums, it may be a scam. Avoid this by comparing several plans before choosing one.
- Most individual policies require significant medical screening for preexisting conditions, so be wary of short and simple applications.
- If someone says you qualify for cheap group coverage as part of a union or trade association you don't belong to, resist the convincing sales pitch.

- Scammers use business names that sound familiar and terms, such as "assurance" and "mutual," that sound official. Some claim they don't need to be licensed or that health insurance is unregulated. Legitimate companies and insurance agents will encourage you to check up on them.

    If you have bought insurance from an illegal plan, you may have trouble later on. That's because if you were ill or injured during the time you thought you were covered, any medical condition you still have may be excluded from your new policy as a preexisting condition. It will depend on the type of policy you buy and the state regulations where you live.

    Inoculate yourself from this rash by spending some time checking into your health care coverage. You'll find information on choosing solid insurance companies at the end of this chapter.

Fee-for-Service Health Insurance

One type of health insurance that's gone the way of affordable medical care is fee-for-service. It is still available, but managed care is more the norm. With fee-for-service, you choose doctors and hospitals and can refer yourself to specialists without permission. Plus, you—not the insurance company—get to decide whether a doctor visit is necessary.

Of course you'll pay for all this freedom. There is often an annual deductible starting around $200 before insurance kicks in, and then insurance covers about 80 percent of any medical bills and you pay the rest. There is usually a limit to your out-of-pocket expenses, though, and the insurance company will pay 100 percent above it. Also, you may have to pay for services and then be reimbursed. If you're shopping for this type of insurance, check to be sure preventive care is covered because not all insurance policies include it.

You'll hear the phrase "reasonable and customary" bantered around with fee-for-service insurance. It's the amount the insurance company will pay for care after taking into account what health care costs are in your particular region of the country. If your doc charges $150 for a procedure but the insurance company says it should only cost a hundred bucks, you'll probably need to make up the difference.

Managed Care Floats in the Mainstream

Managed care is a fact of life for most of us. It can be frustrating to work within the rules enforced by the insurance companies, mainly because they don't always seem to make much sense. If you've ever had to switch pharmacies to comply with insurance company whims, had your claim for chiropractic care refused, or been denied coverage because you inadvertently went to the "wrong" doctor, you know what we mean. On the other hand, managed care strives to do what its name implies. To manage costs and care, the insurance company negotiates contracts and fees with health care providers in its network, which is why you need to follow their rules. In exchange you pay a relatively small copayment for office visits, prescriptions, hospital stays, and the like, depending on your coverage.

There are three levels of managed care, each with its own set of restrictions. The more freedom you have, the more you will pay. Which route you go depends on how much you want to pay in relation to how much flexibility you require.

The Preferred Provider Organization (PPO) is the least restrictive form of managed care. You can go to doctors outside of the PPO network if you want, but there's a financial incentive and less paperwork if you choose care inside the network. Visit a doctor in the network and make a copayment. Go outside and you'll pay the entire bill and get reimbursed by the insurance company for a certain percentage of the cost. A PPO is similar to fee-for-service health insurance in that you can refer yourself to specialists without prior approval, but preventive care may not be covered.

A Point-of-Service (POS) plan is middle-of-the-road managed care. As with a PPO, you can select care outside of the network, but there are incentives not to. And you need to choose a primary care physician who will make referrals to specialists for you. If you refer yourself, you'll pay for the services, but if your primary physician refers you to someone outside the network, it will be covered. POS generally offers preventive care services to its members.

The Health Maintenance Organization (HMO) is the most restrictive type of managed care, but the costs are lower too. Preventive care is covered in an HMO. A primary care physician is required in the land of HMOs, and you'll need to stay in the network of doctors when you pick one. In fact, any doctor you see must be in the network if you want the care to be covered. And you'll need a referral before seeing a specialist. What's more, before you receive care in an emergency room you have to get clearance in most cases. There are exceptions to that rule, of course. We're guessing you've got to call ahead for treatment on a hangnail, but you're authorized to rush to the ER no questions asked if there's a certain amount of blood.

HERE'S A PERK THAT COULD REDUCE YOUR INCOME TAXES

Does your employer have flexible spending accounts employees can use for medical expenses? If so, the money is taken from your salary before income taxes are withheld, and you can use it for miscellaneous medical expenses throughout the year.

Here's how it works: Decide how much money you want deducted from your paycheck in pretax dollars for expenses not covered—either partially or completely—by your health, dental, or other benefits plans. Allowed expenses include prescription copays, contact lens solution, orthodontia, acupuncture, prescription sunglasses, laser eye surgery, chiropractic care, hearing aids, doctor-recommended weight-loss programs, flu shots, and crutches. The list could go on, but we don't want to get into bodily functions here. Some over-the-counter medications qualify too, such as pain relievers, antacids, and cold and allergy medications. For a complete list of what you can use the money for, see IRS Publication 502, "Medical and Dental Expenses."

The maximum amount you can have deducted is subject to limitations, so check with your employer, but it's usually at least a couple thousand bucks. You don't pay federal, state, or FICA taxes on the money. What's more, you pay less current income taxes overall because your contribution is deducted from your gross salary before taxes are calculated. What's not to like about a plan that reduces your tax bill? You don't have to wait until the money accumulates in your account to spend it either. Talk about icing on the cake! The only drawback is that if you don't use the money in your account each year, you lose it. Unclaimed dollars go to your employer to offset the costs of administering the program.

Most employers offer dependent care accounts too, which work about the same way and are good for things like childcare expenses, preschool, elder care, and private sitters. Some employers offer such accounts for transportation costs too.

THE UPSIDE OF BEING DOWN FOR THE COUNT

Imagine not being able to perform the regular duties of your job. Maybe you're jumping for joy. But what if it's because of a disabling injury or illness, and you not only can't jump for joy, you also can't jump through the usual hoops at work? You're probably scoffing at the mere suggestion that you'll ever be injured to the point you can't work. But consider that at age 40, the average worker faces only a 14 percent chance of dying before age 65, but a 22 percent chance of being disabled for 90 days or more, according to the Insurance Information Institute in 2002 (www.iii.org). Your chances are greater than one in five that you'll spend some time unable to jump through work hoops, or any others, for that matter.

Can you go three months or more without income? If not, you should probably protect yourself against that risk with disability income insurance. Many people consider it a luxury, but disability coverage should be considered a necessity if you don't have financial resources you could depend on if illness or injury prevents you from working. To clarify, we're not referring to sick days or short-term disability plans offered at work. We're talking about long-term protection during serious downtime.

You might already have some disability insurance from your employer. In fact, many people use that as an excuse not to explore buying additional coverage. But most employer plans cover just 40 percent to 60 percent of your gross annual income and don't kick in right away. Or they may only pay benefits for a short time. Plus, the benefits would be income taxable if the employer pays the premiums, which means you won't see anywhere close to 60 percent of what you're used to getting on payday. We don't know about you, but it's difficult for us to imagine living on less than half of what we're currently earning.

If you're self-employed, do you have a disability insurance policy? If not, you may want to flip back to Chapter 1 and reread the babble about procrastination in "'Plan' Is a Four-Letter Word." We're guessing your job security would suffer dramatically if you became disabled and unable to keep that self-employment income coming in. You might want to add buying disability coverage to your to-do list. Maybe we should call it a to-spend list.

Some argue that they will rely on Social Security disability benefits if necessary. We can tell you that it's difficult to qualify for government benefits, and you shouldn't count on them. For starters, eligibility is based on being unable to hold *any* job, not just the one you have at the time you're disabled. Before you can apply for benefits it must be determined (by a real-life medical doctor and not a loan shark) that the disability is going to last 12 months or result in death. What a clever way for the government to cut down on paperwork from unqualified applicants.

Have we convinced you to consider disability coverage or are you simply reading on auto pilot? Your reward for getting this far is a brief, yet dull overview of what to look for when shopping disability income insurance.

There are three renewability options to consider. The most expensive is *noncancelable and guaranteed renewable,* which means the policy can't be canceled nor can the premiums increase as long as premiums are paid. *Guaranteed renewable* policies can't be canceled if premiums are paid, and premiums can only increase if they go up for an entire class of policyholders. *Optionally renewable* is the cheapest—and least appealing—option because the insurance company can cancel coverage or charge higher premiums.

Look for a broad definition of disability. Some policies pay benefits if you can't perform the duties of your current occupation, while others pay only if you are unable to do *any* job. And some policies define disability based on your own occupation at first but after a few years they continue to pay only if you're unable to hold any job. You'll pay more for a pure "own occupation" policy, but its flexibility may be worth it.

Disability insurance polices may pay residual or partial benefits to make up for lost income if you're only able to work part time. It's a standard feature of some policies and optional coverage on others. It's handy in cases where after an accident you can't work at all for a year but then can rejoin the workforce on a part-time basis while you continue to recover.

The amount of income you'll receive from the policy will vary but benefits from all sources usually range from 60 percent to 80 percent. Insurance companies don't pay full lost wages because it may tempt some policy owners to stay home even after they regain their health.

You can expect to pay between 1 percent and 3 percent of your salary for disability insurance. That's a lot of coin, and it may prompt you to play the I-can't-afford-it card. Perhaps you're quick with numbers and figure that estimate is nearly double what you're paying for homeowners insurance. And you'd be correct, depending on where you live, the value of your home, and a bunch of other factors. The reason has to do with how insurance companies calculate what to charge for a product based on the likelihood of having to pay claims. The probability that you'll become disabled and unable to work is fairly high, based on the statistics we tossed out at the beginning of this section. The probability that you'll ever have to file a major claim on your homeowners insurance is fairly slim, on the other hand.

The younger you are when you buy disability income insurance, the lower your premiums will be. The cost will vary based on how much coverage you buy, your age, gender, health history, and occupation. The riskier your work, the more you'll pay. Buy a noncancelable and guaranteed renewable policy and your premiums will stay the same and your insurability will remain guaranteed, provided you continue coverage by paying your premiums on time and you smile while writing the check. Buy a guaranteed renewable policy and your premiums could go up, and with an optionally renewable policy, of course, there's no guarantee where your insurability is concerned.

Other factors that will affect the cost of a disability income insurance policy are the elimination period and the benefit period. They boil down to how long you're willing to wait to begin receiving benefits and how long you'll get them once they start. You can choose an elimination period anywhere from 30 days to two years, with longer translating to cheaper. One thing to note is that if you pick 90 days, you won't get a check on day 91 but rather right around day 120—at the end of the month the claims start. Insurance companies tend to round up when it comes to writing claim checks. With the benefit period, you can choose to receive benefits for two years, five years, to age 65, or for the rest of your life, in some cases. Longer in this case translates to more expensive.

LIFE INSURANCE IS FOR THE LIVING

Do you see yourself in any of these scenarios?

- Chris and Terry just bought a house, and they want to do what they can to ensure it would be paid for so one of them could continue living there if tragedy strikes and the other one dies.
- Kaana's college education made it possible for her to land a high-paying job, and she said "thank you" to her alma mater by naming it as a beneficiary of her life insurance policy. She can add beneficiaries over time, should she get married or have children.

- Robert and Jackie are saving money to adopt a child. If they borrow the cash value that's accumulated in their life insurance policy, they may have the money they need. They intend to pay back that loan in a few years, but if the loan is not repaid, the policy death benefit will be reduced or the policy could lapse. And there could be some income taxes to pay, depending on several factors we won't bore you with.
- As co-owners of a growing business, Morgan and Taylor want to keep focused on their work and not have to worry about whether the business will survive if one of them suddenly dies.

Sure, the most traditional use of life insurance is to provide a death benefit to financially assist a surviving partner and/or dependents when the insured is no longer starring in his or her own motion picture (i.e., dead). If drama is what you're looking for, however, you might want to ponder the possibilities for the aforementioned death benefit, such as providing for your family, making charitable gifts, or ensuring that your business continues without you. Certain kinds of life insurance policies may also provide cash values you can access through loans and withdrawals to help with college costs or retirement needs. All of this comes at a cost, of course, and we'll discuss the related fees and expenses later.

To be sure, there are as many reasons to buy life insurance as there are types of insurance to buy. And there are twice as many excuses for not buying life insurance as there are products on the market. Whether you're the business owner or new parent in the scenarios above, you have your own reasons for buying insurance or rationalizing your decision not to. Whether you need life insurance is a question with no correct answer, so all we'll do is present the facts and let you decide.

WE DARE YOU TO STAY AWAKE WHEN READING THIS

The two main types of life insurance are term and cash value. Term insurance is straightforward coverage without the extra features you may not need or be able to afford. It is designed to pay an income tax–free death benefit to a chosen beneficiary or beneficiaries but only if you die during the specified term. If only we could get politicians to agree to those term limits. Most people find they can buy large amounts of term insurance at affordable premiums, which can mean a lot if you are supporting a young family or building a business.

A more expensive type of life insurance is cash value insurance, which provides current cash values in the policy in addition to the death benefit. Cash values come from the premiums you pay in early policy years that exceed the actual cost of insurance. In later policy years, these cash values may increase, so the premium you pay can remain level. You may use the cash value for emergencies and other needs, or it can be used as supplemental retirement income. We'll get into the details of accessing cash values in a few paragraphs.

Types of Term Insurance

We're going to get a little more detailed here, so prop up those eyelids with toothpicks. Keep in mind that term insurance premiums increase as the policyholder ages. That ought to keep you awake.

With *level term insurance*, the death benefit and premiums remain level for a specific time, usually 5, 10, 15, 20, or 30 years. This coverage may be suitable if your children will be dependent on you for a number of years. *Decreasing term insurance* has a death benefit that decreases each year, even though premiums remain level. This type of policy is frequently used to cover a mortgage or other loan with a decreasing balance. With *annual renewable term insurance*, the death benefit remains level and premiums increase annually or at certain age brackets. This policy is for people with short-term insurance needs, typically fewer than five years. For example, if you intend to pay off a business loan in a short period of time.

Types of Cash Value Insurance

The original type of cash value life insurance is *whole life*, which provides lifetime protection. It has a guaranteed death benefit and policy premiums that remain level for the whole time you're paying them. (At the end of this chapter we talk about choosing a life insurance company based on its financial strength and claims-paying ability. It's important, considering any guaranteed death benefit would depend on it.) The next generation is *universal life insurance,* and it was created in the late 1970s with greater flexibility as its goal. Keep in mind that policyholders pay more in fees the more sophisticated the insurance policy. Policyholders can increase or decrease premiums within limits or even skip payments without losing coverage, as long as the cash values are adequate to cover insurance costs. Loan and withdrawal features may provide liquidity when you need it. Both options will reduce the death benefit and policy cash values. Plus, they could generate an income tax liability, or the policy could lapse if the loan is not repaid.

Variable life insurance is a form of insurance that combines insurance protection with an investment component, and *variable universal life insurance* takes it one step further to allow more flexibility of face amount and premium payments. With both types of variable insurance you allocate the cash value part of the policy in variable investment options based on your goals and objectives and ability to handle risk. Those variable investment options are invested in underlying funds managed by various fund companies. There is potential for greater gains than with other types of cash value insurance, but the cash value and death benefit aren't guaranteed and can vary based on how the investment options perform. In short, you could lose money. Why would anyone buy a life insurance product that could lose money? If you're investment minded and want the potential for more gains, you probably know the answer to that question. And you're also willing to accept the risks involved with products that don't offer guarantees in exchange for that potential.

A type of life insurance commonly used in estate planning is called *survivorship,* or *second-to-die insurance.* It is a single policy that insures two lives and may allow for the insurance of one individual who would otherwise be uninsurable with a single life policy, as long as the other one is healthy. No benefit is paid when the first person dies. The policy is still in effect and the premiums still need to be paid until the second one dies, and then the policy's death benefit is paid to the named beneficiary.

There's also a *first-to-die life insurance* policy, which insures a limited number of people under the same policy with the death benefit payable on the first death. First-to-die policies are often used to protect business partners, with the death benefit being used by the surviving partner(s) to buy the deceased partner's share of the business and/or keep the business running during the transition following the death of a partner. It's the concept of business continuation we mentioned at the beginning of this enthralling section on life insurance.

How Much Might You Need?

Your lifestyle can help you identify an adequate amount of life insurance. If you have low housing payments, little or no debt, or no children, spouse, or parents to care for, some experts suggest that you have life insurance equal to one to three times your salary. Buying life insurance when you are young may mean you pay less because important factors considered in determining cost are age and health. As debt or mortgage costs increase and you have children or a spouse as dependents, you may need between three and seven times your salary in life insurance. You also may start to feel like you're sinking into a black hole, but remember, it's only a feeling. Parents with young children, significant mortgages, and a spouse may need the greatest amount of life insurance protection, equivalent to at least seven to nine times their salary. You're also now sure you're in that black hole.

Say you're wondering about buying life insurance to replace income and provide for your family. To determine how much, if any, life insurance you need, you might find this simple equation helpful. Consider buying $100,000 of life insurance for every $500 of pretax income your family would need per month. Let's say they would need $3,000 a month ($36,000 per year) to cover expenses. You would need $600,000 of insurance coverage to support them indefinitely.

$$\$3,000/\$500 = 6$$
$$6 \times \$100,000 = \$600,000$$

Your survivors would invest the $600,000 at, say, 6 percent interest. That would generate $36,000 a year in interest before taxes. Assuming they would only use the interest and not the principal, the income would last a long, long time. Keep in mind that this hypothetical math problem was included for pure enjoyment. It doesn't represent any specific insurance product and it doesn't take into account sales charges or other expenses that may be required.

LONG-TERM CARE INSURANCE PREPARES TODAY FOR TOMORROW

Long-term care insurance is similar to other insurance in that it allows the policyholder to pay a premium over time that could offset the risk of much larger expenses down the road. It's also similar to other insurance in that you can't buy the coverage once you have a problem that requires long-term care. That would be like buying auto insurance at the scene of your car crash. The cost of long-term care insurance varies

YOU'RE INSURED AT WORK, SO WHY BOTHER?

Many employers provide insurance coverage equal to an employee's annual salary. One benefit of such group coverage is that you aren't required to have a physical exam to qualify, which makes the insurance accessible to employees who may not be able to buy life insurance on their own. But, depending on your particular circumstances, you may need more protection than what your employee benefits provide. Also, the life insurance coverage offered by your employer may last only as long as your job does. Contact your human resources department to see whether your coverage is portable, enabling you to keep the coverage should you leave the company. If the coverage isn't portable and you develop health problems, you may have a hard time buying life insurance when you leave your job. Cross your fingers that your next employer offers group coverage too.

dramatically based on all sorts of factors, most notably your age at time of purchase and the amount of coverage. But that's not all. Other things that affect the cost are duration of benefits, the length of any waiting period before benefits are paid (called the elimination period), and whether policyholders can retain a partial benefit if they let their policy lapse for any reason.

If you plan on growing old, you could be a candidate for long-term care insurance, especially if you're living a middle-income or upper-income lifestyle. Because it's expensive, long-term care insurance isn't typically a product lower-income individuals are able to buy. If you're middle-class, you're likely to be hit the hardest by the high cost of long-term care, because you're likely to spend most of your assets if you required extended long-term assistance. You may not qualify for Medicaid assistance, yet paying your own bills for long-term care could break you. If you've got a lot of dough (assets of $1 million or more), you probably can pay for your own long-term care, although you might want insurance anyway to preserve your estate for your kids or grandkids or that favorite charity if the kids don't deserve it. This is also the reason some people buy long-term care insurance for their parents—to preserve the inheritance they might receive one day.

Long-term care insurance usually covers the costs for care that aren't picked up by regular health insurance or Medicare, the government health program for people age 65 and over. Many long-term care policies will pay benefits based on need demonstrated by the inability to perform a specific number of personal activities of daily living, such as bathing, dressing, eating, and mobility, or when care is needed due to Alzheimer's disease or other cognitive impairment. The types of services vary, depending on the policy you choose, but most cover skilled, intermediate, and custodial nursing home care. Most policies also cover home health care with skilled or nonskilled nursing care, personal care, physical therapy, assisted living, adult day services, alternate care, and respite care for the caregiver. It goes without saying that you'll pay more for a long-term care policy that covers more expenses. Which causes us to wonder, why do statements that could go without saying get said in the first place?

LONG-TERM CARE INCOME TAX FAVORS

You may be able to deduct your long-term care insurance premiums from your taxable income, up to a maximum limit. Unreimbursed expenses for qualified long-term care services may also be deductible. As with most medically related income tax deductions, this one only works if you itemize your deductions and have medical costs in excess of 7.5 percent of adjusted gross income, and there are other limits imposed on the deductibility of premiums based on your age.

Shop Features First, Price Second

When you're considering long-term care insurance, be careful to decide on policy features first and then look at the price. Buying a policy based purely on cost could end up being worse than having no protection at all. How? Paying premiums over time for what turns out to be inadequate coverage would be what we call a "lose/lose" situation. You're out the money you've paid in premiums, and then you don't end up with suitable care when you need it most. Once you've selected a policy with the features you require, you may be able to lower the premium cost by choosing a longer waiting period before the insurance benefits kick in. Or you might reduce your premiums by selecting a lower daily benefit. Make those sorts of decisions after you have found a policy that fits your needs.

When to Buy Isn't an Easy Decision

Long-term care insurance costs less the younger you are when you buy it. It makes sense, then, to buy it when you're young, right? Not necessarily. It's true you pay less for premiums at a younger age, but presumably you'll pay for that coverage for a longer period of time, so the costs could even out in the end. You may choose to set money aside for long-term care insurance that you'll purchase at a later date, but who knows if you'll earn enough interest to make up the difference. Also, the older you get, the more likely you may be to have medical conditions that make it tough to qualify for a long-term care policy. On the other hand, if you buy this type of insurance coverage at a young age to qualify for lower premiums, be sure all your other financial bases are covered first. Do you have enough health, life, and disability income insurance to protect you before you commit to long-term care insurance premiums?

The only conclusion we can reach is that there's no easy answer as to when or if you should buy long-term care insurance. The premiums will add up whether you pay less over a longer period of time or more because you've reached an older age bracket. As with most financial decisions, you must weigh the pros and cons against your age, health history, timeframe, ability to handle risk, and resources.

CHOOSING AN INSURANCE COMPANY

If you're shopping for insurance, now may be the time for us to step in and wake you. Let's face it, insurance products just aren't that exciting. Downright boring, in fact. One consideration when choosing insurance, then—whether it's health, disability, life, long-term care, or pet insurance—should be the company that stands behind the product. Still pretty boring, but since you could be a customer of that company for years, if not decades, you want to pick one with credibility. How are you supposed to know one insurance company from the next? Take a look at their ratings. In the interest of full disclosure, we haven't a clue how pet insurance companies are rated, if at all, nor are we offering an opinion about pet insurance as a product. We'll stick to other types of insurance from now on.

Insurance companies are rated by respected third-party rating services like Standard & Poor's, Moody's, and A.M. Best. They rate companies based on their history, claims-paying ability, and financial stability, among other factors. These ratings are subject to change based on a company's history, claims-paying ability, and financial stability, among other factors. Are you starting to see why it's important to enlist the expertise of the ratings agency and not rely on your own impressions of the company's logo?

You can check the current and historical rating of insurance companies you may be considering by contacting these services:

Standard & Poor's	www.standardandpoor.com	212-438-2400
Moody's	www.moodys.com	212-553-0377
A.M. Best	www.ambest.com	908-439-2200

Get health care quality ratings from the National Committee for Quality Assurance, www.ncqa.org.

GET YOUR QUOTES HERE

If you're inclined to shop for insurance on your own, you can find price quotes on just about any type of policy at these Web sites. Keep in mind that quotes given online tend to apply to people in perfect health. Before a company will sell you a policy, you'll probably need to endure a comprehensive underwriting process, and information that comes up then may boost your premium. And as we said earlier, you'll want to check up on an insurance company before committing to any purchase.

Insurance Buyers Guide (insbuyer.com)
1st Insured (1stinsured.com)
Insurance.com
ehealthinsurance.com, 1-877-EHEALTH
digitalinsurance.com, small group and individual health insurance

10

Lifestyles of the Ready and Willing

There's a popular misconception that estate planning is only for the rich and famous. Truth is, estate planning is for anyone who wants to make sure their wishes are carried out if they are unable to speak for themselves. We know how opinionated you are, so we'll be bold and say that estate planning is for you. What the rich and famous do with their possessions doesn't concern us. What we care about is how people just like you handle important issues such as keeping your beneficiary designations current on your retirement accounts and establishing a healthcare directive so you're prepared and having a will so your stuff ends up where it's supposed to. But if by some chance you happen to be rich and famous, can we have your autograph?

It's incredible what a few legal documents can do in terms of providing peace of mind for you and some logical direction for those people you care to entrust with the decision making. In this chapter we'll outline a few basic legal documents you'll need in order to leave instructions about how you want to be cared for if you are unable to communicate your wishes, and to financially and physically protect your loved ones if you die. There are some snappy checklists at the end so you can quickly note how much estate planning you're in for based on your stage of life. There's no right or wrong answer, needless to say, but there are questions that need to be answered. And you owe it to yourself and those you love to be ready and willing to make those decisions.

FORMS HELP YOU FUNCTION

One task we'll recommend is that you waste a few minutes calculating in dollars and cents just how much you're worth using the net worth worksheet in Chapter 1, "'Plan' Is a Four-Letter Word." When tallying your net worth, keep in mind it's a dynamic figure that will change over time as your financial situation evolves. It's really a painless exercise and you might end up discovering you're worth more on paper than you ever imagined. Not quite like winning the lottery, but it may generate warm feelings as you contemplate your estate plan and who gets how much of what you've got.

Considering this is Chapter 10, you may have already filled in the blanks on that worksheet a long time ago. We're guessing, however, that a certain percentage of readers with an inclination to put off until next week what they should have done last year would welcome a second chance to use the net-worth worksheet, no questions asked. We'll hold your page while you take a moment now to flip back to Chapter 1. Not that we're pointing fingers or anything. If nothing else, take this opportunity to avoid digging deeper into estate planning, a topic that's easy to resist.

WHERE THERE'S A WILL YOU'VE FOUND A WAY

A will formally and legally declares your wishes about who gets what and how much after you have died. That includes naming a guardian who will be responsible for your minor child or children after your untimely death. Your will is only good at that time and has no significance during your life, other than the peace of mind it provides. Hey, it's the only way you'll be sure that your wishes are carried out when you're gone. To be blunt, you may have blood relatives who have no business raising your child, but to prevent it from happening, something needs to be in writing. Estate laws vary by state, so make sure your will abides by the laws where you live.

If you're thinking of bypassing this essential element of estate planning, think again. Die without a will (eloquently called "dying intestate"), and your property is passed on to heirs according to state laws, regardless of your personal wishes. A will is especially essential if you have a spouse and children. If there's no will and you die, some of your assets could go directly to your kids. That may not seem like a big deal—especially if you're looking for excuses for not having a will—but a problem with a direct inheritance to the children could arise if the surviving parent needs to get permission from the court to use that money. In most families that's a waste of time. You probably want to spare your spouse any of those potential hassles.

Just because a will is a legal document doesn't mean you need an attorney to draft one for you, depending on your situation. It may be smart to hire a lawyer if you own a small business, your property is worth a lot of dough, you need to make arrangements for the long-term care of a beneficiary, you want to disinherit someone, or you have complex wishes for your estate. We'll leave it up to you to put a dollar fig-

Poll

What's your favorite excuse for not having a will?

I have nothing to leave to anyone	35%
I'm not going anywhere	15%
I hate lawyers	14%
I won't need a will until I have a family	13%
I already have a will	23%

Poll conducted by ihatefinancialplanning.com

ure on "a lot of dough." Some people are comfortable with the nitty gritty of researching and writing a will, while others would prefer paying a lawyer to write even the simplest of wills. Most people, unfortunately, don't take either approach and the document goes unwritten. Do yourself a favor and remove yourself from that last category by putting your wishes on paper in a legally sound document.

If you'd rather skip the legal advice (and fees) made possible by hiring a lawyer, and write the will yourself, there are some essential components you'll need to include to ensure that your will is valid. For starters, you need to be at least 18 years old and of "sound mind" to draft a will. Don't let the sound-mind requirement scare you, as it isn't tough to prove, mainly because it's usually assumed and rarely questioned that the will writer is playing with a full deck. There goes that excuse. The document must expressly state that it's your will. Provide your full name and place of residence, as well as the names of your spouse, children, or other beneficiaries, including their relationship to you. You may want to include a brief summary of your property, but it's not required for the will to be valid. You may choose to use a catchall clause, which generally states, "I give the remainder of my estate to [insert name here]." Without this clause, items not specifically mentioned will be distributed in accordance with state law.

Your will must include at least one provision, which is basically the details of who gets what and how much. A simple declaration that all of your property be left to one person qualifies, as does a statement appointing a personal guardian for your minor children. We're guessing you'll want to include more provisions than those examples, however. You may choose to be specific and name recipients of certain pieces of your personal property. It's also a good idea to name an alternative guardian, in case your first choice is unable or unwilling to take care of your kids. Likewise when naming the executor, which you should appoint in your will. The executor is responsible for managing the distribution of your property in probate after your death and making sure your debts and any taxes due are paid. Most states will appoint an executor if you fail to name one.

Finally, you must sign and date the will in the presence of at least two witnesses. Most states require that witnesses not be named in the will to receive property, so keep that in mind when asking someone to witness the big event. Some states do allow wills that have no witness signatures, but other strict rules apply so you're better off just finding two people to watch. Most states don't require that your witness be a notary public. Once all these details are covered, you don't need to file your will with the court or anything like that. Just be sure to keep it in a safe place and let your executor know where it is. You can keep the will in your safe deposit box, but be aware that some states will seal your safe deposit box upon your death, so it may not always be the smartest place to store it.

There are many resources available for assistance with your will project. Simple software programs and fill-in-the-blank forms are available to buy. You can also visit www.nolo.com, a law center with a broad range of legal tools for everyone but lawyers. From what we've heard, lawyers who attempt to log-on to that Web site are forced to watch their computers self-destruct in five seconds.

RETAIN CONTROL WITH POWER OF ATTORNEY

A will is just the beginning of estate planning for most people. A power of attorney (POA) is a written document that allows another person to act on your behalf while you're still alive. Say you're taking an extended road trip and need someone to file your income taxes or represent you at the closing on the sale of your home. The person you name is called the attorney-in-fact and you are called the principal. A POA can be as specific or as general as you designate. Back to that hypothetical road trip. You can legally authorize your attorney-in-fact only for the income tax filing, or you can stipulate that he or she may also pay your bills and sign for you at the closing—and any number of other tasks, for that matter. The POA may be revoked at any time, and it is automatically terminated if you become incapacitated, unless noted otherwise in the POA.

That's what a *durable* power of attorney is for. It specifically authorizes your attorney-in-fact to act on your behalf in the event you become ill or incapacitated. Leave it to the legal world to mandate multiple legal documents for you to lose or forget to secure in the first place. A durable POA can come in quite handy when the time is right, so we shouldn't poke fun. With one, your financial life will be allowed to con-

WHEN A WILL BECOMES A WON'T

You probably own property that falls outside the terms of your will, assuming you've got one. We're referring to life insurance or annuity death benefits, employer-sponsored retirement accounts, individual retirement accounts, and in some cases, bank accounts or securities. Your will usually has no effect on those types of assets, and naming beneficiaries for them in your will does not supersede previous beneficiary designations you may have made. Say you enrolled in your employer's retirement plan, named your spouse as beneficiary, and have since divorced and remarried. Naming your current spouse in your will won't cut it. If for any reason you change your mind about which beneficiaries should receive these types of property, you need to complete change of beneficiary documents with the life insurance company, plan administrator, bank, and such. It's especially important to review your beneficiary designations after major events such as marriage, birth of a child, divorce, or death of a spouse or child, to ensure that your designations are current. We apologize if we've added more line items to your to-do list, but we're just looking out for you.

tinue even if you're unable to tend to it due to illness, injury, or some other form of incapacitation. You may not *want* to keep paying bills, managing your investments, or paying taxes, but a durable POA ensures that a person you designate will be authorized to do so.

MAKE YOUR HEALTHCARE WISHES KNOWN

You may have heard healthcare directives mentioned in the media whenever there's a heart-wrenching news story about a comatose person whose family is fighting about whether to remove life support. About the only thing the family, the courts, and the media can agree on in situations like this is that it's too bad the person didn't have a living will. By any of its names—healthcare POA, living will, healthcare directive, healthcare proxy, durable medical power of attorney—this legal document could end up being a vital part of your estate plan. (It's important to note that a living will is not related in any way, shape, or form to the conventional will we discussed earlier or a living trust, which is used to leave property at death.) With the document you designate your attorney-in-fact to make medical decisions for you when you are unable to do it yourself. You also declare which life-sustaining medical procedures you want performed if necessary and which you do not. It's easy to procrastinate getting a healthcare POA because it forces questions like, "Who do I want to make life-and-death medical decisions for me?" or "How long do I want to stay on life support if my condition won't improve?" Hard questions like these deserve thoughtful answers. They deserve legally binding answers.

It's not necessarily easy making decisions required in a healthcare directive, but it is easy to get your hands on the necessary documents. Each state has approved forms you can download for free on the Web site for the nonprofit group Partnership for Caring (www.partnership-forcaring.org). Or you may request the forms by calling Partnership for Caring at 1-800-989-9455. Talking with your loved ones about your wishes is just as important as getting the forms and filling them out. Make sure there's a copy on file with your doctor too. It's essential that you make your wishes known, or you never know whose wishes will be carried out.

WHAT PROBATE IS AND WHO NEEDS IT

Probate may seem as mysterious and awkward as its name, but it's simply a legal process for distributing your estate after your death. When you die, any property that is not jointly owned or distributed by a beneficiary agreement, such as a trust or life insurance policy, becomes probate property. Your estate is then distributed by a personal representative you have named—called the executor or administrator—with some level of super-

FINANCIAL JARGON MADE EASY

Our friend Richard's mother died eight years ago. Richard's dad remarried a year later and his new wife moved into the home where Richard and his sisters had grown up. Three short years later, his dad passed away. Stories like this occasionally lead to hurt feelings and legal battles, but thankfully this is not one of those stories. Richard's dad had established a *life estate* for the property, allowing for his new wife to stay in the house as long as she lives, at which time the house and its contents will be inherited by Richard and his sisters. As a life tenant of the home, wife number two is responsible for general upkeep but she has no rights to sell it or make any sort of profit from the house in any way. A life estate can be created in a property deed, will, trust, or prenuptial agreement, with the best method being determined by the situation. It's fairly common to establish a life estate naming a charitable organization to receive the property instead of heirs, in which case the property owner may benefit from an income tax deduction in the year the life estate is established. Consult a tax advisor or attorney for the scoop.

We've got even more tales to tell—and financial terms to define—in the glossary at the back of the book.

vision by a probate court. If it still sounds mysterious and awkward, that's understandable, but you really needn't fear probate. Besides, you won't be around for the procedures, so what's the big deal?

A number of things happen in probate to ensure the equitable and thoughtful distribution of your money, property, and any valuables. The validity of your will is determined, if one exists. (Hint: write a will!) If you don't have a will or an executor, the court will appoint someone to oversee the distribution of your assets based on laws in your state. Your assets are identified, and your heirs are located, which isn't too difficult considering that it seems wherever assets are, heirs are soon to follow. At least that's what we've concluded after years of watching made-for-televisions dramas.

A key aspect of probate is that debts you owe at death get paid. Creditors are notified and have a certain length of time to make their claims on your estate. Creditors who don't do so within the timeframe may no longer collect. And let's not forget taxes. During probate any income taxes or estate taxes you owe are paid to Uncle Sam. Small estates usually go through probate in a matter of months, depending on your state's court system. Every state has its own definition of "small estate," by the way, and different rules offering shortcuts through probate for estates that qualify. Taxable estates may take more than a year because of their complexity and the IRS's need to dot every "i" and cross every "t."

Some people mistakenly believe that avoiding probate means you avoid some of the mumbo jumbo we mentioned in the previous paragraph. Taxes are usually top on the list of things they want to avoid, as well as costs and delays in selling property and settling the estate. Depending on how big your estate is, however, proper administration of your assets and subsequent distribution to heirs will take time. Probate can actually enhance the process, so the costs, which vary by state and size of the estate, can be well worth it.

COMMON ESTATE PLANNING TOOLS

After that brief overview of what awaits in probate, we've got some suggestions of ways you can avoid it. These common estate planning tools make for a smooth distribution of your assets after you leave this world. Some of them are quick and easy to arrange and others take some planning and usually some assistance from an estate planning attorney or financial professional.

Payable-on-Death Accounts

One of the easiest ways to keep your money out of probate is with a payable-on-death account, or POD, for your bank accounts. Oh yeah, it's free too, which makes it hard to overlook. Simply fill out a POD form at your bank naming a qualifying beneficiary to inherit those assets. While you're alive you maintain full control—close your bank account, change your beneficiary, whatever. When you die you maintain some control in that the adult you have designated gets whatever money is in the account. And probate court will have nothing to say about it, which is just fine. POD accounts are different than joint bank accounts in that the other person on those accounts has equal rights to the money, but a POD beneficiary has no such access—until you're gone, of course.

Transfer-on-Death for Securities

A transfer on death (TOD) works much like a POD, but instead of allowing someone to inherit your bank accounts, it allows them to inherit your stocks, bonds, and brokerage accounts without probate. You complete paperwork with the stockbroker or company itself naming a beneficiary for your securities. That person has no rights to them as long as you are alive but can transfer ownership at your death.

Retirement Accounts

When you establish an Individual Retirement Account or employer-sponsored retirement plan such as a 401(k) or 403(b), you name a beneficiary for those accounts. After you die, the money in those retirement accounts won't pass through probate before the named beneficiary can claim them from the account custodian. If you're single, you may choose anyone you want to be the beneficiary of your retirement accounts. If you're married, depending on your state of residence your spouse may have rights to some or all of the money, unless he or she agrees, in writing, to your choice of a different beneficiary.

Joint Tenancy (with Right of Survivorship)

This agreement may be something you and your spouse already do—with your home, for example. If one of you dies, the surviving joint tenant becomes the property owner without that property going through probate. Whew, no one gets kicked out of the house. Joint tenancy works well when couples acquire real estate, vehicles, bank accounts, securities, and other valuable property. Joint tenants don't have to be married couples, either. Any two or more people may own property in joint tenancy.

Living Trusts

A revocable living trust is a flexible tool you can use to pass your assets to heirs when you die. You specify in a trust document, which is similar to a will, who you want to inherit which property, and at your death that transfer occurs without probate. While you're alive and kicking, the trust has no effect, and you can revoke it or make changes at any time. Though the property in the trust isn't part of your estate for probate purposes, it is considered as part of your estate when federal estate tax collectors come calling. Trusts can be more costly and time-consuming to establish and maintain than other estate planning tools, so it may be a good idea to get advice from a tax advisor or attorney about your individual situation.

Life Insurance Death Benefits

Life insurance is an entire topic unto itself in Chapter 9 but it's worth mentioning here because it can provide your beneficiaries an immediate source of cash after your death. Many estates don't have readily available cash to pay bills and taxes that follow a death. For instance, federal estate taxes are due nine months after the date of death. Apparently that's the period of mourning allotted by good ol' Uncle Sam. If your estate includes life insurance, which is not subject to probate, your beneficiaries will have money on hand and won't be reduced to selling your antique armoire to drum up the dough. You should know that life insurance may be subject to estate tax, if the total value of your estate exceeds certain federal and state limits. The upcoming discussion of federal estate taxes is guaranteed to make that topic clear as interstate highways on a holiday weekend.

AVOID FEDERAL ESTATE TAXES—IF YOU CAN FIGURE THEM OUT

A sizeable portion of your life holdings could be snatched away by the government through estate taxes if you decide to do nothing about an estate plan. In 2004 every estate owner is entitled to a unified credit that permits up to $1.5 million of assets to pass free of federal estate and gift taxes. That figure is scheduled to increase through 2009 when it maxes out at $3.5 million, based on the Economic Growth and Tax Relief Reconciliation Act of 2001. That law is complicated, which isn't surprising considering it's legislation related to the tax code. Current law calls for the federal estate tax to be repealed or phased out in 2010. Thanks to a bizarre twist made possible by bickering politicians, however, the estate tax is scheduled to come back in 2011. Of course, Congress could vote to extend the repeal or change its mind on the estate tax a hundred different ways between now and then.

What you need to know about the federal estate tax is that it affects only those individuals who die and leave a taxable estate greater than the figures listed in the table below. Unless, of course, the laws have changed by the time you read this. We're not commenting at all on state death taxes, as they're called, because every state has its own set of laws and is compensating for changes to the federal estate tax laws in its own way.

Federal Estate Tax Unified Credit	
Year	**Estate Exclusion**
2004–2005	$1,500,000
2006–2008	$2,000,000
2009	$3,500,000
2010	Estate tax phased out
2011	Estate tax returns

Should your estate be within the $1.5 million to $3.5 million range, read on because there are ways you can reduce the size of your estate while you are living to avoid estate taxes after you've died. You may wish to consult with a tax or financial advisor for additional ideas on reducing your potential estate tax burden, but first, consider these deductions:

- The marital deduction (unlimited for the value of property left to a surviving spouse, who must be a U.S. citizen).
- Unlimited charitable deductions.
- Debts and expenses related to the estate distribution, funeral, and burial.
- State death taxes may have certain limits (any inheritance tax paid is credited against the federal tax due).
- Gifts of property. You are entitled to give annual gifts (maximum amount in 2004 is $11,000) to as many people as you choose, for as many years as you wish, without incurring a gift tax.

ORGAN DONATION: THE ULTIMATE WAY TO SPREAD YOUR ASSETS

We're going to talk body parts now, so turn your head if you don't want to look. But by all means, keep reading because this is information you should know. The absence of logic in the previous sentences is an intentional attempt to send a clear message that we are not suitable brain donors. Speaking of which, medical advances have made organ donation cheaper, easier, and safer. These days it's common to transplant corneas, hearts, kidneys, pancreas, skin, bones, bone marrow, livers, and lungs. You may know someone whose life has been extended by an organ transplant. Perhaps someone you love has been an organ donor. There are thousands of people waiting for transplants and a growing number of willing donors, but in order for those two to come together, there's paperwork to be completed.

If you're interested in donating any of your organs should the situation present itself, all you've got to do is fill out the proper paperwork. Don't let the necessary effort deter your selfless decision to share. You can easily get a donor card from most hospitals, community eye banks, and the local offices of the National Kidney Foundation. In most states you can sign up to be a donor at the local Department of Motor Vehicles. It's smart to also inform your friends and relatives that you're a willing organ donor. Think of it as part of your estate plan.

ESTATE PLANNING CHECKLISTS

Depending where you are on the continuum of life, you'll have different estate planning needs. And those needs will change as your life does, which is convenient for us because you'll want to revisit this book from time to time. To get a handle on where your current estate plan should be, just select a checklist below suited to your situation, then plan accordingly. We tried to keep them short so you're not overwhelmed by an endless list of things to put off even longer.

Young and Unattached or Otherwise Preoccupied

We'd say you're too young to even be thinking about estate planning, but when we were 25 one of our best friends died in a car crash, so we know there's no such thing as too young to die. You're young, but you may have a car, a mortgage, some possessions, and whatnot. Or you might have none of that. In either case, there's probably a lot of life ahead of you and no need to rush into an estate plan. However, consider these simple ways to ensure a smooth passage—financially speaking anyway.

- Payable-on-death accounts so your bank balance can readily pass to whomever you choose. Assuming there's a balance in your accounts.
- Beneficiary designations on your employer-sponsored retirement accounts (this is basically just one more chance for us to point out that you're not too young to be saving for retirement).

- Healthcare directive to ensure that your wishes be carried out should you become incapacitated and unable to make medical decisions for yourself.
- A will if you don't want whatever you leave behind to go to your parents, which could be fine with you or a mistake in your mind, for all we know.

More Than a Couple Things for Unmarried Couples

You may only have eyes for each other, but you're complete strangers in the eyes of the law. Financially speaking that could be a good thing, a nuisance, or disgustingly unfair, depending on your circumstances. We'll leave it up to you to choose the description that applies to your relationship. Where estate planning is concerned, you're foolish not to create a legal paper trail that will make your union binding, unless you truly want to keep your partner on the outside looking in should anything happen to you. We'll leave that up to you to decide.

- Payable-on-death bank account, especially if you and your partner don't establish a joint bank account.
- Durable power of attorney so your partner can manage your finances (pay bills, deposit checks, and so on) if you become incapacitated.
- Healthcare directive to ensure that your partner will be authorized to make medical care decisions on your behalf in case of emergency.
- Die without a will and laws in most states dictate that your possessions will most likely go to blood relatives. You need a will. Period.
- Joint tenancy with right of survivorship on property such as real estate, cars, bank accounts, or other valuable property, so when one of you dies the survivor will own it.
- In lieu of joint tenancy, establish a life estate on your home allowing your partner to keep living there until he or she dies. Read more about these arrangements earlier in this chapter.
- Make sure someone knows where your important papers are located. We're talking will, trusts, bank accounts, real estate deeds, life insurance policies, investment accounts. If you have a safe deposit box, be sure your partner has access to it.

- If you have any advisors, such as an attorney, accountant, insurance agent, or stockbroker, document their contact information and keep it with your other important papers.

Minor Children Are a Major Consideration

Kids change everything, especially where your money is concerned. Assuming you have firsthand knowledge of how children can complicate life, we'll skip right to the list of things you need to consider. Needless to say, it's not a good idea to put this off until your kids grow up.

- Write a will. It doesn't need to be fancy, but it should name a guardian for the kids and also document who gets your property. Failure to name a guardian could mean your offspring end up with a court-appointed caregiver. We hope our word choice in the previous sentence accomplished our goal of making that process sound terribly sterile, almost offensive. Maybe that will motivate you.
- Healthcare directive, especially if you're unmarried. If you're married, your spouse will automatically make medical decisions on your behalf, but it's wise to talk about your wishes before you're unable to do so. Better yet, make your wishes official with a living will.
- Life insurance should be a consideration when children are in the picture. Refer to Chapter 9 for more than you care to know about this type of risk protection.
- Take a look at the description of trusts in this chapter to decide if you need to consider creating one for your children or other dependents.
- Make sure someone knows where your important papers are located. We're talking will, trusts, bank accounts, real estate deeds, life insurance policies, investment accounts. If you have a safe deposit box, be sure someone knows where it is and is authorized to access it.
- If you have any professional advisors, such as an attorney, accountant, insurance agent or stockbroker, document their contact information and keep it with your other important papers.

Middle Age Is No Time for Middle of the Road

By this stage of your life you may have bought and sold some property, have a family to care for, been married and/or divorced, and endured a bad haircut or two. You've been around the block, in other words. There's no time like the present to make thoughtful decisions regarding the assets you've acquired.

- You need a will, for all the reasons we detailed earlier in the chapter. If you've already got one, review and update it.
- Ditto for durable power of attorney and healthcare directives.
- Take a look at the section on trusts to determine if your circumstances require one, especially a living trust that allows you to eliminate the need for probate.
- Review your beneficiary designations on any retirement accounts, life insurance policies, annuities, and payable-on-death bank accounts you may have, especially if you've had children, gotten married, or divorced since naming them.
- If you have considerable assets and need to think about federal estate taxes, see that section in this chapter and/or consult an estate planning attorney or tax professional.
- Make sure someone knows where your important papers are located. We're talking will, trusts, bank accounts, real estate deeds, life insurance policies, investment accounts, divorce decrees. If you have a safe deposit box, be sure someone knows where it is and is authorized to access it.
- If you have any professional advisors, such as an attorney, accountant, insurance agent, or stockbroker, document their contact information and keep it with your other important papers.

Approaching the Finish Line

We're not saying whether it's the 100-meter dash or a marathon, but for whatever reason you know the end is coming. If you're elderly or ill, it's time for an estate plan.

- Review and update your will.

- Create a durable power of attorney for financial matters and a health-care directive if you haven't already. It will put your mind at ease to declare your wishes and to appoint someone to carry them out.
- If your estate will be subject to probate, make sure the executor you have named is still ready and willing to play the important role.
- Make sure someone knows where your important papers are located. We're talking will, trusts, bank accounts, real estate deeds, life insurance policies, investment accounts. If you have a safe deposit box, be sure someone knows where it is and is authorized to access it.
- If you have any professional advisors, such as an attorney, accountant, insurance agent, or stockbroker, document their contact information and keep it with your other important papers.

SUGGESTIONS FOR SURVIVORS

What do you do now? When you lose someone you love—whether suddenly or after an illness—the last thing you can think about is day-to-day bills and other financial concerns. And that is fine. We can't pretend to understand your loss or presume to tell you how to act in the weeks and months and years following your loved one's death. When you are ready, there are some financial issues you will need to address, but don't pressure yourself to rush into anything. The financial consequences of your loss are as unique as the loved one you're forced to live without.

We have several suggestions that may make it easier for you to handle the task at hand when you are ready. They are meant to serve as a guide and resource for you, but they won't answer all your questions. If you are in a position to consult with a financial professional or lawyer, you may want to consider it. Perhaps you have an ongoing relationship with one or both already. If that is the case, they can help you sort out the necessary paperwork.

Save Major Decisions for Later

You are probably experiencing a great deal of stress after the death of your loved one. For that reason, delay making any major decisions if at all possible. Selling property, moving to another location, switching jobs or getting a job, and giving away personal belongings are better left for a time when you are ready to handle them. Be cautious about signing any financial documents until you've had them reviewed by your financial professional, an attorney, or someone you trust.

Important Papers You Will Need

You will need a death certificate whenever you must prove that you are a survivor or executor of an estate and will be receiving property or other assets because of the death. One death certificate will probably be needed for each insurance policy and financial institution. It's smart to get many copies because you'll easily need as many as 20. You can order them from the funeral director or your county health department.

Understand Which Benefits You're Eligible For

You may be eligible to receive certain benefits through insurance policies, Social Security, the Veterans Administration, and your loved one's employers. Insurance benefits can generally be processed quickly and simply with proceeds being paid directly to the beneficiary or beneficiaries. Contact your insurance company or insurance agent for information on filing a claim. Look for policy documents for life insurance, mortgage insurance, employer insurance, and credit card insurance when going through your loved one's financial papers. Study checkbook registers for possible premium payments if you can't locate actual policies.

For information about Social Security benefits, go to ssa.gov or call 1-800-772-1213. If your loved one was receiving Social Security benefits, don't cash any checks received after his or her death. For information about veterans' benefits, including burial benefits, contact the Department of Veterans Affairs at va.gov or 1-800-827-1000.

If your loved one was employed at the time of death, contact the employer for information on benefits. If your loved one was retired and receiving a pension, you may also be eligible for benefits. Your financial professional or lawyer can help you determine eligibility.

Titles, Ownership, and Beneficiary Changes

You may need to transfer titles and ownership for your loved one's vehicles, personal property, real estate, and financial accounts. You may also need to adjust your insurance policies and change beneficiaries. The following documents should be reviewed:

- Insurance policies: beneficiaries and other policy changes
- Automobile(s): titles and loans
- Investments: stocks, bonds, and other investments
- Banking: checking accounts, savings accounts
- Credit cards: outstanding payments; cancel accounts in only your loved one's name

Taxes Will Come Due

You may be responsible for filing final federal and state income tax returns for the year of death and previous years as well. You may also need to consider estate, inheritance, business, and property taxes. We recommend that you work with a professional tax advisor for these filings. You can learn more in the IRS's Publication 559, "Information for Survivors, Executors and Administrators," which you can find at irs.gov.

CAN WE TALK YOU INTO A *NON-PLAN* FOR YOUR ESTATE?

We'll understand if you've read this entire chapter but still get a little queasy thinking about establishing an estate plan. We know it's easy for us to tell you what to do, but it's another thing altogether to actually do it, and tougher still to discuss your wishes with those you love. Hey, it's not fun to talk about, but if you expect your friends and family to take care of things following your death, you owe it to them to tell them what those things are.

Maybe you know where all your important financial papers are, but you're carrying that information in your head. Guess what? Nobody will be able to tap into that knowledge after the fact. The "fact" in this case being your untimely demise. Consider the consequences of your inaction: Stocks, bonds, bank accounts, real estate, insurance policy benefits, and a bunch more in your name could go unclaimed. Fortunately, losses like these can be avoided with just a little advance planning and organizing. We're not saying it will be an easy task, but if you do one thing at a time, you can accomplish the job. Skip any full-blown estate planning if you must, but do yourself—and your loved ones—a favor by thinking through the following recommendations.

Make a List

Grab a piece of paper and write down what you own. We're talking stocks, bonds, bank accounts, real estate, insurance policies, employer pensions. Take a breath and continue reading. We're also talking anything you have in a safe, safe deposit box, shoebox, or other hidden places. Do you own family heirlooms, valuables, or irreplaceable items? Add them to the list.

Simplify

Now look at your list to see if you can consolidate or eliminate anything. Do you have more than one savings account? Is there a good reason for that? Do you own real estate you should have sold years ago? Is it time to simplify your finances for your sake and for the sake of your heirs?

Name Names

We'll assume you have a will, even though we bribed you into reading this section of the chapter by saying it's a non-plan. Do the names in your will match your named beneficiaries on things like your house, retirement accounts, and the like? If you own a house jointly with right of survivorship, the other owners will usually inherit the property, even if you leave the home to somebody else in your will.

Tell Somebody

Tell your spouse and/or family members and/or trusted friends where your important papers are. You do know where your important papers are, don't you? You may also want to inform your heirs in a general way what you've got. Imagine Junior's surprise when he learns you're donating your art collection to the local gallery.

Keep It Safe

If you've actually gotten this far, we hope you have things in writing that you want to keep in a safe place. Store papers or a computer disk or CD in a fireproof metal box, file cabinet, or home safe. If you put it in a safe deposit box, be sure someone besides you has access to it or your documents won't be accessible once you're gone.

11

Financial Insecurity

Mary Jones (real person, fake name) discovered a state income tax bill one day when opening her mail. Being a conscientious citizen, it concerned Mary that somebody thought she hadn't paid her taxes. Yet the state of Minnesota was insisting that she had neglected to pay $2,700 on her wages. Simple mistake, Mary thought, especially considering that *she had never lived or worked in Minnesota.* She thought one phone call explaining that she had lived in Michigan her entire life would set things straight, but she was wrong.

Turns out, someone had stolen her mother's purse in Michigan. Among other things, the purse contained Mary's birth certificate. We wish we knew why, but we're just telling the story. The thief sold the birth certificate to someone else entirely, who then used it to open a bank account in Minnesota. That person worked two jobs and had her paychecks deposited directly in the account. She must have wanted more spending money because she requested that no state income taxes be withheld from the paychecks. Then she quit her jobs and skipped town—presumably to set up the next scam.

It's alarmingly easy for someone to steal another's identity. One lousy piece of paper—if it's the right piece of paper—is usually enough. A birth certificate, a driver's license, a Social Security card, even an obscure account number. Mary and her mother probably had a logical explanation why the birth certificate ended up in her purse, but in hindsight, we're guessing they wish they had been a little more careful. Needless to say, charges were never filed against the criminals involved. The silver lining in this story is that Mary was able to prove she had never even been to Minnesota, and the state didn't hold her responsible for the back taxes.

You might not be so lucky.

Identity thieves don't sneak into your home in the dark of night and scrape your identity from the drool on your pillow. They don't rely on high-tech tactics or only target your wealthy neighbors. Identity thieves— like most crooks—aren't nearly that ambitious. They do things like learn your dog's name because it's a common password choice and watch the keypad when you're using a calling card on a pay phone at the airport. They make your name their own after finding your bank statement in the garbage. They use your credit record to open accounts and spend until they have robbed you of your future buying power. Most of the time identity thieves drag your name through the mud before you realize it was raining. By the time you report your losses, the crooks are long gone. They commit crimes simultaneously in multiple jurisdictions, making it difficult for authorities to make a case against them.

The good news? If you've been a victim of such theft, you're not alone. According to the Federal Trade Commission, it's the number one and fastest-growing financial crime. We've got information in this chapter you may find helpful, either to take steps to minimize the risk that you could become part of that statistic or to help you put your finances back in order once they've been stolen. And as an added bonus, we'll toss in tips and ideas for making your daily life more efficient and safe, from banking and shopping online to lowering your own profile by removing yourself from direct marketing lists.

ONE PERSON'S TRASH IS ANOTHER THIEF'S TREASURE

When your identity is stolen, you'll spend 30 hours and $500 to fix the problems caused by such a security breach, so says the Federal Trade Commission (FTC) as a result of its 2003 research on identity crimes. Just add up time spent explaining bounced checks and forged signa-

Poll

What type of identity theft have you endured?

Check fraud	7%
Someone else has used my Social Security number	9%
Stolen credit/ATM cards	20%
So far I've been lucky	64%

Poll conducted by ihatefinancialplanning.com

tures to banks and retailers, contacting the major credit bureaus to report fraud, then multiply that by the fear of being victimized again. And yes, we said "when" your identity is stolen, not "if." Ten million people were victimized in 2002, according to the FTC, and the numbers are only going to increase as more thieves crack the system. Armed with your bank account numbers, driver's license, and other personal data obtained by sifting through trash or sneaking a peek over your shoulder at the ATM, scam artists ruin your credit rating while spending your money.

How can you protect yourself? It's not easy when thieves aren't above digging through your trash. Guard your personal information with your life and monitor your accounts frequently. Blow it off if you want but don't be surprised if we track you down when the time comes just to say we told you so.

- Review your credit report at least yearly. It's easy to get copies of your report from the three major credit agencies, but you'll probably have to pay for them. Get all three individually or a consolidated report. We've got agency contact info in a few pages.
- Try not to carry more than one credit card in your wallet. One side effect of this precaution, of course, is less debt.

- Instead of signing credit cards with your name, write "Ask for picture ID." Many retail outlets, including the United States Postal Service, have stopped accepting unsigned credit cards, so consider writing "ask for ID" next to your signature.
- Avoid using common passwords and PINs, such as the last four digits of your Social Security number, your dog's name, your mother's maiden name, your birth date, and the like. Mix upper- and lower-case letters, include numbers, and don't be afraid to go longer rather than shorter with your passwords. And change them periodically.
- Don't carry credit card receipts. Keep them in a safe place or destroy them, especially if they include your full account number and expiration date. Most merchants have begun printing only part of account numbers on receipts.
- Shred documents with account numbers on them, including credit card offers, old bank statements, medical invoices, and everyday bills. (See the box "What to Keep and What to Toss" if you're wondering how long to hang on to this sort of paperwork.) Where shredders are concerned, buy one that makes confetti of your documents rather than trimming them into thin strips. Thieves love to put those back together like jigsaw puzzles, but cross-cut paper is nearly impossible to reconstruct.
- Don't carry account passwords with your credit cards or write them on the cards. This one wins the prize for stating the obvious.
- When it's time to order more checks, ask that they be mailed to your bank, not your home, and don't have your driver's license or Social Security number printed on them. (And then remember to pick them up!) Thieves can lift a box of checks out of your mailbox and make them their own in no time by forging your name.
- Don't leave outgoing bills in your mailbox; drop them at a post office or secure mail slot. Remember the post office?
- If you move, put creditors on the top of your address-change list. You don't want credit information or credit cards delivered to the old address.
- Review bills carefully for unexplained charges. Note, there's a big difference between unexplained charges and those resulting from an unplanned shopping spree.

WHAT TO KEEP AND WHAT TO TOSS

It's easy for us to tell you to run anything through a paper shredder that may give identity thieves what they're looking for, but how do you know which stack to keep and how much to toss? We've got a list here that might help. Be warned, though, that one side effect of this task may be a general sharpening of your organization skills. The purging process may have a cleansing effect, but just be sure you hold on to the records you need.

- Toss paid bills after one year, but keep receipts for big purchases (computers, furniture, jewelry, and such) indefinitely for insurance and warranty purposes.
- Ditto on paycheck stubs. You only need them until you receive W-2s for the year.
- Purge monthly bank and other financial statements after three years. In this day of online everything, do banks still return canceled checks?
- Save tax returns indefinitely and supporting documents for six years. The IRS has three years to audit you and six to challenge underreported income. But if the Social Security Administration claims you didn't work 20 years ago, stupefy them by pulling out your tax returns.
- Pitch monthly/quarterly investment and retirement plan statements annually, but keep year-end statements and other records as long as you own the securities.
- Keep nondeductible IRA records to prove you already paid income taxes on the contributions.
- Store wills; trusts; powers of attorney; birth, marriage, and death certificates; adoption and custody papers; investment records; insurance policies; car titles; and property deeds in a safe place (as in, not in the glove

compartment of your car). It can take months to replace lost originals, and the resulting frustration will far outweigh the effort of being organized enough to know where they are. Scanning documents into your computer will work for quick reference but won't make them legally useful. You're still going to need the originals.

REPAIRING THE DAMAGE

So some thieves stole your life. What do you do now? If you've happened on this chapter and there's a fairly recent theft in your past, we've got some steps you can take to reclaim your life. Nothing we can offer will take away the paranoia you may be feeling, unfortunately. Perhaps you've never been robbed of your identity, but taking the statistics about the chance that you will be to heart, you may want to mark this section for future reference.

If you haven't done so already, contact the fraud departments of the three major credit reporting agencies. Request a credit report, which is free to identity theft victims. Ask that your file be flagged with a fraud alert and find out how long the alert will remain on your record. That's so you know when you need to contact them again if fraudulent activity continues. After a few months have passed, request another free copy of your credit report to ensure that fraudulent activity has stopped.

Equifax

To report fraud: 1-800-525-6285
To order credit report: 1-800-685-1111
www.equifax.com

Experian

To report fraud: 1-888-397-3742
To order credit report: 1-888-397-3742
www.experian.com

TransUnion

To report fraud: 1-800-916-8800
To order credit report: 1-800-888-4213
www.transunion.com

Keep a log of all conversations, including dates, names, and phone numbers. Make a note of your time and expenses. Keep photocopies of all letters and other documents you send to banks, other financial institutions, creditors, and law enforcement. This isn't just busywork to take your mind off the task at hand. Mistakes occur and, down the road, you may need proof all this stuff happened to you.

Contact all creditors to inform them of the theft. You may have to fill out fraud affidavits. Get replacement credit cards with new account numbers. You may be surprised how quickly they arrive, but creditors want you to resume spending as soon as possible. If your ATM or debit card has been stolen, report it immediately. Thieves have probably already accessed your account, and you may be liable if the fraud isn't reported quickly. Get a new card, account number, and password.

Report the crime to your local police department and the police department where the crime occurred, if it's different. Make sure the police report lists the account affected by fraud. Better yet, make sure there is a police report! Some police departments don't document these crimes (too much paperwork and very little chance of catching the perp). Get a copy of the report because credit card companies and banks may request that you show the report to verify the crime.

You may need to change your driver's license number if someone uses yours as ID to pass bad checks and for other fraud. Contact the Department of Motor Vehicles in your state or visit your local DMV to put a fraud alert on your license.

If you've had checks stolen or fraudulent bank accounts established in your name, notify the bank and put stop payments on any outstanding checks. Cancel the account(s) and open new ones, but have any new checks mailed to the bank, not your home. Report the theft to check verification companies. They do their work over the telephone because they need to speak to you in person and verify several pieces of information.

CheckRite	1-800-766-2748
CrossCheck	1-800-843-0760
Chexsystems	1-800-428-9623
SCAN	1-800-262-7771
TeleCheck	1-800-710-9898

If you suspect that your mailing address has been changed by thieves to accommodate their scams, notify the postal inspector of the fraud. You may also need to contact your local post office to ensure that any mail being forwarded to the changed address is sent to your own address. Call 1-800-275-8777 or go to www.usps.gov/websites/depart/inspect.

Contact the Social Security Administration to report any fraudulent use of your Social Security number. If the fraud is extensive and continues, you may have to change your number, but that is only as an absolute last resort. Be warned that it will potentially screw up the rest of your financial life (retirement accounts, etc.) to have a new Social Security number. Luckily the government knows this and will only issue new numbers in worst-case scenarios.

You might be tempted to pay a stray credit card bill just to put the theft behind you. Don't do it. Don't pay any bill resulting from identity theft. Don't cover any checks that were written or cashed fraudulently. Your credit rating should not be permanently affected and no legal action should be taken against you. If any merchant, financial institution, or collection agency suggests otherwise, report them immediately to the Federal Trade Commission (www.ftc.gov). And then say, "Book 'em, Danno."

Finally, see a physical therapist to deal with the kink in your neck from looking over your shoulder. Hey, you gotta laugh about this junk or you'll lose your mind.

WHAT ABOUT FRAUD PROTECTION?

When there's a buck to be made, entire industries are soon to follow, and the business of protecting yourself from identity thieves is no exception. Whether you should purchase any sort of fraud protection depends on whether you believe you can purchase peace of mind. The only thing that's certain is that as this industry expands, so too will your opportunities to spend money on it.

FINANCIAL JARGON MADE EASY

When your identity is robbed, you need to contact the major credit agencies and request a *fraud alert*. It's a statement put on your credit report to alert creditors that your personal financial information has been compromised. But fraud alerts are advisory in nature, and lenders aren't legally obligated to act on them. In other words, if a lender wants to extend credit so as to make a buck, said lender can ignore the fraud alert. Some lenders approve loans without reviewing a full credit report, which makes it possible for the phrase "fraud alert" to mean the same thing as "moot point."

Go to the glossary at the back of the book for definitions of more terms you'd rather not know.

First, there's identity theft insurance, which basically amounts to buying convenience, because if your identity does get robbed, the insurance company will handle much of the messy work involved. And by that we mean calls and letters to credit bureaus and creditors, among other tasks. Some policies also cover certain fees, such as getting a new driver's license, and legal fees that may be required. You will play an integral role in reclaiming your identity, though, so don't assume that a policy like this will protect you from the headaches. And the credit bureaus have fraud departments that will assist you for free.

Next, there are credit and privacy monitoring services, which essentially are early warning systems that will let you know if and when anyone inquires about your credit or tries to obtain credit in your name. Most services will simply call you or send an e-mail message when some activity is attempted, and depending on the level of protection you buy, those contacts will occur weekly, monthly, or instantly. Some services will also help you get and understand copies of your credit reports or other records pertaining to your identity.

Last, and probably least, you can hire a personal shredding service. If you can't be bothered with destroying your own documents, someone else will haul your paperwork to an industrial-strength shredder and promptly destroy it. For a price. If you can't find such a service in your area, some will sell you packing boxes, and you can ship your sensitive documents to their shredding shop. We're all for procrastination and general laziness, but this cottage industry seems a bit ridiculous. Just invest in a personal shredder and go at it yourself.

DISPUTE LETTERS: WHAT TO SAY WHEN YOU'RE TOO MAD TO SPEAK

If you need to dispute entries on your credit report or with creditors who have charged you for things the thieves are giving as birthday gifts, you may need to send letters stating your claims. Knowing how much you enjoy taking action, the Federal Trade Commission has been kind enough to provide sample letters, which we have reprinted on pages 243 and 244. Thank goodness for the federal government.

IT'S BETTER TO BE SAFE THAN SORRY

Identity theft isn't limited to purse snatching, of course. The Internet has brought thieves into your home through your computer. In this section we're going to give some ideas on making your online experience more safe—from surfing the 'Net and shopping online, to protecting your privacy and blocking Web sites from tracking your every electronic move. We want to warn you ahead of time because that's a lot of info for people like you who usually shy away from too much information.

Consumers spend billions of dollars on the Internet, which is amazing when you consider that not long ago it hadn't occurred to anyone to string together the words "World Wide Web." Maybe you've thrown your two cents in the pile when you bought an airline ticket or renewed your magazine subscription online. Perhaps you bought this book from an e-tailer and had it shipped to your door. It's never been easier to

Sample Dispute Letter—Credit Agencies

Date
Your Name
Your Address
Your City, State, ZIP

Complaint Department
Name of Credit Agency
Address
City, State, ZIP

Dear Sir or Madam:

I am writing to dispute the following information in my file. The items I dispute also are circled on the attached copy of the report I received. (Identify items disputed by name of source, such as creditors or tax court, and identify type of item, such as credit account, judgments, etc.)

This item is (inaccurate or incomplete) because (describe what is inaccurate or incomplete and why). I am requesting that the item be deleted (or request another specific change) to correct the information.

Enclosed are copies of (use this sentence if applicable and describe any enclosed documentation, such as payment records, court documents) supporting my position. Please investigate this matter and (delete or correct) the disputed items as soon as possible.

Sincerely,
Your Name

Enclosures: (List what you are enclosing)

Sample Dispute Letter—Credit Card Issuers

Date
Your Name
Your Address
Your City, State, ZIP

Your Account Number
Name of Creditor
Billing Inquiries
Address
City, State, ZIP

Dear Sir or Madam:

I am writing to dispute a billing error in the amount of $_____ on my account. The amount is inaccurate because (describe fraud or other problem). I am requesting that the error be corrected, that any finance and other charges related to the amount be credited as well, and that I receive an accurate statement.

Enclosed are copies of (use this sentence to describe any enclosed information, such as police report, sales slips, payment records) supporting my position. Please investigate this matter and correct the billing error as soon as possible.

Sincerely,
Your Name

Enclosures: (List what you are enclosing)

shop in cyberspace and it's never been safer either, which may sound preposterous in a chapter called "Financial Insecurity." But the truth is, you can feel confident conducting business on the Web as more and more safeguards are being put in place all the time. Here's how:

- Make sure you're shopping at a secure site. Most e-tailers use encryption technology to scramble your sensitive information, making it unreadable by those who do not have a complete set of digital keys. When you type confidential information, on an online order form, for example, it's scrambled so your credit card number, mailing address, and whatnot don't float unattended in cyberspace. Look for a small padlock in the bottom corner of your computer screen. Also, the address line should start with "https" rather than the usual "http."
- Find out who is behind the Web sites you frequent. There should be a customer service telephone number and/or e-mail address that's easy to find. Be cautious when shopping with merchants that only list a post office box. Look for a street address.
- Use a credit card when shopping online, not a debit card. If someone steals your account number and makes fraudulent charges, it's easier to challenge them on a credit card bill. With a debit card, your account may already be charged before you know about the fraud. Assuming you can prove the theft, you'll eventually get your money back, but meanwhile, that money is spent in the eyes of your bank.
- Avoid doing business on sites that include the full 16-digit account number and/or expiration date in e-mail correspondence with you. The merchant should mask part of your account number. For example, 1234********5678.
- TRUSTe and Verisign are privacy protection programs many Web sites use to protect their users. Be careful if you're using sites that don't make prominent display of their efforts to protect your privacy.
- Finally, read the privacy policy at the sites you frequent to find out how they use the information they gather. Steer clear of sites that don't have a privacy policy or don't put it in an obvious place on their Web pages. Be sure to print warranties, price guarantees, and privacy policies for your records

TAKE YOUR NAME OFF ALL THOSE ANNOYING LISTS

You can take big steps toward protecting your identity simply by lowering your profile. All that unopened junk mail you throw in the trash is waiting for thieves to open and use at their will. If credit card applications multiply in your mailbox like so many dandelions on the lawn, you can do your part to stop the madness without using pesticides. Issuers know who you are, and what you need (namely, more cash), and they make their billions by tempting you until you're begging for cash advances and low-rate balance transfers. You can request that your name be removed from credit card mailing lists.

To opt out, simply make a quick toll-free telephone call to 1-888-5-OPTOUT (1-888-567-8688) and answer the automated questions. Your name will be removed from lists provided by major credit agencies for two years. Some of the junk mail is bound to get through, but it's worth the call to limit those pesky credit weeds from cropping up.

SAVE A TREE (AND YOUR TIME) TOO

Junk mail wastes trees and your time nearly every day of the week. And telemarketing calls and spam e-mail messages are another source of wasted time. You've got better things to do than deal with all the clutter. To stop the madness, contact consumer assistance at the Direct Marketing Association. At the DMA Web site (www.dmaconsumers.org) you can have your name, e-mail address, and telephone number removed from snail mail and e-mail lists, as well as telemarketing lists. The DMA is not the source of those lists, but it distributes requests to be removed from the lists and monitors the lists for compliance. Be advised that if you want to make your removal request on DMA's Web site, there is a charge, but you can send it through the mail for just the cost of a postage stamp. Junkbusters.com is another link you may find helpful.

If you've been on hiatus on an island south of Hawaii and have never heard of the National Do-Not-Call Registry, there's still time to sign up. It seems the rules and regulations governing this list managed by the Federal Trade Commission fluctuate with the whims of politicians, but that doesn't mean you shouldn't sign up if, in fact, you don't want to receive telemarketing calls for up to five years. Simply visit www.donotcall.gov to sign up if you have an active e-mail address, or call 1-888-382-1222 from the telephone number you wish to register.

We're going to wrap up this chapter right where we started it. Identity theft is the number-one and fastest-growing financial crime, which means identity protection is a moving target. Any improvement or security enhancement prompts the next generation of crooks to find an alternate route of privacy invasion. The government can step in with legislation aimed at protecting the average citizen, but what's that they say about laws are made to be broken? Not exactly encouraging words. But then you can't live your life in a vacuum either. What you can do is be alert and protect yourself the best you can.

12

What Makes You Do That Thing You Do?

Imagine you're a contestant on a hot new game show that's replaced reality shows in the ratings. There's never a wrong answer, but you'll be judged—by others and yourself—on which answer you give. The winner is the one who can best balance the consequences of his or her choices and then weigh them against the decisions of the judges.

You'd have 30 seconds to answer three questions:

1. Is it more important to invest in companies that produce double-digit returns every year or to invest in ones that manufacture products you approve of?
2. Do you live to work or work to live?
3. If you had $5,000 to spend on one thing, would you choose to invest it in your family or an investment guaranteed to triple its value in 10 months?

Do you ever get the feeling that your financial life is a game show you just can't win? Either you pay down your debt or you save for your kid's college. Your investments may make beaucoup bucks but you'll be supporting the tobacco industry or child labor or defense spending or the list goes on.

The more attention you pay to the money matters of your life, the more frequently you'll hear words such as "goals," "time horizon," and "risk tolerance." They are three legs of the financial stool. Can you achieve your goals? Well, it depends on your investment choices, how long they will have to grow, and your ability to handle the normal ups and downs of the market. If this sounds familiar, it's because everyone sits on that stool at some point while making financial decisions. More and more people are openly adding a fourth leg to their stool—values. Some would argue that values play a role in most, if not all, of a person's financial decisions. Trouble is, we're not always aware of the impact our values play, or we act contrary to them—either intentionally or otherwise.

You may be in tune with your values or you may never have considered them before. In either case, values have an impact on most every decision you make or choice you ignore. It's important, then, to gain an understanding of your values so you are better equipped to make decisions or ignore certain choices. From a financial perspective, your values say a lot about how you choose to spend your money, how you determine which debts are acceptable, and how you make job and life decisions. We're not attempting to solve all the financial dilemmas you're facing, but this chapter may help you answer some tough questions about what impact your values have on financial decisions. We've got some suggestions about where you can look to find investments that are more aligned with your values. There are no wrong answers, so just keep playing. You may already be a winner!

YOU MIGHT VALUE THIS LITTLE EXERCISE

At the risk of becoming a self-help cliché, allow us to offer up an exercise that can help you get a grip on your values. If you want to skip this for any reason, go ahead. But if you would find some "value" in it, by all means play along just this once. We can offer no guarantees that the exercise will help you get in shape. And there's no cash prize—mainly because there are no wrong answers—so we can't help you with any outstanding debts either. Who cares? Games are fun even when no prizes are awarded.

1. Simply pick your seven top values using the list in the box on the next page as your guide (add others we may have missed).

2. Narrow down the list of seven to the four that matter most to you.
3. Finally, put those four values in rank order, with number one being the value that matters most to you.
4. There's no use looking over someone else's shoulder, because his or her list will be different than yours. And what would cheating say about your values anyway?

So, now what? You've got lists of your top values and then you've got one whopping value on the top of the pile. What does it mean? Take those four values that matter most to you and think about them in terms of how you spend your time and your money. Think of the people that are most important to you and those who are total strangers. How do your values affect how you interact with those people? How do certain aspects of your life contradict your values? If trust

WHAT ARE YOUR PERSONAL VALUES?

Accountability	Faith	Love
Altruism	Family	Obligation
Autonomy	Freedom	Relationships
Beauty	Friendship	Respect
Commitment	Generosity	Responsibility
Community	Harmony	Safety
Compassion	Health	Self-worth
Creativity	Honesty	Spirituality
Duty	Individuality	Support
Empathy	Integrity	Thrift
Equality	Intelligence	Trust
Fairness	Kindness	Truth

is a primary value, for example, and you withhold information about debt from your partner, what does that mean for you in terms of coming to grips with your values?

If you dare ask yourself these tough questions and—more important—if you dare answer them, you may make some discoveries that could enhance your life. And you can go about it more confidently. You can handle your day-to-day transactions with more understanding. You might change the way you do just one thing—whether it's financial in nature or not.

MONEY ATTITUDES AFFECT YOUR RELATIONSHIPS

At the risk of going tabloid on you, we're going to spill a few extremely true tales that just might ring a bell with you. They aptly illustrate that when people say, "it's all about the money," it's hardly ever about the money at all. We've changed the names so don't try to read between the lines to identify anyone. Save your questions until you read all the scenarios.

Poll

What does money mean to you?

Freedom	49%
Security	34%
Control	7%
Obligation	6%
Compromise	1%
Nothing	4%

Poll conducted by ihatefinancialplanning.com

Don't Ask, Don't Tell Doesn't Work

Two buddies—we'll call them Mutt and Jeff—bought a limousine service with dreams of retiring early to adjacent beach homes. Both childhood chums had college degrees and a lot of experience behind the wheel and behind the desk. The business cruised along at the start, but suddenly limo traffic came to a standstill (something about a teachers' strike forcing school officials to cancel prom). On the way to the bank to borrow money, Mutt told Jeff that his credit wasn't so good and maybe they should put the loan in Jeff's name. No problem, good and trusted friend! To make a long story bearable, the limo service tanked and Jeff ended up declaring personal bankruptcy. Six years later, he's working two jobs and driving a rent-a-wreck reject, thanks to a credit record that's been broadsided.

Honesty Is the Best Policy

Harry and Sally got married after living together for two years. They deposited $9,000 of wedding cash in a joint savings account to fund joint dreams. They funneled money through a joint checking account for mutual expenses but otherwise kept their finances separate. Harry's freelance writing jobs dried up, but he didn't discuss his money woes with his wife. Instead, he quietly transferred money from their savings to their checking account when bills were due. Sally admitted in marriage counseling that she had seen bank statements and knew Harry's ploy. He thought he'd repay the savings account before Sally found out, and she didn't confront him on the situation until they were in counseling. Just 23 months after the wedding, Sally demanded a divorce because, in her own words, she "could have forgiven infidelity but not someone stealing her dreams."

Love Isn't Always What It Seems

Barbie and Ken seem like a match made in Mattel Heaven. They're both from large lower-middle-class families and worked their way through college, where they met. Through hard work and more than a little luck, both ended up earning six-figure salaries by the time their first child was born. Smart living allowed them to save a ridiculous amount of money for a couple their age. Turns out they were doing it for different reasons, which they never discussed. Barbie made double payments on her school loans and never carried a balance on her credit cards because she wanted to quit her job and have another baby. She figured Ken would agree to her plan because they had money in the bank, no debts, and a common desire for a second child. Ken, on the other hand, expected Barbie to continue working and saving money, but his reasoning was more deeply rooted (and harder to admit). Ken's father had been irresponsible and lazy, leaving his mother to support the family financially and emotionally. Ken equated his mother's paycheck with security and love, a reality he uncovered through counseling in a last-ditch effort to save their marriage. He admitted that Barbie's paycheck wasn't about money at all. He believed they "needed" it to survive, even while their bank and investment statements told the opposite story.

Regrettably, these stories aren't shocking. Fascinating, sure, but only because they sound familiar. We'll sooner reveal secrets about sex or our criminal past than admit how we handle our finances. And often we handle finances the way we were raised to handle them. Gender plays a huge role too. If you grew up believing your husband will provide, perhaps you've put off saving for retirement or buying your dream home because you're still waiting for a prince to knock on your apartment door. Perhaps your role model taught you that money is how to keep score or some other moneymaking cliché. If that's the case, you may keep your nose to the grindstone in order to keep adding to your score. What are the consequences in the other aspects of your life? Some grew up watching one parent keep purchases secret from the other, while still others overheard their parents rationalizing shady business practices. Lessons learned in childhood about deceit and shame may manifest themselves in adulthood, and the results aren't pretty.

WHAT'S YOUR MONEY PERSONALITY?

We're not here to help you resolve any deep-seated childhood money issues you may have, but we do want to help you realize that they may play a role in your life. It's important to think through money behaviors that may be causing conflict in your work and personal relationships. Use the financial compatibility quiz in Chapter 5 if you find those types of inventories helpful. Be sure to include your partner and be frank in the discussion it may provoke. Here we've got a short list of questions that can help you determine your money personality. You may find the answers beneficial as you struggle (and succeed) in understanding your attitudes about money. And remember, there are no right answers.

- What is your first memory of money?
- How did your family communicate about money?
- How did you relate to money as a child? ("Nice to meet you, dime, my name is Penny.")
- As a child, did you feel poor or rich or somewhere between?
- What is your happiest moment with money? Your unhappiest? (Besides every month when bills are due.)
- What was your parents or grandparents' situation during the Depression?
- Will you inherit money? How does that make you feel?
- Are you generous? Stingy? Do you treat?
- Could you ask a close relative for a business loan? Money to make ends meet?
- Do you judge others by how you perceive they deal with their money?

These questions show what an intimate topic money can be. They may help you identify your true feelings about money and the events that helped shape those feelings. Even if you know what you think about money, you might not be able to talk about it because of traditions or attitudes you developed as a young child.

CHARITABLE GIVING: THE TAX DEDUCTION IS JUST ONE OF THE BENEFITS

There are several schools of thought on making charitable donations. Giving your money, time, and talents to a worthy cause is good for everyone involved. You feel good, the recipients feel good, programs grow, and people's lives are changed. From a purely financial perspective, charitable giving makes sense if for no other reason than the income tax deduction you can claim every April for gifts made in the previous tax year. As your net worth increases over time, so may your ability to make larger charitable donations. To maximize the financial nature of your charitable donations, keep these tips in mind.

- Document gifts under $250 with a receipt from the organization or your canceled check. This doesn't include multiple smaller gifts that total $250. A canceled check alone isn't sufficient proof for claiming a cash contribution of $250 or more, so always get a receipt. And they say the IRS has gotten more friendly.

- If you make payroll deduction contributions to United Way or similar nonprofit programs, keep your pay stub as proof when claiming the deduction.

- Deduct out-of-pocket expenses associated with your volunteer efforts, such as mileage, long distance phone calls, and supplies. Sorry, but your time doesn't count as a deduction.

- Remember to keep an itemized list of clothing, household goods, tools, and the like you may donate to local homeless shelters or other organizations such as the Salvation Army. If the combined goods total $500 or more, your receipts from the organization(s) should list items given, estimated market value, and date. There are tax guidebooks that put a dollar amount on each item you donate, so it pays to have a list when you're figuring deductions. Your tax advisor may have a current copy of the guidebook.

- Deduct appreciation on property donated to charity. Unfortunately, those worn T-shirts you gave to your kid brother don't qualify, no matter how much he appreciates your kindness.

- Consider contributing appreciated stock to your favorite charity.

- Many employers will match employee contributions to colleges, universities, and nonprofit organizations. It's worth the effort to find out if your employer offers this perk to employees. It's not cash in your pocket or a deduction at tax time, but it's money for something you care about, which is almost as good.

VOLUNTEERING OFFERS GREAT REWARDS

Depending on your financial situation—and energy level—you may want to volunteer your time to a charitable organization, either in addition to your monetary contributions or in place of them. Choose a one-time deal or an ongoing project. Bring a friend or relative along or go planning to meet new friends. Just call an organization in your area and offer your time; we'll guarantee that they can use you. And if you don't have a favorite organization already, these Web sites can give you some ideas:

- The Points of Light Foundation (pointsoflight.org) can help you shine in your neighborhood, with some help from the Volunteer Center National Network.

- VolunteerMatch (volunteermatch.org) is a database that volunteers can use to search thousands of one-time and ongoing opportunities by ZIP code, category, and date.

- The United Way (national.unitedway.org) can link you to its organizations throughout the United States, Canada, and many other countries.

A WORD ABOUT SCAMS

As more people choose to openly integrate their values with their investment decisions, more people are taking the opportunity to hook suckers with scams of all kinds. Fake charities and scams that claim religious backing are on the rise. The cons are getting smarter and more sophisticated while investors are trusting too much and not asking enough questions. Many scammers convince trusting souls to equate religious faith with faith in the investment. Oftentimes, they promise investment returns as high as 30 percent per month. Those sorts of gains would truly require divine intervention.

Most nonprofit groups are completely legitimate, but it pays to be skeptical at first—especially if you're contemplating investing in relatively new or previously unknown organizations. Scammers are counting on the fact that you won't be. If you choose to make charitable gifts using a credit card, be extremely cautious when giving your credit card information to the organization. And don't do it before you have checked that it's a legitimate nonprofit group. Before you make an investment with an organization that claims to have religious backing, ask to see an annual report or make some telephone calls to check it out. Finally, if it doesn't make sense or you've got a bad feeling in your gut, don't invest. You know what they say about too good to be true.

VALUE-BASED INVESTING

Can we change the world one investment at a time? The number of people who think so are making a difference, and the results have been good for the world—and investors' pocketbooks. Socially responsible investing (SRI) grew out of major social concerns of the 1970s, and we're not talking disco. We're talking the Vietnam War, apartheid in South Africa, and the Three Mile Island nuclear disaster, just to name a few. But protests and community action are just part of the equation. Former hippies, yuppies, and groupies also started putting their money where their mouth is to effect social change by hitting the pocketbooks of major corporations and influencing their decisions makers around the world. People committed to SRI aren't willing to sacrifice their principles for the almighty dollar.

What It Takes to Be Socially Responsible

In a nutshell, socially responsible investing involves making investment decisions based on their potential social and environmental impact. It's investing your principal while using your principles, as it were. But SRI is not just about money. It's sweat equity in the form of shareholder activism, which involves using your rights as a shareholder to influence corporate management (get the scoop on that in a few pages). The main approach to SRI is screening your investment portfolio to be sure it is compatible with certain social, ethical, or environmental criteria. Such filters include tobacco, alcohol, gambling, religious affiliation, defense/weapons, animal testing, environment, pornography, human rights, labor relations, employment/equality, and community investment.

To be a social investor does not mean you need to include all of these screens. You may believe a strong military is a good thing. You may think alcohol consumption is a personal choice. In fact, you might be drinking a beer right now while reading this book. You may not care if animal testing is used to make products safe for human consumption. As we've mentioned before, where your values are concerned, there are no wrong answers.

When choosing socially conscious investments, look first at the social agenda to make sure it complements your own. But don't forget to also consider investment style, expenses, and performance just as you would any other investment. You could put your entire nest egg into a company that focused on rainforest preservation, but if it has a five-year history of double-digit losses, you may want to rethink your commitment to that natural resource. Or at the very least, look for an investment with better numbers. Remember, though, that how an investment has performed in the past has no bearing on how it will do in the future. There's no such thing as guarantees, no matter what. Finally, you can be more confident in your socially conscious choices if you invest in something you know—just as conventional investors are. Here are three Web sites that may help you make some decisions:

- Socialfunds.com is easy to use and lets you sort funds by various investing policies. It links you to U.S. mutual funds that are managed with social criteria.
- Social Investment Forum (socialinvest.org) offers data on fund screens and fund returns. It also has links to socially conscious mutual funds in the United States.
- Responsible Shopper (responsibleshopper.org) helps you learn more about the companies behind the products you buy with

reports about workplace and environmental issues at more than 200 companies.

If you think it's tricky screening companies to find some that are worthy of your investment dollar, you're right. It's a lot of work. Lucky for you—and all the socially conscious investors like you—there is a growing number of SRI investment companies that will do the work for you, for a fee, of course. Whether you're opposed to nuclear power or favor a particular religious affiliation, there are investment options for you. And if you refuse to buy energy funds or you're opposed to "sin" stocks like tobacco, alcohol, and gambling, you can invest in the stock market anyway. All you gotta do is find a fund that avoids or embraces the same things you do.

SHAREHOLDER ACTIVISM BRINGS POWER TO THE PEOPLE

If you shop at The Home Depot or use a thermometer to check your temperature (or anyone else's), you are the beneficiary of shareholder activism. In 1999, Home Depot announced its intent to phase out the sale of wood products from endangered forests. Just months earlier, a shareholder resolution calling for a report on phasing out sales of old-growth wood received a vote of 12 percent—more than double the 5 percent average vote for first-year environmental resolutions. This victory was the result of internal pressure from a shareholder campaign.

In 2001, many major pharmacy chains in the United States began phasing out the sale of mercury thermometers. They are the largest source of mercury toxins in municipal solid waste, and combustion of that waste is the second largest source of mercury pollution in the country. By switching to alternative thermometers, pharmacy chains help protect the environment and limit the calls to poison control centers and emergency rooms because of broken mercury thermometers. Remember trying to pick up that slippery mercury after the thermometer broke when you were a kid?

While the corporate world sometimes disregards the criticism of grassroots groups, it pays serious attention to the financial community.

With shareholder activism, a little pressure goes a long way. Someone with 5 percent ownership would be considered a major shareholder, so a resolution receiving a small vote can still be highly effective. That explains why the 12 percent vote at Home Depot had such a huge impact.

Shareholder activists use the power of stock ownership to file resolutions, raise awareness, build coalitions, exert pressure, and create change. Shareholder action first gained national attention in the 1980s with the filing of scores of antiapartheid resolutions asking companies to divest from South Africa. Institutional investors (cities, universities, state pension funds, etc.) were pressured to drop the stocks of companies that continued to do business in that country, which proved to be a major factor in convincing many U.S. companies to leave South Africa.

Because social resolutions never lead to a majority vote by shareholders, some critics argue that shareholder power doesn't influence corporate social behavior. However, shareholder activism may be difficult to determine, as companies may make changes as a result of shareholder resolutions yet not publicly cite shareholder concern and pressure as a reason for making such changes. But even when shareholder activity does not produce immediate results, the actions of concerned and vocal shareholders are an important tool for social change. Over the past 25 years, shareholder activists have filed resolutions that have helped improve wages, benefits, and working conditions. Shareholder initiatives have led to increased representation of women and minorities on corporate boards, have improved disclosure of environmental liabilities, halted environmentally damaging projects, and have compelled companies to cease doing business in countries with human rights abuses.

Every Vote Counts

You can sign petitions, stage boycotts, and march in picket lines, but in order to make your vote count, you need to own shares of stock in a company and send in those proxy vote statements when they come in the mail. If you, your family, friends, or organization hold shares through a 401(k), Individual Retirement Account, or other investment, urge your fund manager to support shareholder resolutions. But it's not just your vote that counts. To get involved at any level of the fight, link to any of these Web sites:

- Friends of the Earth (foe.org) has all sorts of helpful information on how to get started.
- The Shareholder Action Network (shareholderaction.org) unites investors for corporate responsibility.
- As You Sow (asyousow.org) includes lists of current campaigns about genetically engineered food, sweatshop working conditions, recycling, and forestry, among others. The organization promotes corporate accountability and programs for social change.
- The Investor Responsibility Research Center (irrc.org) is an independent firm that provides impartial research, software, and other services.

Congratulations for wanting to base your money decisions on more than making a buck, but be prepared for what lies ahead. Heck, you may find what lies ahead to be a rewarding challenge and a good use of your time. It's perfectly all right, on the other hand, if all this talk about socially responsible investing has proved too much for you. It's a lot of work and takes a huge commitment, and then you still may end up investing in companies that manufacture tobacco-based ammunition for Third World countries. (We smell smoke!) You may have lost the urge to screen your investments that carefully, but we certainly hope you haven't lost the urge to invest your money.

WEALTH AND RICHES ARE TWO DIFFERENT THINGS

We've come to that part of the chapter—and the book, for that matter—that we affectionately call "the end." Far from leaving you in the lurch, we're going to leave you with some thoughts about incorporating your values into your financial life. Those thoughts are similar in a lot of ways with how we started the book in the chapter about financial planning. Set goals and go after them, blah, blah, blah. A budget can help you move ahead while excessive debt will impede your progress, yada,

FINANCIAL JARGON MADE EASY

One option for socially conscious investors is to support *community development financial institutions (CDFI)*. Their mission is to promote economic independence for the hard-to-reach populations. CDFIs direct funds to individuals and organizations that build homes, start businesses, and provide services to disadvantaged communities. Your role is to deposit money with a CDFI and let it lend those funds to people who need money. These financial institutions measure their return in dollars, but more important, in new jobs, good homes, and better neighborhoods. You can locate a CDFI in your area by visiting Web sites for the National Community Capital Association (www.communitycapital.org) or the Center for Community Self-Help (www.selfhelp.org).

You may find some value in learning more financial terms in the glossary in the back of the book.

yada, yada. And if you've read the whole book—besides being one of our parents or our editor—we hope that means you can see some benefit in incorporating some of it into your everyday financial decisions. And like we said at the beginning of this chapter, your values play a role in those decisions. Here are several ways you can intentionally integrate values into your financial life. You probably do some of these things already, whether you realize it or not. But as we like to say, there is no right answer.

Think about It

No, this isn't one more way to procrastinate. You need to know what's most important in your life. What couldn't you live without? If you're working an awful job because it pays well, how do you rationalize spending those 40, 50, 60 hours a week doing something you can't stand? Maybe your self-analysis will show that there's no other choice, considering the job market, and your financial obligations. But thinking about what's important may cause you to look for a different job. Work is just one example of what's important, incidentally.

Evaluate Spending

We've got entire chapters on budgeting and debt, so we won't dwell on those bad boys here, but we do want to emphasize that how you spend your money reflects your values. Or at least it should. It's not bad to buy things, but those things shouldn't replace what you cherish in life or cause you to not afford more "value-able" pursuits. If you're in debt up to your eyeballs, you might be blinded by the bills and unable to focus on the rest of your life. Be methodical about paying off credit cards, college loans, car loans, home equity loans, and loan sharks.

Budget with Values in Mind

Track your expenses and spending for a month or so (see the Spending Record and Spending Plan worksheets in Chapter 2 for some direction). It could reveal some money habits that need changing. And it can help you shape future habits, such as saving for the future, charitable giving, and providing for those you love. If you budget for a trip to visit relatives, you'll be able to maintain those family connections without feeling pinched in the pocketbook. Of course, spending time with your family may be something you want to avoid budgeting for. Wink, wink.

Stay "In Touch" with Money

Plastic credit cards and online shopping have eliminated the touchy-feely aspect of money. Using cash more often may help you stay in touch with what's yours—and what you're willing to give up the greenbacks for. Plus, you'll appreciate the valuable role money plays in your life if you force yourself to watch the quarters, dimes, and 20-dollar bills go from your pocketbook into the cash register.

Protect Future Income

You owe it to yourself and friends and family to protect your earning power with health insurance, disability income insurance, and/or life insurance. Speaking of things people choose to avoid, Chapter 9 on risk protection may be just what you need to read.

Save for Goals

If you want to adopt a child or buy a small business or retire at 55, values-based money management can help you achieve your goals. Whether it's $15 a week in a savings account or 15 percent of your salary in an employer-sponsored retirement plan, you've got to start saving something now. It's easier to stay on track if you have something to shoot for, and it's easier to hold yourself accountable if you can see where you're aiming. See Chapter 1 if you want some guidance on setting goals.

Find a Cause That Counts

If you choose to make charitable (and income tax–deductible) contributions, one way to select a worthy cause is to think about an issue or cause that has touched your life. You'll be more passionate about your involvement and more willing to give. Whether it's a college that had an impact on your life or medical research to cure the cancer that took your loved one, if it matters to you, it counts. And just in case you missed the discussion on the tax advantages of charity, flip back to what we had to say about charitable giving earlier in this chapter.

Be an Example to the Next Generation

You can teach young people you know valuable lessons merely by handling your money responsibly. If they see that you make thoughtful spending decisions and that you save money toward achieving your goals, they may adopt your habits. As long as you continue spoiling them rotten at holidays. Seriously, you can pass on more than just your crooked toes and sense of humor to the next generation.

Enjoy Today

Don't be so focused on gaining wealth that you neglect to live richly now. And take care of yourself. The longer you remain healthy, the longer you'll be able to earn an income, and good health will reduce your medical costs throughout your lifetime. And we're not talking dollars as much as we're talking sense.

Guide to Financial Jargon

All of the definitions are real, but some of the comments are not.

401(k) plan
Employer-sponsored, qualified plan that permits employees to make pretax contributions from their salaries to a profit-sharing plan, a target benefit plan, or a stock bonus plan. The great news is contributions and earnings grow tax deferred until withdrawn. At which time you plan on being in Hawaii.

403(b) plan
A retirement plan for employees of nonprofit organizations, public schools, and churches where employees can contribute a portion of their salary into a mutual fund or annuity. As with a 401(k) plan, the great news here is contributions and earnings grow tax deferred until withdrawn.

457 plan
A deferred compensation program for employees of state and federal governments and agencies. Earnings grow on a income tax–deferred basis and contributions are not taxed until the assets are distributed from the plan, usually in retirement. A 457 plan is similar to a 401(k) or 403(b) plan, except there are never employer matching contributions and the IRS does not consider it a qualified retirement plan. Hmmm, no

matching contributions and fewer tax advantages. What's the saying about close only counts in horseshoes and hand grenades?

adjusted gross income
Also known by its friendlier nickname, AGI. This is the income amount on which a working stiff computes deductions that are based on, or limited by, a percentage of his or her income in order to figure out federal taxable income. AGI is determined by subtracting from gross income any deductible business expenses and other allowable adjustments.

alternative minimum tax
An IRS mechanism created to ensure that high-income individuals, corporations, trusts, and estates pay at least some minimum amount of tax, regardless of deductions, credits, or exemptions. (It seems only fair, doesn't it?) It operates by adding certain tax-preference items back into adjusted gross income.

American Stock Exchange (AMEX)
The second largest stock exchange in the United States after the New York Stock Exchange (NYSE). AMEX has a larger number of stocks and bonds issued by smaller companies than the NYSE.

amortization
It's the kind of word that makes you smile and nod when you hear it because you want people to believe you understand. (Keep reading and you really will understand.) It's the gradual elimination of a liability, such as a mortgage, in regular payments over a specified period of time. Such payments must be sufficient to cover both principal and interest.

annuity
A contract that provides for a series of payments to be made or received at regular intervals. An annuity (say those two words 10 times fast) may be immediate, starting as soon as the premium has been paid, or deferred, starting at a designated later date. Annuities are commonly used to fund retirement.

asset allocation

Investment strategy whose purpose is to enhance total return and/or reduce risk by diversifying assets among different types of stocks, bonds, and money market investments. Variety is the spice of investment life.

asset classes

No, these are not dreary investment seminars for narcoleptics. They're types of investments, such as stocks, bonds, real estate, and cash.

back-end load

A sales charge on an investment that is taken at the time of redemption instead of the traditional front-end sales charge. Back-end load is not to be confused with back-end loader, which is a piece of heavy equipment.

bear market

A big, fuzzy term used to describe the stock market when prices have been declining in value for about as long as a bear hibernates in winter.

bond

Basically an IOU or promissory note of a corporation. A bond is evidence of a debt on which the issuing company usually promises to pay the bond holders a specified amount of interest for a specified length of time, and to repay the loan on the expiration date. In every case, a bond represents debt—its holder is a creditor of the corporation and not a part owner, as is the shareholder.

bull market

A prolonged period in which investment prices rise faster than their historical average. Bull markets can happen as a result of an economic recovery, an economic boom, or investor psychology. You may recall the booming 1990s, and we're not talking Michael Jordan's Chicago Bulls.

catch-up provision

A provision in some retirement savings plans that allows some participants to make contributions over the usual annual limit if they have not maximized their contributions in earlier years. If you're a teacher and your school system offers employees this provision, you are guaranteed to have condiments whenever hamburgers are served for school lunch (i.e., catch-up, mustard, onions).

compound interest

The interest that accrues when earnings for a specified period are added to the principal, so that interest for the following period is computed on the principal plus accumulated interest. Interest is calculated on reinvested interest as well as on the original amount invested. Look, Einstein called compound interest the greatest discovery of the twentieth century, so even if you don't understand it, take advantage of it.

consumer price index (CPI)

An inflationary indicator that measures the change in the cost of a fixed "basket" of products and services, including housing, electricity, food, and transportation. The CPI is published monthly (fascinating reading) by the Bureau of Labor Statistics of the U.S. Department of Labor. Also called cost-of-living index.

Coverdell Education Savings Account

Formerly called the Education IRA, this savings tool allows you to stuff up to $2,000 a year in an account and then use the cash for college costs and qualified K-12 expenses too. Contributions are made with after-tax dollars but any proceeds aren't subject to income taxes if they're used for qualified education expenses of the designated individual. If you don't use the money for its intended purpose you're going to pay taxes on it. Sounds like incentive enough!

death benefit

The payment made to a beneficiary from an annuity or life insurance policy when the policyholder dies. Also called face amount or face value.

deductible

Relating to health insurance, a predetermined amount the insured person pays for medical treatment before the health insurance coverage kicks in. "Kicks in" is a common expression for "takes effect."

deferred compensation

A contractual agreement between an organization and an employee wherein the organization makes an unsecured promise to defer the compensation of the employee to some future date for services currently performed by the employee. We'd like to see more deferred work programs wherein you get paid now for a job you'll actually do at a later date. All in favor?

defined benefit plan

A company retirement plan in which a retired employee receives a specific benefit based on salary history and years of service, and in which the employer bears the investment risk. Contributions may be made by the employee, the employer, or both.

defined contribution plan

A company retirement plan, such as profit sharing, money purchase pension, 401(k), or 403(b), in which each participant has an individual account within the plan with benefits based solely upon amounts contributed and the past performance of that account. The participant bears the investment risk.

deflation

It's the opposite of inflation, which means it's the antonym of that word. (We love tossing vocabulary terms out there for you to enjoy.) Back to the topic at hand, deflation is a fall in the general level of prices. It can be a very bad thing, since businesses and consumers make plans based on the expectation that prices will remain stable or climb. When prices fall, it sets off a potential domino effect in the overall economy.

diversification

Spreading investments (without spreading yourself thin) among different companies in different fields. Another type of diversification is offered by the securities of many individual companies because of the wide range of their activities.

dividend

The part of a company's net income paid to stockholders at the discretion of the board of directors. Dividends are usually paid in cash but they're sometimes paid in stock. Dividends may be omitted if business is poor or the directors withhold earnings to invest in plant and equipment.

dollar-cost averaging

A system of buying securities at regular intervals with a fixed dollar amount. Under this system you buy by the dollar's worth rather than by the number of shares. If each investment is the same number of dollars, payments buy more shares when the price is low and fewer when it increases. Makes sense when you think about it. Keep in mind that periodic investment plans do not assure a profit or protect against loss in declining markets. Consider your financial ability to continue purchases through periods of low price levels.

Dow Jones Industrial Average

You've heard it a million times. The most widely used indicator of the overall condition of the stock market, the DJIA is a price-weighted average of 30 actively traded blue chip stocks, primarily industrials. It's figured by adding up the prices of all the stocks in the index and then dividing by 30. We'll leave math problems like that to the experts.

durable power of attorney

A legal document allowing individuals to grant others general or specific powers for managing financial or medical decisions in the event that the individual becomes incapacitated and unable to make decisions. To make the document even more durable, consider typing it on burlap.

estate taxes

IRS tax rates that apply to the estate after the death of the holder. Often portfolios are managed to reduce this substantial tax burden. At least the smart ones.

executor

An individual or institution nominated in a will and appointed by a court to settle the estate of a deceased.

Federal Deposit Insurance Corporation (FDIC)

A federal agency that insures deposits in member banks and thrifts up to $100,000. Look at bank and other financial-company ads. You'll often find "FDIC" at the bottom. This is what it refers to.

Federal Housing Administration (FHA)

A government agency whose primary purpose is to insure residential mortgage loans. Sort of like the roof over the roof over your head.

FICA payroll taxes

FICA is an acronym for Federal Insurance Contributors Act, and is the federal law that requires employers to withhold a portion of employee wages and pay them to the government trust fund that provides retirement benefits (more commonly known as Social Security). If you want us to fax you the facts on FICA tax, leave your name and number at the tone.

front-end load

The initial sales charge or front-end load is a deduction made from each investment in a fund. Think of it as money off the top. The amount of the charge is generally based on the amount of the investment.

full retirement age

The age at which someone is eligible for full retirement benefits from the government. The magic number isn't 65 for all Americans anymore, folks. If you were born after 1942, your full retirement age is 66, and it's 67 if you were born after 1960.

individual retirement account (IRA)

A tax-deferred personal retirement account set up through a bank, brokerage, or other financial institution in which annual contributions may be invested in many types of securities.

inflation

The general upward trend in price of goods and services in an economy, usually as measured by the Consumer Price Index. As prices go up over time, the value of a dollar is going to fall because a person won't be able to buy as much. If you still have questions, call the Federal Reserve.

initial public offering (IPO)

The first offering of stock of a company to the public. We're not sure if a Subsequent Public Offering (SPO) exists or not. Doesn't sound like it, anyway.

interest

Amount charged by a lender to a borrower for the use of money. Interest rates are normally expressed on an annual basis. Sisters, however, are often found charging interest on a daily basis to their little brothers (and in potential violation of federal usury laws, we might add).

intestate

Fancy word for dying without a legal will and therefore a fancy word meaning your property will be distributed according to state law and not your wishes.

irrevocable trust

First, a pronunciation guide: ear-REV-uh-cuh-bull. Now that we've got that out of the way, it's a trust that cannot be changed or canceled once it is set up without the consent of the beneficiary.

liability insurance

Coverage to protect against the liability the insured becomes legally obligated to pay due to bodily injury, property damage, or professional liability or libel. This can really come in handy when your steering wheel unexpectedly comes off in your hands while driving.

lien

A claim by one person on the property of another as security for money owed. Think of it this way: "If you don't pay me what you owe, I will lean on your house until you do."

line of credit

The maximum preapproved amount that a person may borrow without completing a new credit application. And anything you have to do to avoid completing a new credit application is a good thing.

living will

A document that enables a person to declare his or her wishes in advance concerning the use of life-sustaining procedures in the event of a terminal illness or injury when the person has become incompetent. It is a documented fact, however, that some people become incompetent without the terminal illness or injury. Different rules apply here.

long-term capital gain or loss

A capital gain or loss on an investment that was held for at least some minimum amount of time (often a year and a day). A long-term gain usually results in a lower tax rate than a short-term gain. If we were talking about politicians who won or lost an election, we would spell it capitol gain or loss.

long-term care insurance

An insurance policy that provides benefits for the chronically ill or disabled over a long period of time.

look-back period

Relating to long-term care, it's the timeframe during which the government may check whether you gave any cash or property gifts during that window that would affect your eligibility for benefits. You can't fool Big Brother, brother.

management fee

The fee paid to the investment manager of a mutual fund. It is usually about one half of one percent, or maybe one percent, of average net assets annually. Not to be confused with the sales charge, which is the one-time commission paid at the time of purchase as a part of the offering price. Not to suggest that you would be confused or anything.

Medicaid

A program, funded by the federal and state governments, that pays for nursing home and in-home health care for those who can't afford it. Not to be confused with those who merely say they can't afford it.

Medicare

A federal program that pays for certain health care expenses for people age 65 or older. Driver's licenses are accepted for proof of age. Birth certificates, too, if you can find them.

Medigap

The feeling of falling through the insurance cracks. Seriously, Medigap, or Medicare supplement policies, are private insurance policies that pay for care that is approved but not paid by Medicare. Medigap policies will not pay for services not covered by Medicare.

money market

Portfolios of high-quality, short-term securities. Marked by high liquidity and returns that are generally higher than a traditional savings account, they're an alternative to bank savings accounts. And an even better alternative to shoeboxes. However, they are not guaranteed and could lose value.

mutual fund

An open-end investment company that continuously offers new shares to the public in addition to redeeming shares on demand as required by law. And if you invest in one, believe us, the feeling is mutual.

Nasdaq Composite Index

A market-value weighted index of all common stocks listed on Nasdaq, which dates back to 1971. The index is used mainly to track technology stocks, so it's not a good indicator of the market as a whole. As the dot-bomb era proved, tech stocks aren't all there is.

net asset value (NAV)

A term usually used in connection with mutual funds, meaning net asset value per share. It is common practice for mutual funds to compute their net asset value daily by totaling the market value of all securities owned, deducting liabilities, and dividing the balance by the number of shares outstanding. The resulting figure is the net asset value per share. This is why they stress adding, subtracting, multiplying, and dividing in school so much.

points

The amount paid either to maintain or lower the interest rate charged. Each point is equal to one percent of the loan amount. For example, two points on a $100,000 mortgage would equal $2,000 (and three points would be a field goal).

power of attorney

A legal document giving another the power to act as one's attorney or agent in handling all personal affairs. The power may be general or specific (that pretty well covers the waterfront) and is revoked upon the death of the principal.

price-earnings (P/E) ratio

The price of a share of stock divided by earnings per share for a 12-month period. For example, a stock selling for $100 a share and earning $5 a share is said to be selling at a price-earnings ratio of 20 to 1. (Until we saw that example, we didn't get it either.)

private mortgage insurance (PMI)

Paid on loans that are not government insured and whose loan-to-value is greater than 80 percent. When you have accumulated 20 percent of your home's value as equity, your lender may waive PMI at your request. In your request, be sure to use the words "pretty please with sugar on top." Please note that such insurance is not a form of life insurance that pays off the loan in case of death.

probate

A judicial procedure to test the authenticity and validity of an estate, will, guardianship, or trust agreement. Reprobate, on the other hand, is something else altogether and should not be confused with the financial term.

qualified domestic relations order (QDRO)

In divorce proceedings, a QDRO is an order from the court (as opposed to order in the court) to the retirement plan administrator, which allows one spouse to receive benefits from the other spouse's company-sponsored retirement plan.

reverse mortgage

An arrangement in which a homeowner borrows against the equity in his or her home and receives regular monthly tax-free payments from the lender. Also called reverse-annuity mortgage or home equity conversion mortgage. You've gotta be 62 or older to be eligible, so Gen Xers (and quite a few baby boomers too) need not apply.

revocable trust

A trust that may be changed or canceled by its grantor or by another person. Does not avoid estate taxes as an irrevocable trust does. Just in case you thought you could get away with something there.

risk tolerance

Technically, it's the measure of an investor's ability to accept risk. Investors are often categorized as risk indifferent, risk averse, or risk seeking. In practical terms, it's the degree to which you feel either nauseous or giddy or somewhere in between at the prospect of certain types of risky investments.

Roth IRA

A type of individual retirement account that allows taxpayers, subject to certain income limits, to save for retirement while allowing the savings to grow income tax–free. Taxes are paid on contributions, but withdrawals aren't taxed at all if requirements are met.

S&P 500 Index

Standard & Poor's value-weighted index of 500 U.S. domestic stocks, mostly NYSE-listed companies, with some others. For those of you even further in the dark, NYSE is New York Stock Exchange. And for the record, there was never an Old York Stock Exchange.

SEP (simplified employee pension plan)

A retirement program for self-employed people or owners of small companies, allowing them to defer taxes on investments intended for retirement. And if this is the simplified plan, you don't want to tangle with the complicated version.

security

An investment instrument, other than an insurance policy or fixed annuity, issued by a corporation, government, or other organization that offers evidence of debt or equity. The SEC has ruled that a security blanket does not qualify as a security.

share

Certificate representing one unit of ownership in a corporation, mutual fund, or limited partnership. The saying about "share and share a like" has very little, if anything, to do with this term in the financial arena.

short-term capital gain or loss

A capital gain or loss on an investment that was held for less than some minimum amount of time (often a year and a day). A short-term gain usually results in a higher tax rate than a long-term gain.

short-term investments

Relatively stable investments that can be easily changed into currency, such as a checking account, Treasury bills, a money market account, or even a short-term bond fund. Unlike with typical human children, maturity typically occurs in less than three years.

stock

Ownership (called equity) of a corporation representing a claim on a company's earnings and assets. Ownership in the company is determined by the number of shares a person owns divided by the total number of shares outstanding. Stock may be issued in different forms, including common and preferred.

tax deductible

An item or expense subtracted from adjusted gross income to reduce the amount of income subject to tax. Examples include mortgage interest, state and local taxes, unreimbursed business expenses, and charitable contributions. Claiming your dog as home-office manager seldom goes through unchallenged.

tax deferral

Paying taxes in the future for income earned in the current year, such as through an IRA, 401(k), SEP IRA, or Keogh Plan. Save now, pay later,we always say.

title insurance

Protection for lenders or homeowners against financial loss resulting from legal defects in the title. Unfortunately, title insurance offers no protection when you get demoted at work.

Treasury bill

U.S. government security with a maturity of under one year. Pays no interest, but yields the difference between its par value and its discounted purchase price. Now there's two more terms to look up.

Treasury bond
U.S. government security with a maturity of more than 10 years. Pays interest periodically. Assuming no government overthrows have occurred.

Treasury note
U.S. government security with maturates between 1 and 10 years. Pays interest periodically. Assuming no nuclear holocaust has taken out Washington, D.C.

trusts
A legal arrangement in which an individual (the grantor) gives fiduciary control of property to a person or institution (the trustee) for the benefit of beneficiaries. And if you think the phrase "benefit of beneficiaries" is redundant, it's not. It's just how legal and financial people have to talk.

yield
Also known as return. The dividends or interest paid by a security expressed as a percentage of the current price. A stock with a current market value of $20 a share that is currently paying dividends at the rate of $1 a year is said to return 5 percent ($1/$20). The current return on a bond is figured the same way. Just get out your calculator and have fun.

Index

Note: glossary words in **bold**

Adjustable rate mortgage (ARM),
    106–107, 114
Adjusted gross income, **268**
Age
    average net worth, 12
    estate planning, 224–228
    long-term care, 207–208
    of retirement, 143
    retirement savings, 132–133, 137
Aggressive investment portfolio,
    170–171
Alimony, 103–104
Alternative minimum tax, **268**
American Stock Exchange (AMEX), **268**
Amortization, **268**
Annual operating expenses, 177
Annual report, 185
Annuity, **268**
ARM (adjustable rate mortgage),
    106–107, 114
Asset classes, **269**
Assets
    allocation of, 169–171, **269**
    divorce, 97–101
    net worth, 10–11
ATM cards, 66

Back-end load, 177, **269**
Balanced mutual funds, 176
Balloon loans, 107
Bank certificates of deposit (CDs),
    175–176
Banking accounts, 38, 88, 175–176
Bankruptcy, 50–51
Bear market, **269**
Beneficiary designations, 216, 220, 224,
    230
Biweekly mortgage payment, 116–117
Bond mutual funds, 176
Bonds, 181–184, **269**
Budgeting, 25–41
    blowing it, 36
    gross and net income, 32–34
    job change, 76–77
    plan, 35–39
    realistic numbers, 34–35
    spending record, 26–32
    steps to consider, 39–40
    wedding planning worksheet, 86–87
Bull market, **269**

Calculators, saving and spending, 32
Cash advances, 48
Cash value life insurance, 201, 202–205
Catastrophic health coverage, 192
Catch-up provision, **269–270**
CDFI (community development financial
    institutions), 263
CDs (bank certificates of deposit),
    175–176
Change, coping with, 73–104
    divorce, 95–104
    job change, 73–82
    marriage, 82–95
Chapter 7 bankruptcy, 51
Chapter 13 bankruptcy, 51
Charge-off, 68
Charitable giving, 255–257
Checking accounts, 88
Child support, 103–104
Children and estate planning, 226
Claims, homeowners insurance, 124–125
Classes of mutual fund shares, 178
CLUE (Comprehensive Loss Underwriting
    Exchange), 125–126
COBRA (Consolidated Omnibus Budget
    Reconciliation Act of 1985),
    191–192
Commission-only financial professionals,
    22
Community development financial
    institutions (CDFI), 263
Compound interest, 14–16, **270**
Comprehensive Loss Underwriting
    Exchange (CLUE), 125–126
Conservative investment portfolio, 170
Consolidated Omnibus Budget
    Reconciliation Act of 1985
    (COBRA), 191–192
Consumer price index (CPI), **270**
Contract for deed, 107–108
Contribution limits, retirement plans, 149
Conventional mortgage loans, 106
Copying wallet contents, 46
Corporate bonds, 182
Counseling service, 50, 57
Coverdell Education Savings Account, **270**
CPI (consumer price index), **270**
Credit cards, 44–47, 63, 66
Credit counseling, 67–71
Credit rating and reporting, 59–71
    annual review, 235
    boost your score, 64–65

Credit rating and reporting (*Cont.*):
  correcting incorrect information, 65–67
  credit counseling, 67–71
  creditworthiness score, 59–64
  identity theft repair, 238–240
  professional advice, 70–71

Death, estate planning, 228–232
Death benefit, **270**
Debit cards, 66
Debt, 43–57
  bad debt, 47–48
  bankruptcy, 50–51
  cash advances, 48
  credit cards, 44–45
  debt-to-income ratio, 52–54
  divorce, 100
  good debt, 43–44
  home equity loans, 46–47
  marriage, 84–85
  payday loans, 48–50
  steps to address, 55–57
  warning signals, 54–55
Debt-to-income ratio, 52–54
Deductible, **271**
Deferred compensation, **271**
Defined benefit plan, 102, 145, **271**
Defined contribution plan, 102, 145, **271**
Deflation, **271**
Designations, financial professionals, 21
Disability insurance, 197–200
Dispute
  credit reporting, 65–67
  identity theft, 242–245
Diversification, **272**
Dividend, **272**
Dividend reinvestment plans (DRIPs),
  180–181
Divorce, 95–104
  alimony, 103–104
  child support, 103–104
  debt division, 100
  house, 100–101
  initial steps, 96–97
  property division, 97–100
  retirement savings, 101–102
  single parenting, 104
  taxes, 101, 102, 103
  (*See also* Marriage)
DJIA (Dow Jones Industrial Average),
  272
Document management, 236–238
Dollar-cost averaging, 14, 162, 171–172,
  173, **272**
Dow Jones Industrial Average (DJIA),
  272

DRIPs (dividend reinvestment plans),
  180–181
Durable power of attorney, **272**

Early retirement, 156–157
Employer-sponsored retirement plans, 138
Equity mutual funds, 176
Estate planning, 211–232
  beneficiary designations, 216, 220,
    224, 230
  checklists, 224–226
  death and survivors, 228–232
  healthcare directives, 216–217
  list of intentions, 230–232
  organ donation, 223–224
  planning tools, 219–222
  power of attorney (POA), 215–216
  probate, 217–219
  tax issues, 222–223, 230
  will, 212–215, 217–219
Estate taxes, **273**
Executor, **273**

FDIC (Federal Deposit Insurance
  Corporation), **273**
Federal Deposit Insurance Corporation
  (FDIC), **273**
Federal Emergency Management Agency
  (FEMA), 120
Federal Housing Administration (FHA),
  107, 119, **273**
Federal Insurance Contributions Act
  (FICA), 142
Fee-for-service health insurance,
  194–195
Fee-only financial professionals, 21–22
Fee-plus-commission financial
  professionals, 22
Fees, mutual funds, 177–179
FEMA (Federal Emergency Management
  Agency), 120
FHA (Federal Housing Administration),
  107, 119, **273**
FICA (Federal Insurance Contributions
  Act), 142
FICO score, 60–62
Financial accountability, marriage, 85, 88
Financial compatibility quiz, marriage,
  90–93
Financial planning, starting, 1–23
  compounding, 14–16
  current situation quiz, 2–6
  goals, 6–9
  net worth, 9–12
  procrastination, 12–15
  professional advice, 16–23

Financial planning, starting (*Cont.*):
  spending, 26–32, 35–40
  (*See also specific topics*)
First-to-die insurance, 203–204
Fixed income mutual funds, 176
Flexible spending accounts, health
  insurance, 196–197
Flood insurance, 120
457(b) plan, 148–150, **267–268**
401(k) plan, 80–81, 144–149, 151–152,
  267
403(b) plan, 144–149, 151–152, **267**
Fraud alerts, 241
Fraud protection, identity theft, 240–242
Front-end load, 177, **273**
Full retirement age, **273**

Global mutual funds, 176–177
Goals
  financial planning, starting, 6–9
  investments and investing, 161–162,
    166
  retirement savings, 134, 135
Good-faith estimate, 108
Gross income, 32–34

Hardship withdrawals in retirement
  savings, 148, 150
Head of household, 103
Health insurance, 190–197
  catastrophic coverage, 192
  COBRA, 191–192
  fee-for-service, 194–195
  flexible spending accounts, 196–197
  insurance, 190–197
  managed care, 195–196
  short-term, 190–191
Health maintenance organization (HMO),
  196
Healthcare directives, estate planning,
  216–217
HELOC (home equity line of credit),
  47
HMO (health maintenance organization),
  196
Home equity conversion mortgage, FHA,
  119
Home equity line of credit (HELOC), 47
Home equity loans, 46–47
Home improvement, 127–129
Home ownership and mortgages, 105–130
  ARM loans, 106–107, 114
  balloon loans, 107
  contract for deed, 107–108
  conventional loans, 106
  divorce, 100–101

Home ownership and mortgages (*Cont.*):
  FHA loan, 107, 119
  home improvement, 127–129
  homeowners insurance, 119–127
  jumbo loan, 108
  mortgage mistakes, 110–113
  mortgage shopping, 108–109
  piggyback loans, 122
  PMI, 121–123
  prepayment, 115–117
  property taxes, 117
  refinancing, 113–115
  reverse mortgage, 108, 118–119
  selling, 130
  VA loans, 107
Homeowners insurance, 119–127

Identity theft, 233–247
  dispute letters, 242–245
  documents management, 237–238
  fraud protection, 240–242
  opting out of junk mail, 246–247
  protection, 234–236
  repair, 238–240
Income
  average net worth, 12
  debt-to-income ratio, 52–54
  expectations and retirement savings,
    136–137
  gross and net income, 32–34
  net income worksheet, 33
Income mutual funds, 176
Index mutual funds, 176
Individual retirement accounts (IRAs),
  153–155
  defined, **274**
  rollover, 78–79
  Roth, 149, 154–155
  SEP IRA, 149, 152–153
  SIMPLE IRA, 149, 152
  (*See also* Retirement savings)
Inflation, 140–141, 163–164, **274**
Initial public offering (IPO), 164, **274**
Insurance, 119–127, 189–209
  CLUE, 125–126
  disability insurance, 197–200
  flood insurance, 120
  health insurance, 190–197
  home ownership and mortgages,
    119–127
  homeowners, 119–127
  life insurance, 200–205, 221
  long-term care, 205–209
  mortgage life/disability/unemployment
    insurance, 120
  personal property insurance, 121

Insurance (*Cont.*):
  PMI, 121–123
  title insurance, 120–121
  umbrella liability, 120
Interest, **274**
  (*See also specific topics*)
Interest rate lock, mortgage, 109
International mutual funds, 176–177
Intestate, **274**
Inventory, homeowners insurance, 126
Investment risk, 163
Investments and investing, 159–187
  annual report, 185
  asset allocation, 169–171
  bonds, 181–184
  dollar-cost averaging, 14, 162,
    171–172, 173
  DRIPs, 180–181
  goals, 161–162, 166
  inflation, 163–164
  liquidity, 174–175
  mutual funds, 175–179, 184–185
  portfolio rebalancing, 172, 174
  prospectus, 184–185
  risk, 160–161, 162–171
  risk tolerance quiz, 166–169
  savings bonds, 183–184
  socially responsible investing (SRI),
    258–262
  stocks, 179–181, 184–185
  Treasury Inflation-Indexed Securities
    (TIPS), 165
IPO (initial public offering),
  164, **274**
IRA (*See* individual retirement account
  ([IRA])
Irrevocable trust, **274**

Job change, 73–82
  dealing with job loss, 74–75
  new job and new budget, 76–77
  relocation, 81–82
  retirement rollover, 78–81
  unemployment benefits, 76
Joint tenancy, with right of survivorship,
  220–221
Jumbo loan mortgage, 108
Junk mail, opting out of, 246–247

Keogh plan, 153

Liabilities, net worth, 10–11
Liability insurance, **275**
Lien, **275**
Life estate, 218
Life expectancy estimates, 139
Life insurance, 200–205, 221

Line of credit, **275**
Liquidity of investments, 174–175
Living trusts, 221
Living will, **275**
Load, mutual funds, 177–179
Loans
  home equity loans, 46–47
  retirement, 146–148, 150
  (*See also* Home ownership and
    mortgages)
Long-term capital gain/loss, **275**
Long-term care insurance, 205–209, **275**
Look-back period, **276**

Managed care health insurance,
  195–196
Management fee, **276**
Markowitz, Harry, 169
Marriage, 82–95
  banking and checking account, 88
  debt, 84–85
  financial accountability and
    partnership, 85, 88
  financial compatibility quiz, 90–93
  name changes, 89–90
  prenuptial agreements, 93, 95
  wedding planning, 82–83, 86–87
  (*See also* Divorce)
Marriage penalty, taxes, 94–95
Medicaid, **276**
Medicare, 142, **276**
Medigap, **276**
Miller, Merton, 169
MIP (mortgage insurance premium),
  107
Moderate investment portfolio, 170
Modern Portfolio Theory, 170
Money market, 175–176, **276**
Mortgage-backed bonds, 182
Mortgage insurance premium (MIP), 107
Mortgage life/disability/unemployment
  insurance, 120
Mortgages (*See* Home ownership and
  mortgages)
Municipal bonds, 182
Mutual funds, 175–179, 184–185, **277**

Name changes, 89–90
Net asset value (NAV), **277**
Net income, 32–34
Net worth, 9–12, 30–31

One-time financial plan, 22
Opting out of junk mail, 246–247
Organ donation, 223–224
Ownership changes, estate planning,
  230

P/E (price-earnings) ratio, **277**
Payable-on-death (POD) accounts, 219–220, 224
Payday loans, 48–50
Personal property insurance, 121
Personal values, 249–255
Piggyback loans, 122
Plan loans, retirement, 146–148, 150
Planning (*See* Financial planning, starting; *specific topics*)
PMI (private mortgage insurance), 114, 115, 122–123, **278**
POA (power of attorney), **207**, 215–216, **272**
Point-of-service (POS), 195–196
Points, **277**
Portfolios, asset allocation, 170–171, 172,174
POS (point-of-service), 195–196
Power of attorney (POA), **207**, 215–216, **272**
PPO (preferred provider organization), 195
Preferred provider organization (PPO), 195
Prenuptial agreements, 93, 95
Prepayment, home mortgage, 115–117
Price-earnings (P/E) ratio, **277**
Private mortgage insurance (PMI), 114, 115, 122–123, **278**
Probate, 217–219, **278**
Procrastination in financial planning, 12–15
Professional advice
    credit counseling, 50, 57, 69–71
    credit rating and reporting, 70–71
    financial planning, starting, 16–23
Property division, divorce, 97–100
Property taxes, 117
Prospectus, 184–185
Protection from identity theft, 234–236

Qualified domestic relations order (QDRO), 101, **278**
QuickPlan, 18

Real estate (*See* Home ownership and mortgages)
Redemption fee, mutual funds, 177
Refinancing of home mortgage, 113–115
Relocation, job, 81–82
Renovation and home improvement, 127–129
Repair of identity theft, 238–240
Retirement savings, 131–157
    age and time, 132–133
    beneficiaries, 220

Retirement savings (*Cont.*):
    catch-up provisions, 146, 148
    divorce, 101–102
    early retirement, 156–157
    errors, 135, 137–141
    457(b) plan, 148–150
    401(k) and 403(b) plans, 144–149, 151–152
    goals, 134, 135
    hardship withdrawals, 148, 150
    income expectations and amount needed, 136–137
    Keogh plan, 153
    plan loans, 146–148, 150
    planning, 134–135, 136
    rollover, 78–81
    SEP (simplified employee pension) IRA,149,152–153, **279**
    SIMPLE (Savings Incentive Match Plan for Employees) IRA, 149, 152
    small business, 181
    Social Security, 141–144
    Solo 401(k), 149, 151–152
    tax, 138–139
    TSP plan, 149, 150–151
    (*See also* individual retirement accounts ([IRAs])
Reverse mortgage, 108, 118–119, **278**
Revocable trust, **278**
Right of survivorship, 220–221
Risk, investment, 160–161, 162–169
Risk tolerance quiz, 166–169
Rollover, retirement plan, 78
Roth IRA, 149, 154–155, **279**
Rule of 72, 17

Savings account, 38, 175–176
Savings bonds, 183–184
Savings Incentive Match Plan for Employees (SIMPLE) IRA, 149, 152
Second-to-die insurance, 203
Sector mutual funds, 177
Security, **279**
Selling house, 130
SEP (simplified employee pension) IRA, 149, 152–153, **279**
Series EE savings bond, 183–184
Series I savings bond, 183–184
Share, **279**
Sharpe, William, 169
Short-term capital gain/loss, **279**
Short-term health insurance, 190–191
Short-term investments, **280**
SIMPLE (Savings Incentive Match Plan for Employees) IRA, 149, 152

Simplified employee pension (SEP) IRA, 149, 152–153, **279**
Single parenting, 104
Small business retirement savings, 181
Social Security
    composition, 142
    estate planning, 229
    ex-spouse, 102
    identity theft repair, 240
    marriage, 83
    retirement income estimates, 135
    retirement savings, 141–144
    taxed at retirement, 138
Socially responsible investing (SRI), 258–262
Solo 401(k) Plan, 149, 151–152
S&P (Standard & Poor's) 500 index, **279**
Spending and planning, 26–32, 35–40
SRI (socially responsible investing), 258–262
Standard & Poor's (S&P) 500 index, **279**
Stocks, 179–181, 184–185, **280**
Survivors, estate planning, 228–232
Survivorship insurance, 203

Tax deductible, **280**
Tax-deferral, **280**
Taxes
    capital gains, 167
    divorce, 101, 102, 103
    estate planning, 222–223, 230
    long-term care, 207–208
    marriage penalty, 94–95
    name changes, 89
    property taxes, 117
    retirement savings, 138–139
    (*See also* Social Security)
Term life insurance, 201–202
Thrift Savings Plan (TSP), 149, 150–151
TIPS (Treasury Inflation-Indexed Securities), 165
Title changes, estate planning, 230

Title insurance, 120–121, **280**
Transfer on death (TOD), 220
Treasury bill, **280**
Treasury bond, **281**
Treasury Inflation-Indexed Securities (TIPS), 165
Treasury note, **281**
Trusts, **281**
TSP (Thrift Savings Plan), 149, 150–151
12b-1 fees, mutual funds, 177

Umbrella liability insurance, 120
Unemployment benefits, 76
Universal life insurance, 203
Unmarried couples, estate planning, 225–226

VA mortgage, 107
Value system, 249–266
    charitable giving, 255–257
    money considerations and living, 262–266
    personal values, 249–255
    scams, 257–258
    socially responsible investing (SRI), 258–262
Variable life insurance, 203
Vesting, retirement plan, 81
Volunteering, 257

Wallet contents, copying, 46
Wealth managers, 22
Wedding
    financial compatibility quiz, 90–93
    planning, 82–83, 86–87
    (*See also* Marriage)
Whole life insurance, 202–203
Will in estate planning, 212–215, 217–219
Withdrawals from retirement savings, 146–148, 150

Yield (return), **281**

About the Author

Suzanne Hunstad Olson earned a degree in English and journalism from Augustana College in Sioux Falls, S.D. She held a range of writing jobs before landing in financial services nearly 15 years ago. She found her niche when her employer sought writers to put a witty spin on life insurance, dollar-cost averaging, and other dry topics for ihatefinancialplanning.com. Suzanne lives in Minneapolis.